HIGH-TABLE DIPLOMACY

HIGH-TABLE DIPLOMACY

The Reshaping of International Security Institutions

KJELL ENGELBREKT

Georgetown University Press | Washington, DC

Library of Congress Cataloging-in-Publication Data

Engelbrekt, Kjell, author.
   High-table diplomacy : the reshaping of international security institutions / Kjell Engelbrekt.
     pages cm
   Includes bibliographical references and index.
   Summary: Today, great-power and middle-power diplomacy take place at two high tables, one using a well-known fixed address on First Avenue in Manhattan and the other at varying summit locations where heads of state and government meet. This book examines the growing importance of minilateral summit diplomacy in the management of international security problems. Kjell Engelbrekt contrasts the "GX" summitry of the G7 (and the G8 1998–2014) and G20 clubs with the older and more formal UN Security Council. He examines whether or not this new form of GX high-table diplomacy offers a more effective alternative to, or whether it simply complements, traditional institutions. One defining feature of GX diplomacy has been the diversification of countries with a seat at the table, as seen by contrasting the G20 with the five-member UN Security Council. A second feature of GX summits are their relative informality and flexibility, which has helped put nontraditional security threats on the agenda. Engelbrekt conducted research in primary-source documents of the G7, G8, G20, and UN Security Council to examine and contrast how these institutions have deliberated on three policy areas: conflict management, counterterrorism cooperation, and climate change mitigation.
   ISBN 978-1-62616-312-6 (hardcover : alk. paper) — ISBN 978-1-62616-313-3 (pbk. : alk. paper) — ISBN 978-1-62616-314-0 (ebook) 1. Summit meetings. 2. Diplomacy. 3. International relations. 4. Security, International. 5. Conflict management—International cooperation. 6. Terrorism—Prevention—International cooperation. 7. Climate change mitigation—International cooperation. I. Title.
   JZ1305.E54 2016
   355'.031—dc23   2015025235

♾ This book is printed on acid-free paper meeting the requirements of the American National Standard for Permanence in Paper for Printed Library Materials.

17 16   9 8 7 6 5 4 3 2
First printing

Printed in the United States of America

Cover design by Jen Huppert. Cover image by Robert Michael/picture-alliance/dpa/AP Images.

Disaster may be the price of failure to achieve One World in terms of a moral and political ideal.

—Inis L. Claude, *Swords into Ploughshares*

And so the way I see the struggle that's starting to emerge between the U.S., Europe on the one hand and rising states on the other is a struggle for voice, for authority. It's the global political hierarchy that's being contested, who gets to sit at the table, how many votes you get.

—G. John Ikenberry, "The Emerging Powers and the Future of the Global Order"

CONTENTS

ILLUSTRATIONS

ACKNOWLEDGMENTS

This book is dedicated to two categories of people without whom it would not have come into existence. The first category consists of individuals who spend most of their days solving or working around hard problems in the realm of international security. There are hundreds of thousands of nongovernmental organization (NGO) staff members, international civil servants, military personnel, and national diplomats whose work requires them to be exceptionally resilient and creative in order to overcome challenges that most of us would find overwhelming in terms of scale and institutional capacities available as remedy. In many cases these people become committed far beyond the limitations of their job descriptions and levels of remuneration. And yet these problem solvers rarely pause, let alone relent, in their attempts to alleviate the difficult situations that confront them.

The second category of people to which this book is dedicated is made of up problem preemptors, for lack of a better descriptor. These are not seldom individuals with some experience of work in the former category who subsequently engaged in creating prerequisites for international security problems to arise less frequently, to arise less dramatically, or to be handled more effectively. Their commitment to such causes takes the form of articulating proposals for preventive measures, improved institutional capacities, enhanced legal arrangements, or fresh funds addressing issues that so far have been ignored or underestimated. This second category of people operate not only in academic environments and think tanks but also within large NGOs and international organizations, combining desk or field jobs with innovative thinking about generic issues and institutional processes.

I have through the course of researching this book sat down to entertain conversations with scores of individuals from either category, characteristically ready to generously share their experiences and views with anybody who has taken an interest in security problems that cross borders. Some of my students at the Swedish Defense University in Stockholm, in fact, are problem solvers who spend a year or two reflecting on problem preemption owing to their own experience of what works in the type of situation in which they frequently operate. At the Chicago Council on Global Affairs, where I found an ideal environment to finish this project, I had the privilege of meeting some of America's most capable problem preemptors, who have extraordinary insights into problem solving at the international, national, and municipal levels, working on projects or appearing on the roster of visiting speakers.

Aside from this general dedication to internationally minded public servants, my deepest gratitude for hosting me and my busy laptop goes to all colleagues, partners, and friends in those two great American cities where my research began and ended. It was during a sabbatical semester to New York and Columbia University, facilitated by Timothy Frye at the helm of the Harriman Institute, that the early stage of the project took form. Robert Jervis invited me to his seminar on security and diplomacy, and Michael C. Doyle commented generously on my nascent project. Had my 2010 stay in Manhattan not been generously sponsored by the Wenner-Gren Foundation, I may not have been able to conduct so many interviews at the United Nations Headquarters, as many were agreed to on short notice owing to the relative inflexibility of the schedules of many senior diplomats.

In the final stage of my work, America's Second City offered me a stimulating intellectual environment in which to complete the manuscript, ranging from the Chicago Council on Global Affairs as the city's preeminent think tank to the Program on International Security Policy (PISP) seminar at the University of Chicago and the staff seminars at the Department of Political Science and the Office of International Affairs at the University of Illinois at Chicago (UIC). My special thanks go to Rachel Bronson, Dina Smelz, and Ivo Daalder at the Chicago Council and Dennis Judd, Evan McKenzie, Seung-Whan Choi, Petia Kostadinova, and Diplomat in Residence Ian Kelly at the UIC for hosting me and making me feel welcome. As a visiting fellow to the Chicago Council and the UIC, I could benefit from the combined insights of visiting policymakers and fellow scholars with regard to my research topic, and the city's outstanding flight connections made it an ideal launching pad for a final set of interview trips to New York and Washington, DC.

Not entirely unexpectedly, the US capital also eventually came to play a significant part in bringing this project to a successful close. Apart from everything I learned speaking to Washington-based academics and think tankers in recent years, I have in Georgetown University Press (GUP) found an especially encouraging and reliable partner. To publish with an American university press associated with one of the world's most outstanding academic programs in the related fields of international relations, diplomatic studies, and security studies is a highly satisfying experience for any European scholar. I owe Donald Jacobs, Richard Brown, Kathryn Owens, Julie Kimmel, and the anonymous reviewers of GUP a deep debt of gratitude for taking on this project and for patiently working to overcome all the impediments toward the finished product.

Last but not least, I would like to thank my colleagues at the Swedish Defense University for unwavering support and encouragement in this endeavor, and most emphatically, Magnus Ekengren, Jan Hallenberg, and Col. Jan Mörtberg, who in various ways provided critical input and thereby made this book possible. Johan Eriksson at the Swedish Institute for International Affairs and Jonas Tallberg at the Department of Political Science at Stockholm University, my two co-conspirators in making the Joint Seminar in International Relations the most exciting venue for visiting colleagues in this field, similarly deserve credit for their tireless efforts in reaffirming cross-departmental collaboration in "Scandinavia's Venice." Indeed, the Swedish capital has constituted a stable home base for me and my wife during the past two decades and for my daughter during the sixteen years she has been a precious part of our lives.

INTRODUCTION

In setting out to research the topic of this book a few years back, my overall interest was in current and anticipated changes in the global power configuration, the "polarity" of international relations in conventional terminology, and the likely repercussions of those changes on the diplomatic relations of great powers and the international security institutions to which the latter belong. The original idea was to contrast how swiftly informal institutional arrangements, such as the summits of the Group of Seven (G7), Eight (G8), and Twenty (G20), adjusted to a power shift in the making as opposed to the formal, regularized, and inflexible United Nations (UN) and its Security Council (UNSC). At the time a particularly vivid illustration of this discrepancy was the rapid transformation of the informal G20 from a meeting of finance ministers to a summit of heads of state and government in 2008–9, versus intergovernmental negotiations on a formula for reforming and expanding the formal UNSC, which got off to an excruciatingly slow and cumbersome start.

Yet, in the next few years, some of that vibrant political energy embodied by the G20 floated back into the UNSC. As the mapping of responses by informal and formal institutional arrangements to changing power relations made progress, not least through interviews with diplomats of G20 countries serving at the UN Headquarters in New York,[1] my curiosity turned toward the more intricate workings of security-related diplomacy lodged within, respectively, informal and formal settings. Especially intriguing, I found, was the tendency of formal settings to generate space for governance that relies on informality and of formal structures to crystallize inside informal diplomatic contexts. In recognizing that great-power diplomacy in the realm of international security takes place at two principal high tables—one using a well-known fixed address on First Avenue in New York and the other situated wherever the participating heads of state and government meet as a collective—I also decided that the existing literature grossly underestimated the degree to which institutional arrangements associated with the two high tables operate as horizontally organized, communicating vessels.

Equally striking was that the summitry of the G7, G8, and G20 was chiefly attending to nontraditional threats, risks, and challenges and that the member states of those informal institutions were wary of trespassing into traditional international security, which since the end of the Second World War has been the legitimate domain of the UNSC.[2] Being the centerpiece of a unique international institution created to rid humanity of the scourge of war and large-scale conflict, the UNSC is not equipped to transcend the international laws and rules that regulate its work at the same time as informal summits of heads of state and government enjoy flexibility to engage whatever issues they agree to raise among themselves. Because of the partial overlap between the UNSC and the major states partaking in informal summitry as well as what appears to be a political agreement to respect the existing division of labor, the boundary between traditional and nontraditional security matters for the most part continues to be upheld.

To probe the plausibility of my initial hunch that the two principal high tables actually do address nontraditional as well as traditional issues in international security, and that they furthermore exploit their respective status as informal and formal institutions to achieve results without jeopardizing existing arrangements, I first turned to the official records of both bodies. Seeking evidence that high-table diplomacy is becoming increasingly influential at the expense of policies pursued by either set of institutional arrangements or major powers, I examined all available official documents from the years 1990, 2000, and 2010. The reinvigoration of international security institutions in the immediate aftermath of the Cold War is well researched, and even a cursory analysis of this sample could confirm that the US government in 1990 was very much in control of the international security agenda, regardless of whether specific agenda items belonged to the traditional or nontraditional kind. The latter was evident in what was then the G7, where the desires of the Soviet and European leaders for American policy concessions went virtually unheeded by the administration of George H. W. Bush. At the UN Headquarters in New York, meanwhile, US policies providing political cover for heavy-handed actions against Palestinians by Israelis, additionally setting back an already stalled peace process, did face widespread criticism. However, when Iraq attacked Kuwait in the late summer, the Bush administration handily deflected such objections and built an impressive coalition to eject Saddam Hussein's army from Kuwaiti territory. Most important, under US leadership the UNSC acted decisively and in unison for the first time in decades.[3]

The year 2000, second in my three-part sample, further showed that the US government by that time was less in control of the international security agenda, or did at least not want to be seen as holding all the cards. UNSC Resolution 1322, adopted in October 2000, was one of few the US permanent representative abstained from vetoing. The resolution censured Israeli coercive actions against the Palestinian population in the Occupied Territories, thereby exposing Tel Aviv to an implicit American rebuke as well as sharp criticism outside the council. At the G8 Okinawa summit, furthermore, Japan organized an extraordinarily encompassing agenda, exceeding that of all previous holders of the G7/G8 presidencies. There is evidence that Tokyo consulted with the administration of then–US president Bill Clinton so as to prepare a summit poised to accomplish significant joint agreements; still, the extensive nature of the preparations clearly reflected growing Japanese strides to strengthen Japan's own profile in international relations, partly by opening up top-level summits to non-Western views and values.[4] The practice of extending invitations to a wide variety of international organizations, and to countries serving as chairs of regional organizations, was a significant novelty that Tokyo introduced.

By 2010, finally, there were several indications that the agenda of the UNSC was not being driven by the US government as single-handedly as in the past two decades. Brazil and Turkey's attempt to engineer a solution that would obviate the need for an embargo against Iran due to its nuclear technology program suggested that Washington could no longer suppress independent proposals, and the greater inclination of all five veto powers to refrain from using their vetoes suggested a more consensual way of doing business at the council. Concerning the civil war in Syria, which erupted in 2009 and worsened over the next several years, the US position in favor of intervention was even met with vehement opposition to any active involvement beyond humanitarian relief, primarily but not exclusively from Russia.[5] Within the context of top-level summitry, which was undergoing the biggest transformation since its inception in the mid-1970s, the role of Western states was clearly diminished as a result of the handover of core economic and financial issues from the G7/G8 to the G20. By not disbanding the G7/G8 in 2009–10, though, the US government, together with the UK and France, could continue to harness an agenda-setting role on international security affairs.

Albeit only a modest investigation, the outcome of my plausibility probe into the official records of the UNSC and the G7, G8, and G20 summitry for 1990–2010 thus largely resonated with the claims of scholars who in recent years have observed the waning of the "unipolar moment" of US preeminence proclaimed in the early 1990s.[6] Not least when it comes to international security, it is becoming a commonplace that agenda-setting and bargaining leverage no longer resides solely with the United States and its close allies but has been gradually diffused to a greater number of actors, a trend that has persisted since the end of the Cold War. The year 1990 is in this respect a useful baseline from which to extrapolate trends that some view as steep and others as climbing only slowly.[7] For the purposes of this study, it suffices to accept that more voices had come to the fore at the two high tables by 2000, as exemplified at the G8 Okinawa summit and by the decisions made that year at the UNSC. And by 2010 the number of engaged stakeholders able to shape the agenda had expanded, as reflected by the rise of the G20 summit and the contentious deliberations of the UNSC on issues such as Syria.

Five years after I had completed the initial probe using a limited sample, the finished book is a study of international security institutions through the prism of great- and middle-power diplomacy at a time characterized by global redistribution of resources and an increasingly level playing field among major states. This phenomenon, which I propose to call high-table diplomacy, is most clearly manifested in institutional arrangements in which great powers constitute the decisive stakeholders but middle powers, once seated, also wield influence. In terms of empirical substance, the full-fledged study maps organizational, political, and above all, diplomatic practices in three separate policy areas of international security, systematically investigating the years 2009–14. Chapters covering this period analyze conflict management, counterterrorism cooperation, and climate change mitigation as individual policy areas in which high-table diplomacy was influential. Taken together, these three policy areas encompass formidable challenges that belong to narrow, traditional as well as broad, nontraditional understandings of international security. Overall, it can be argued, there are in the beginning of the twenty-first century few, if any, greater tasks facing humanity as a whole.

NOTES

1. See the appendix.

2. For integrative accounts of traditional and nontraditional security, see Morgan, *International Security*; Buzan and Hansen, *Evolution of International Security Studies*; M. E. Smith, *International Security*; Hameiri and Jones, "Politics and Governance."

3. Risse-Kappen, "Long-Term Future," 44–60.

4. Hook, *Japan's International Relations*, 378.

5. In light of this trend spanning two decades, it is the weak pushback against Washington on the 2011 Libya intervention, not the strong and consistent objections on Syria, that represents the exception. See Engelbrekt, "Why Libya?"

6. Haas, "Age of Nonpolarity"; Foot and Walter, *China, the United States, and Global Order*; Posen, *Restraint*.

7. Overall, analysts emphasizing economic indicators often regard the leveling of the playing field as happening faster than do those who pay more attention to military and political capabilities.

ABBREVIATIONS

ADB	Asian Development Bank
AF	Adaptation Fund
AMISOM	African Mission in Somalia
APSA	African Peace and Security Architecture
ASEAN	Association of Southeast Asian Nations
ASF	African Standby Force
AU	African Union
AWG-KP	Ad Hoc Working Group on Further Commitments for Annex I Parties under the Kyoto Protocol
AWG-LCA	Ad Hoc Working Group on Long-Term Cooperative Action under the Convention
B20	Business 20
BIS	Bank for International Settlements
BRICS	Brazil, Russia, India, China, and South Africa
C20	Civil 20
CAR	Central African Republic
CDM	Clean Development Mechanism
CEWS	Continental Early Warning System
CO2	carbon dioxide
COP	Conference of the Parties
CTAG	Counter-Terrorism Action Group
CTC	Counter-Terrorism Committee
CTED	Counter-Terrorism Executive Directorate
CTG	Counter Terrorism Group
CTITF	Counter-Terrorism Implementation Task Force
DPRK	Democratic People's Republic of Korea
E10	Elected 10 (UNSC member states)
ECOSOC	Economic and Social Council
ECOWAS	Economic Community of West African States
EU	European Union
EUFOR	European Union Force

FATF	Financial Action Task Force
FSB	Financial Stability Board
G7	Group of Seven
G8	Group of Eight
G20	Group of Twenty
G77	Group of Seventy-Seven
GATT	General Agreement on Tariffs and Trade
GCTF	Global Counterterrorism Forum
GHG	greenhouse gas
HTCSG	High-Tech Crime Subgroup
IASB	International Accounting Standards Board
ICANN	Internet Corporation for Assigned Names and Numbers
ICAO	International Civil Aviation Organization
ICCAT	Interagency Climate Change Adaptation Task Force
IEA	International Energy Agency
IGCC	Investors Group on Climate Change
IIGCC	Institutional Investors Group on Climate Change
IMF	International Monetary Fund
IMO	International Maritime Organization
INCR	Investor Network on Climate Risk
Interpol	International Criminal Police Organization
IPCC	Intergovernmental Panel on Climate Change
IPEEC	International Partnership of Energy Efficiency Cooperation
ISCO	International Standard Classification of Occupations
ISIL	Islamic State in Iraq and the Levant
KFOR	Kosovo Stabilization Force
MAP	Mutual Assessment Process
MINURCAT	United Nations Mission in the Central African Republic and Chad
MINUSTAH	United Nations Stabilization Mission to Haiti
MONUC	United Nations Mission in the Democratic Republic of the Congo
MONUSCO	United Nations Stabilization Force in the Democratic Republic of the Congo
MRV	measurement, reporting, and verification
NAM	Non-Alignment Movement
NATO	North Atlantic Treaty Organization
OAS	Organization of American States
OECD	Organisation for Economic Co-operation and Development

OPEC	Organization of the Petroleum Exporting Countries
OSCE	Organization for Security and Co-operation in Europe
P5	Permanent 5 (UNSC member states)
PBC	UN Peacebuilding Commission
REC	Regional Economic Communities
S5	Small Five Group (of UN member states)
SBI	Subsidiary Body for Implementation
SBSTA	Subsidiary Body for Scientific and Technological Advice
SCO	Shanghai Cooperation Organisation
SDR	Special Drawing Rights
SLM/A	Sudanese Liberation Movement/Army
SPLM-N	Sudan People's Liberation Movement–North
UN	United Nations
UNAM	United Nations Assistance Mission in Iraq
UNEP	United Nations Environment Programme
UNFCCC	United Nations Framework Convention on Climate Change
UNGGE	United Nations Group of Governmental Experts on Developments in the Field of Information and Telecommunications
UNHCR	United Nations High Commissioner for Refugees
UNMIK	United Nations Interim Administration Mission in Kosovo
UNMIS	United Nations Mission in the Sudan
UNMISS	United Nations Mission in the Republic of South Sudan
UNODC	United Nations Office on Drugs and Crime
UNSC	United Nations Security Council
UNSMIS	United Nations Supervision Mission in Syria
USAID	US Agency for International Development
WEOG	West European and Others Group (of UN member states)
WFP	World Food Program
WHO	World Health Organization
WTO	World Trade Organization

Chapter 1

A Puzzle and Conceptual Framework

What is high-table diplomacy, and what is its appeal in the early twenty-first century? Why do leaders of established and emerging great powers reshape international organizations and arenas of negotiation in the realm of international security, promoting institutions that lack universal legitimacy and accountability mechanisms, yet fail to reform those to which the latter properties are ascribed? Furthermore, how do contemporary great and middle powers employ existing formal and informal institutional arrangements to address the major challenges of our time, encompassing traditional and nontraditional concepts of security in conflict management, counterterrorism cooperation, and climate change mitigation? Does high-table diplomacy provide a solution to complex governance issues in the realm of international security so promising that the experience can be emulated in other policy areas? In other words, is the theory of a "stakeholdership of the few" plausible?

These are the most straightforward and central questions that this book seeks to answer, and the argument will unfold in this sequence in five chapters and a conclusion. The normative query at the end of the list will be addressed only in the conclusion, taking into consideration the results of this study as well as relevant work by other authors. The core of the book is made up of three analytical chapters that examine policy areas within international security, starting with conflict management, moving on to counterterrorism cooperation, and ending with climate change mitigation. As will be argued later in this chapter, contemporary international security issues extend from traditional to nontraditional types, depending on the character of the potential threat they pose and the resources required for an effective response.

Chapters 1 and 2 both deal with the concept of high-table diplomacy, the latter in historical context and in relation to changing relations among great and middle powers. The former sets out to describe the contemporary phenomenon and its key characteristics and further to justify its use in the study of international relations. It also explains the rationale for promoting international security institutions that rely on informality, such as summits of heads of state and government, without undermining their formal and legally grounded counterparts. Today's high-table diplomacy very much revolves around the summits of heads of state and government; nonetheless, the United Nations Security Council (UNSC) remains critical to institutional arrangements in the realm of international security.

Introducing the Concept

This study identifies, explores, and renders visible the growing significance of high-table diplomacy in international security and in international relations more widely. High-table diplomacy is conducted within institutional arrangements in which great powers enjoy special status and to which they have privileged access. From well-established historical accounts we are aware that the phenomenon of "concert diplomacy" helped to hold balance-of-power dynamics at bay in nineteenth-century, post-Napoleonic Europe and "served as a device for identifying and advancing membership in the great power club."[1] Predating this experience in diplomatic history are instances of non-Western great powers forging security institutions in the premodern era, a particularly successful one underwriting the sophisticated trade and transport system linking Southeast and South India from the Indian Ocean to the Persian Gulf coast region in the 1400s and another helping to sustain the intricate political economy encompassing China and most of East Asia in the same period and several centuries ahead.

Part of what constitutes high-table diplomacy today is in the scholarly literature referred to as summit diplomacy, or more precisely, serial summit diplomacy.[2] More recently, scholars began using "minilateralism," the notion that major actors can "bring to the table the smallest possible number of countries needed to have the largest possible impact on solving a particular problem."[3] High-table diplomacy is compatible with minilateralism (which will be further discussed later), though the former term more poignantly expresses agnosticism about the format of deliberations and an evolving overlap of institutional arrangements across adjacent policy areas.

High-table diplomacy involves meetings of heads of state and government, encounters that are part of a process to which the parties have committed in advance, or an open-ended series of meetings between especially skilled and trusted diplomats who continuously brief heads of state and government and consult them on major decisions. High-table diplomacy is thus a regularized diplomatic practice, often accompanied by meticulous preparations regarding which issues to address and how to try to accomplish a desired result or prevent an undesired outcome. From time to time, though, high-table diplomacy is undoubtedly a crisis-driven phenomenon.[4]

This study is not chiefly concerned with unofficial (secret), or track II, diplomacy aimed at advancing negotiations without committing governments to a particular outcome of a political process.[5] Nor is it primarily preoccupied with ad hoc activities that non-diplomats engage in to further diplomatic ends. But the institutional arrangements, diplomatic practices, and governance mechanisms that I seek to identify, highlight, and theorize are nonetheless at variance with methods and techniques that belong to the orthodox repertoire of diplomatic activities. The high-table diplomacy envisaged here constitutes deliberate practices that are performed within international security institutions, at the nexus of formal and informal governance and that of traditional and nontraditional security. The former is typically conducted with the aim of rendering institutional arrangements in the realm of international security more legitimate, more effective, or both. Practices pertaining to the latter nexus encompass measures that are mainly coercive, are mainly noncoercive, or do not rely exclusively on either mode of operation to maximize the prospects for success.

By the way, the concept of an "institution" is employed here primarily for the sake of achieving comparability of two analytical units that in several respects do not share the same properties. As will be elaborated later, the UNSC is a principal formal organ of the world's core international institution solidly entrenched in international law, with wide-ranging prerogatives, whereas the serial summitry of great and middle powers is an informal practice of modern diplomacy without such legal foundation or established rules of procedure. The point is that the diplomatic practices and policies emanating from the latter are in the individual case not necessarily less consequential in the realm of international security than those of the former. The use of the term "institution" is therefore an outgrowth of a conceptual choice that hopefully results in novel descriptive statements and theoretical insights, not a claim put forward for its normative connotations regarding the status of informal summits.

The Nexus of Formal and Informal Institutional Arrangements

The expansion of diplomatic activities that pertain to international security matters at the UNSC in the first half of the 1990s is regarded as having made that institution more directly relevant to world affairs.[6] But what was not given much attention in the early 1990s was the long-standing evolution of informal cooperation on specific missions and issues that helped underpin the activities decided on by the UNSC and that allowed for UN-mandated peacekeeping operations and other types of missions to grow beyond the boundaries of what was considered feasible during the Cold War era.[7] To offset some of the deleterious implications of a highly formalized setting, diplomatic practices that preserve or reinsert political flexibility allow the most powerful actors to apply their considerable informal resources as leverage.[8] As will be further explained later, I propose to refer to such informal diplomatic practices, when developed within a formal setting, as "nested informality," a space for informal governance lodged within a formal institutional arrangement.[9]

An illustration of, and an especially productive precedent to, nested informality in the UNSC was the collaboration of diplomatic missions of the permanent five UNSC member states (P5) in Phnom Pen during the UN-led political and peacekeeping missions to Cambodia, which emerged in 1989–90.[10] The variety of informal diplomatic practices relevant for the work of the UNSC, also before 1990, should of course not be underestimated. Unofficial bilateral consultations among the P5, and extending to the elected ten countries that hold rotating seats, form a significant portion of those activities.[11] There are also the "good offices" of the secretary general, used since the 1950s for diplomatic facilitation in order to pursue the main goal of the UN at large: international peace and security.[12] When the secretary general was lacking tools to reach the parties in a particular conflict, he could frequently rely on "contact groups," "groups of friends," or looser networks of intermediaries to explore avenues toward mitigating or resolving conflicts.[13]

In the years following the Gulf War, which ejected the Iraqi army from Kuwait in 1990–91, the number of institutional arrangements that helped to realize the decisions adopted by the UNSC multiplied. In some cases the UN secretary general and his team were able to play a direct role.[14] In other instances mediation and stabilization efforts went ahead with strong support from regional organizations, with local knowledge and a commitment to address the causes of the conflict.[15] This is not to say that the vast majority of dispute settlements mediated by state actors on behalf of the UN secretary general or a regional security organization consistently produced enduring results, a claim some scholars say is incorrect.[16] But a diplomatic process legitimately "owned" by the council allowed for other players to step forward and contribute their skills and resources, as long as they kept the P5 and the Secretariat informed and consulted closely if and when a breakthrough seemed feasible.[17]

Group meetings of the P5 and various coalitions of the ten elected UNSC member states (E10) over the past two and a half decades also became more regular, forming other instances of nested informality. These meetings may take place between permanent representatives of UNSC member states or between their deputies or political coordinators.[18] In recent years an increasing amount of council work has been conducted via electronic correspondence, a practice turning the second or third in command of each diplomatic mission into a master coordinator of time management and policy planning.[19] That coordinating role is enhanced and rendered exceedingly more complex when the same individual, as his or her mission assumes the rotating chair of the council, also organizes the entire work program of the body. Although non-P5 missions can rely on auxiliary staff in New York to carry this temporarily enhanced workload, the senior diplomats are much helped by earlier investments in intimate knowledge of working methods, issues, and actual individuals who make up the council and its counterparts in the Secretariat.

Another innovation toward enhanced informal, nonbinding practices evolved at the UN Headquarters in New York is today well established. The so-called Arria formula, pioneered by the Venezuelan permanent representative in 1992 and later integrated into UNSC practice, has proved to be, in the words of James Paul, "an interesting mixture of informality and formality."[20] Under the current practice an Arria event is not an activity of the council but an informal meeting convened at the request of an individual council member state, with invitations sent to the other fourteen permanent representations, and sometimes to the entire UN membership. The meetings are held in a regular conference room, not in the UNSC Consultation Room, and they are neither announced nor recorded in any official manner. This opportunity for discussions whose content is not vetted by professional diplomats in advance will give rise, on occasion, to sharp controversies among council member states. On the other hand the information conveyed via outside parties is widely appreciated for adding perspectives and helping to establish a baseline of key facts regarding a diplomatic challenge that the council is facing.[21]

Conversely, however, there are instances of nested formality—that is, formal governance lodged inside an informal institutional arrangement—in the summitry of the Group of Seven (G7), Group of Eight (G8), and Group of Twenty (G20). Since the summits of heads of state and government lack a permanent secretariat, official meeting protocols, rules of procedure, and formal political commitments in the shape of international law, all of which characterize the UNSC, other diplomatic practices are used to make up for the absence of organizational and normative structure.[22] These practices in some ways differ among the three summits, yet the summits frequently borrow solutions from each other and put organizational units and individuals to double or triple use. There is clearly a close family resemblance regarding the diplomatic mode of operation across all serial summits.

Instead of a permanent secretariat, the participating governments have decided to leave the planning of summits and recurrent meetings between government officials to a troika consisting of the country holding the rotating presidency, together with its predecessor and successor in that position.[23] At the national level each head of state or government leading the delegation has further assigned a so-called Sherpa, a contact person in his or her closest entourage charged with planning and liaising with national counterparts. In several countries it is the same person who performs this duty for all top-level summits, but in recent years there has been a trend toward differentiating the roles also owing to the increasingly varying character of issues raised in each format. In fact, in all attending countries there are so-called sous-Sherpas serving alongside the ranking official who works most closely with the political leader in question.

Another example of nested formality is the increasingly fixed character of several of the working groups that meet to prepare summits in some fields of policy. Especially prominent among these in the G20 context are the International Financial Architecture Working Group, the Development Working Group, and the Anti-Corruption Working Group. Besides official government networks, there is the Business 20 (B20) working group, in which the most influential national business federations and major corporations take part. Civil society organizations attended the 2010 Toronto summit for the first time, and in 2013 in St. Petersburg the Civil 20 (C20) was established as an acknowledged arena adjacent to the G20 summit.

There is nevertheless a history of informal working groups dating back several decades in the G7/G8 setting. The analysis in chapter 4 will discuss the increasingly structured cooperation on counterterrorism that evolved after the end of the Cold War through the participation of senior official and experts poring over foreign affairs, organized crime, justice, and home affairs issues along with terrorism proper. But problems concerning transnational trade, the environment, employment, energy, science and technology, and agriculture were from time to time addressed at a meeting of the ministers of all G7 or G8 countries. In many cases these ministerial meetings were associated with the setting up of temporary working groups assigned to identify solutions that could be implemented across the board or submitted to a formal international institution.

The Nexus of Traditional and Nontraditional Security

Along another dimension high-table diplomacy cuts across another nexus, namely, that between nontraditional and traditional concepts of security. The precise delineation between the two notions is contested on theoretical and normative grounds, and the debates are unlikely to be settled anytime soon. But nontraditional security is widely characterized as encompassing nonmilitary ends, means, or so-called referents of security. In a 2013 article by Shahar Hameiri and Lee Jones, the list of relevant real-world manifestations included "terrorism, environmental degradation and climate change, infectious disease, transnational crime and illegal migration."[24] By logical extension, therefore, traditional security is primarily preoccupied with military, symmetric conflicts, and state coercion relying on the deployment of a wide range of national resources.

It is easy to see that the predominantly informal summitry of heads of state and government is grappling with nontraditional security in several forms, while the predominantly formal UNSC addresses traditional security challenges arising from political actors resorting to violence or the threat of violence across borders or directed at some portion of the domestic population. This is the conventional division of labor in international security institutions, as understood by the political leaders of the twentieth century who established the UN and a host of regional organizations similarly assigned to handle political disputes with a significant potential to generate military conflict. As informal summits engage in international security, they do so with a view of not trespassing into the legitimate domain of the UNSC.

Yet the consistent maintenance of a boundary across this nexus is no longer possible. According to Hameiri and Jones, security is increasingly perceived as nontraditional "because states are also becoming 'non-traditional.'"[25] A political process is contributing to the rescaling of the space, discourses, and management of security, they argue, inevitably prompting the regulatory state to expand into areas where national authorities in the past were not (considered) accountable. By highlighting the transnational character of nontraditional security threats, this observation serves to justify the use of new, unorthodox, and nonmilitary measures to combat the associated phenomena.[26]

As a result there is today a significant degree of overlap between top-level serial summitry and the UNSC. Conflict management remains almost exclusively the legitimate domain of the UNSC at the same time as environmental degradation and climate change are considered by informal summits. Counterterrorism cooperation, however, has gradually evolved from something the G7 and the G8 used to handle within specialized institutional arrangements to a matter in which the subsidiary organs of the UNSC play an increasingly critical role.

The institutional arrangements that accompany high-table diplomacy in the realm of international security can therefore be depicted in a straight-

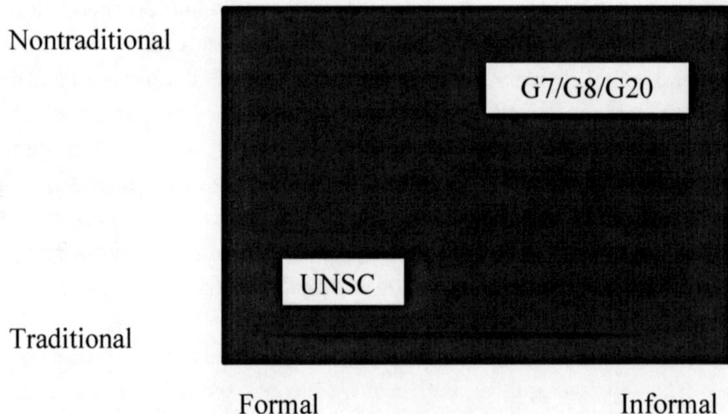

Figure 1.1. International Security Institutions in High-Table Diplomacy

forward way as situated along two axes or dimensions, where informal serial summits and the UNSC occupy different positions.

As described previously, however, the international security institutions that operate along the lines of high-table diplomacy are thereby tempted to try to offset some of their respective weaknesses—*effectiveness* in the case of the UNSC and *legitimacy* when it comes to serial summits—by "shopping" or "shifting" the forum in search of a workable formula for a particular issue.[27] At the same time international security institutions must rely on continuity in order to harness and sustain such values over time.

Waning Multilateralism

The appeal of high-table diplomacy and minilateralism in the early twenty-first century is a complex phenomenon with several components and underlying causes. An obvious but incomplete explanation behind recent developments is the sagging reputation of the latter's more ambitious counterpart: multilateralism. Among decision makers as well as in the public opinion of many countries, multilateralism has since the late 1990s increasingly been associated with gridlocked international political arenas, oversized bureaucracies, and lofty social ideals. Some commentators even view multilateralism as a victim of its own success, in the sense that multilateral institutions gave rise to a cycle of self-reinforcing interdependence that "helped create conditions that, ironically, now impede their effectiveness."[28]

In his widely cited 1993 definition, John Ruggie spelled out the concept of multilateralism by way of three elements: generalized principles of conduct, indivisibility of members of a collectivity, and expectations of diffuse reciprocity, the latter term directly borrowed from Robert Keohane.[29] Multilateralism, Ruggie elaborated in a Keohanean vein, is an institutional form that

> coordinates relations among three or more states on the basis of generalized principles of conduct: that is, principles which specify appropriate conduct for a class of actions, without regard for the particularistic interests of the parties or the strategic exigencies that may exist in any specific occurrence.... Two corollaries follow ... an indivisibility among the members of a collectivity with respect to the range of behavior in question ... multilateralism in practice generate ... expectations of diffuse reciprocity.[30]

While the qualities of Ruggie's definition earned it a prominent place in contemporary international relations research, the definition did downplay the inclusive, if not universalistic, ambition inherent in the concept and the legitimacy claim derived from it. On the latter view multilateralism is above all an inclusive form of international cooperation that places the burden of proof on anyone who seeks to restrict participation to a narrower group of stakeholders than necessary. It follows that the multilateral approach makes most sense when all mutually recognized parties affected by an international institutional arrangement are invited to participate actively in its establishment, which is what post-1945 diplomatic negotiations frequently aspired to in the realms of peace and security, the environment, and trade.[31]

As just alluded to, however, the diplomatic practice of international relations in recent years indicates that multilateralism no longer offers a sufficiently flexible and effective model for addressing some of the major challenges facing the early twenty-first century. In his study of international trade negotiations that since 1994 have failed to produce a binding agreement for nearly two hundred countries with disparate interests, Chris Brummer wrote,

> Multilateralism ... has been supplanted by an array of more modest and seemingly less ambitious joint ventures—from regional clubs like the (shaky) European Union and (rising) Association of Southeast Asian Nations to more geographically diverse and less understood initiatives like the G-20, Basel Committee on Banking Supervision and Financial Stability Board.... More modest in size, formality, and even inclusiveness, they play small ball on the court of international affairs and embrace what can be described as distinctively *mini*lateral strategies of economic statecraft.[32]

If full-fledged multilateral negotiations on crucial matters such as world trade, UNSC reform, and climate change failed to deliver in the past two decades, it is hardly surprising that alternative approaches began to be explored. Bogged down by ever-expanding agendas, government leaders and officials understandably felt there was a limit to how much time and effort should be spent on piecing together the views and interests of all nation-states by diplomatic means, as if laying a jigsaw puzzle the size of a football field in order to bring multilateral negotiations to a successful end. The concept of minilateralism, at least in the restricted sense of a "multilateralism of small numbers,"[33] does not assume that more modest ambitions regarding inclusiveness inevitably betray the norms of the loftier notion.[34] As Lisa Martin suggested in the same volume that featured Ruggie's definition two decades ago, leaders can "overcome the difficulties of multilateral decision making by delegating urgent issues to a smaller set of actors or allowing such a subset to exercise agenda control under certain conditions."[35]

By concentrating on the functionalist logic of the argument, though, we risk underappreciating the significance of the legitimacy claim that underpins most institutional arrangements in international relations. A less obvious explanation for the waning appeal of multilateralism is associated with opposition to the perceived hegemony of the United States, seen as embodied by American preeminence in the military realm, and that of the West more broadly. Since the mid-1990s the leaders of several non-Western great powers have at times voiced their unease with what they regard as the illegitimate leadership status of the United States.[36] Parts of the foreign policy and defense establishment of the Russian Federation, while still reeling from the collapse of the Soviet empire, avoided direct confrontation with the West and the United States but apparently experienced humiliation after the retreat from Central and Eastern Europe. China, India, and several Latin American, Arab, and Islamic countries have also in the post–Cold War period sought to counter US and Western political influence out of a desire to assert their own autonomy.[37]

Milder forms of criticism aside, overt opposition against US preeminence in world affairs has been expressed more frequently since the turn of the twenty-first century. From one point onward non-Western leaders of great powers such as China and Russia began promoting what they referred to as "multipolarity," although the phrase was still used in rather vague terms.[38] The concept of multipolarity only gradually acquired a distinctive definition, involving bilateral agreements or organizational arrangements from which the United States was excluded that were entered into on the part of non-Western great powers. A striking example of an arrangement with such objectives was the Shanghai Cooperation Organisation (SCO), rather modestly set up with

China as the Shanghai Five in 1996 and then rebranded as SCO with a higher profile in 2001. Another symptomatic development has been to qualify the term "multilateralism," for instance, in Russia's promotion of "effective multilateralism," and then apply it with reference to institutional arrangements in which non-Western great powers are highly influential.[39]

To be sure, the preeminence of the United States in the 1990s was reinforced as a result of its being the sole so-called superpower left standing at the end of the Cold War. But America exerted influence around the world on the basis of a combination of factors, and not exclusively by virtue of its economic and military might. The United States was especially reinvigorated in the early 1990s in terms of soft power and its strengthened credibility as advocate of liberal society and expanding trade relations on a global scale. Realizing that its influence highly depended on America's attraction as "a benevolent empire," most senior decision makers were wary of not overplaying Washington's hand.[40] In the realm of international security in particular, Washington almost invariably sought affirmation from one, if not both, high tables (and often from lesser regional players) before taking decisive political or military action. This could be seen in the George H. W. Bush administration's handling of the first Gulf War against Iraq in 1990–91, as well as in cases of direct American military involvement in Bosnia-Herzegovina (1993–95) and Kosovo (1998–99) by way of the UN, the North Atlantic Treaty Organization (NATO), and the so-called Contact Group.[41]

The September 11, 2001, terrorist attacks against New York and Washington clearly prompted a departure from the latter pattern in that Washington militarily engaged enemies and suspects on a unilateral basis and sometimes without robust justifications in international law.[42] The preemption doctrine of the George W. Bush administration and the 2003 decision to invade Iraq, despite criticism from France and Germany at the UN, represent the most striking illustrations of this approach. But American leaders even in this period sought approval and support from their counterparts at high tables when it came to significant auxiliary international security activities, such as the antiterrorist financing instruments put in place by UNSC Resolution 1373 (2001) and followed up by measures reinforcing conflict management and counterterrorism cooperation at the global level. In the years that followed, US leaders also placed more emphasis on G8 cooperation in a number of policy areas relevant to international security, such as the safety of air travel, than they had before 2001.[43]

It was eventually the sharp financial crisis of 2008–9 that made clear to American and Canadian as well as to European and Japanese governments that the world economy had become significantly less based on Western economies and societies than many previously had realized and that political resources corresponding to the ongoing power shift were beginning to accrue in large, formerly developing nations. For efforts to coordinate the actions of the most consequential economies of the world to succeed, it was deemed insufficient to exclusively turn to the G7/G8 constellation of countries to offset the severe damage done to the international financial system and avert a deep, worldwide recession. The large emerging economies, in other words, needed to participate in financial burden sharing if the stimulus effort were to have enough credibility as well as material effect.[44] And so, as a gesture to prospective stakeholders of the highest order, a much broader group of states was invited and offered at least provisional seats at the diplomatic high tables.[45]

Platforms and Institutional Arrangements as Units of Analysis

Regarding the institutional arrangements at the center of this study, it is readily assumed that the most prominent high-table platforms at which security-related diplomacy nowadays takes place are the UNSC, the G7/G8, and the G20. It is convenient to speak about two principal high tables in a spatial sense: one consisting of a flexible summitry structure that convenes wherever the presidency determines and another with a fixed address on First Avenue along the East River in Lower Manhattan. But the recurring congregation of world leaders at the annual opening session of the UN General Assembly, held at the UN Headquarters in New York in September, is also a relevant platform to consider, if not on a par with the UNSC and serial summits. The viability of the assembly as a high-table platform is in part derived from the largely uncontested supranational status of the UN system nearly seven decades after its establishment and in part a consequence of the UNSC and the assembly operating under carefully circumscribed mandates and procedures. While the effectiveness of the main UN organs is frequently disputed, their legitimacy remains a major asset, as alluded to previously.[46]

In contrast, the major asset of the G7, G8, and G20 is the potential effectiveness of commitments made at summits of major powers.[47] A summit of political leaders can at any point in time decide to broaden the scope of its activities, though it will as a consequence grapple more intensely with issues of legitimacy.[48] Some contemporary commentators do not seem to mind the legitimacy deficit associated with great-power summits, as they believe that vulnerability is offset by other values, for instance, that of facilitating a future transition from American preeminence to a more polycentric (or "multipolar") world order.[49] Others attribute greater significance to the whole array of informal great-power summits, the "GX summitry," viewing it as a high table whose institutional arrangements have considerable potential to reinforce effectiveness and even mitigate the legitimacy deficit on the basis of its greater representativeness of global heterogeneity.[50] "GX summitry" will be used later to denote all serial summit formats.

In delimiting this research interest to high-table platforms that either focus almost all of their attention on challenges in the realm of international security (as in the case of the UNSC), or devote at least a significant portion thereof (as in the case of the GX summitry and the UN General Assembly), this study takes a global view. It pays only fleeting attention to national or regional platforms and institutional arrangements. Even though NATO has adopted an out-of-area policy, it remains a body with a regional mandate focused on the transatlantic community from North America to the borders of European states with the Russian Federation. As demonstrated in the direct challenge to Ukrainian sovereignty by the Russian Federation in early 2014, the core task of defending the autonomy and territorial integrity of NATO member states remains relevant even a quarter century after the end of the Cold War and the disbandment of the Moscow-led Warsaw Pact. For the same reason only marginal attention is paid to the Organization for Security and Co-operation in Europe (OSCE), the African Union (AU), the Organization of American States (OAS), the SCO, and the Association of Southeast Asian Nations (ASEAN), the latter having launched a "political-security community" as late as in 2004.

At the overarching international level where high-table diplomacy takes place, there are just, as already suggested, a handful of platforms of consequence. The UNSC, associated with an array of institutional arrangements often well-entrenched in legal rules and diplomatic practices, is undoubtedly the most visible and durable such platform. Having existed for nearly seven decades in the format laid out in the UN Charter and the Provisional Rules on Procedure and conditioned by international law, the UNSC occupies a unique position in contemporary international relations. It operates in accordance with rules handed down in previous council decisions as well as international agreements, international law jurisprudence, customary law forged through the actions of sovereign states, and mutually recognized principles of interstate behavior.[51]

Less obvious is that the norms of multilateralism and minilateralism are both inherent in the UNSC, namely, in the stark division of membership into two distinct categories with different rights and responsibilities.[52] The P5 countries, vested with veto rights, make up a de facto minilateral institutional arrangement at the apex of the UN system. The E10 countries, holding rotating seats for which they need to compete, are at a disadvantage vis-à-vis the P5 not only because they lack veto rights but also because their two-year mandates barely allow diplomats to get up to speed on the issues before they leave the body. The working methods of the council, confirming the P5 as "the masters of [council] procedure," further enhance what prominent E10 representatives continue to characterize as an "enormous asymmetry" between the two categories of membership.[53] Already a decade ago, Kishore Mahbubani of Singapore, himself a former permanent representative to the body, sarcastically remarked that the UN Charter had given the P5 "power without responsibility" and the E10 "responsibility without power."[54]

At the same time, there is no denying that the E10 countries are selected on the multilateral principle of equal representation of the wider UN membership, as stated in article 24 of the UN Charter.[55] The selection takes place in accordance with article 23 of the UN Charter, which means that two countries are drawn from each of five groups (African, Asia-Pacific, Eastern European, Latin American and Caribbean, West European and Others [WEOG]) to ensure "equitable geographic representation." Any UN member state, in other words, is eligible to serve as an elected member state in the UNSC and together with its peers represent the entire community of UN members. Furthermore, since the establishment of the UN, most member states with a significant diplomatic capacity and an active interest in international relations have at least once served in that capacity.[56]

When it comes to informal institutional arrangements generating nonbinding commitments in international security, the situation is, as one might expect, more opaque and unsettled. But given the proven durability of their existence, it is reasonable to highlight two such informal arrangements. One is the recurrent, multilateral event in which virtually all UN member states partake in late September, namely, the general debate that marks the opening session of the UN General Assembly. The event constitutes the world's greatest gathering of heads of state and government on a regular basis and prominently features security issues in the vast majority of speeches. Besides the mere fact of coming together to address issues of common concern, the leading representatives of individual UN member states are only in this context guaranteed a platform from which to articulate their concerns and aspirations directly to their peers in the General Assembly.[57] In addition, the annual event provides national leaders with a rare opportunity to conduct bilateral meetings with their counterparts from all over the world. It is in that sense the only high-table platform in international security premised on the equality of sovereign states.

The inclusiveness of the General Assembly and its opening session debate stands in stark contrast to the exclusiveness of the GX summitry, looming large in the early twenty-first century. Originally established in the mid-1970s,

Table 1.1 Institutional Logics of High-Table Diplomacy in International Security

	Multilateral (inclusive)	Minilateral (exclusive)
Formal (binding commitments)	UNSC (ten elected, non-veto member states drawn from all UN countries)	UNSC (five permanent veto member states)
Informal (nonbinding commitments)	UN General Assembly opening session general debate	GX summitry (G7/G8/G20)

GX serial summits were initiated among the world's major economic powers in order to attend to the deficit of energy resources, fluctuating exchange rates, and incoherence in the approach to international trade and macroeconomic management. The summits continued after they had dealt with the upheavals of the 1970s, and their agendas expanded from the setting of parameters for global economic growth to policy coordination on development, the environment, and nontraditional security issues associated with counterterrorism, nonproliferation, and peace building.[58] The GX summitry, whether taking place in the original G7, the G8 (from 1998 to 2014), or the G20 (after 2009) format, today constitutes the informal minilateral high table par excellence. Its exclusive character is reflected in that the name itself indicates that "the club" refuses to accept additional members.

The Overlapping Practices of High-Table Diplomacy

The study of the UNSC, the GX summitry, and the diplomatic activities that accompany them has so far paid little attention to the formality-informality nexus of institutional arrangements or that of traditional-nontraditional security. In fact, most studies examining diplomacy within either the UN system or the GX summitry have had very little overlap. One reason is presumably a facile academic compartmentalization of research that relates to the apparent thematic differentiation in that the UN and its Security Council are charged with peace and security as their primary objective, whereas the GX summitry is geared toward finance and institutional governance of the global political economy. Consequently, separate communities of observers and scholars are preoccupied with the principal two high tables and the institutional arrangements that emanate from them.

However, a quick glance at the fourth column of Table 1.2, in relation to columns 1–3, suffices to suggest that a strong, albeit implicit, connection

Table 1.2 Political Entities Seated at High Tables, Informal and Formal

	G20	G8	P5	E10 2009–14	Nuclear powers	GDP (billion $)
United States	X	X	X		X	16,770
China	X		X		X	9,240
Japan	X	X		X		4,920
Germany	X	X		X		3,730
France	X	X	X		X	2,806
United Kingdom	X	X	X			2,678
Brazil	X			X		2,246
Italy	X	X				2,149
Russia	X	X	X		X	2,097
India	X			X	X	1,877
Canada	X	X				1,827
Australia	X			X		1,560
Rep. of Korea	X			X		1,305
Mexico	X			X		1,261
Indonesia	X					868.3
Turkey	X			X		822.1
Saudi Arabia	X					748.4
Argentina	X			X		609.9
South Africa	X			X		350.6
European Union	X	X				17,960

Source: Data from World Bank, *World Development Indicators 2013* (Washington, DC: World Bank, 2013).

between the two sets of institutional arrangements does exist and that attempts to accommodate the aspirations of emerging great powers were redoubled after the 2008–9 financial crisis. How could we otherwise explain that every single G20 country that was not a P5 or a G8 member state in 2009–14 served on the UNSC in the E10 category? Emerging great and middle powers must have (1) actively pursued non-permanent seats on the council, (2) received "clearance" from the P5 countries, and then (3) successfully canvassed the UN General Assembly. This confluence of a perceived shift in informal influence on the part of rising powers with the readiness of the wider UN membership to accommodate formal institutional arrangements cannot have been coincidental. Non-G8 members of the G20 were, in other words, tapped for temporary high-table status in a formal institution immediately after being elevated to the top informal forum.

To briefly elaborate on the formality-informality nexus in relation to this confluence of circumstances, only a few scholars have so far examined the nested informality of highly formalized and rule-driven bodies such as the UNSC. But many of the council's decisions could not have been carried out without commitments by non-P5 and non-council UN member states to fund, train, and equip specific missions.[59] Conversely, the literature on GX constellations of bodies has, with few exceptions, not explored the nested formality of institutional arrangements that predominantly operate as informal settings, notwithstanding the fact that serial summits have existed for four decades. For instance, this neglect pertains to the function of Sherpas serving as liaison officers between national leaders and across government offices, as well as of the quasi-permanent working groups associated with serial summits. In this study, in other words, I assume that there is a broader significance to these features of high-table diplomacy—especially as they concern major challenges in the realm of international security.

A substantial share of diplomatic institutions is manifestly structured along a formality-informality nexus (or divide), either side of which cannot be reduced to the other. Diplomatic activities would be ineffective, perhaps even inconceivable, without a sometimes rigid, and sometimes fluid, reflexivity between formal and informal settings.[60] High-table diplomacy, as an activity carried out among an exclusive group of countries at the top levels of decision making, can therefore be expected to offer venues where the formality-informality nexus plays out more powerfully than in politically peripheral and less influential institutions. The practice of diplomacy illustrates, contrary to what some analysts suggest, that the formality-informality nexus often encompasses a productive, yet inherently fractious, relationship.[61] In fact, the parallel existence of a predominantly formal institutional arrangement in the realm of international security, the UNSC, and that of an overwhelmingly informal institutional arrangement, the GX summitry, indicates that a historically unique bifurcation of the two types of settings may have arisen in the post-1945 period.

The same can be said for the traditional-nontraditional security nexus, which similarly is reflected in sharp distinctions between institutions dealing with hard military security matters and those that pursue peace and stability through economic, political, and cultural cooperation. The UNSC, NATO, the OSCE, and the OAS evidently belong to the first category, and the Organisation for Economic Co-operation and Development (OECD), the European Union (EU), and ASEAN to the latter. As a general point of departure, both nexuses clearly warrant more penetrating as well as more nuanced analysis than hitherto undertaken if we are to understand the more intricate dynamics of how institutional arrangements operate, not least in the realm of international security.

The overlapping functions of the UNSC and the GX summitry in international security become visible only if we acknowledge a broader view of that realm and avoid assigning the former to a "realist" dimension of diplomacy and the latter to a "liberal" (or narrowly "economic") one. From the vantage point of individual great powers, whether they are incumbent or emerging, these are two different instruments that need to be approached according to their inherent characteristic traits. By conceptually and analytically separating the two sets of institutional arrangements, outside observers run the risk of not fully grasping the combined contribution to the patterns of interaction that make up contemporary international relations. More specifically, they will inevitably have a difficult time identifying and appreciating the rise of the phenomenon of minilateralism and high-table diplomacy in the early twenty-first century.

The Analytical Framework

The primary layer of conceptual building blocks of this study consists of high-table diplomacy, the formality-informality nexus, and the traditional-nontraditional security nexus. As stated at the outset, a basic objective of the research is to acquaint the reader with this conceptual approach to contemporary international relations, which interprets recent developments through an analytical prism that combines power- and rule-oriented theoretical perspectives. In analyzing the GX summitry and the UNSC as horizontally organized, communicating vessels, a nascent phenomenon in international relations is rendered visible.

If "two-table diplomacy" was not so easily confused with the vertically organized "two-level games," famously coined by Robert Putnam, it might have been an alternative conceptualization to that chosen here.[62] But another semantic advantage of "high-table diplomacy" is that the concept does not focus exclusively on deliberations at the very apex of the institutional arrangements and allows for considering practices within the subsidiary organs of the UNSC and working groups directly associated with serial summits. Especially when restricted to the realm of international security, the "club character" of the institutional arrangements and the inevitable overlap in deliberations cannot be ignored. An executive council of great powers is the "prototype of a modern international organization," as Claude famously stated more than half a century ago.[63] A quality of the contemporary G20, Andrew F. Cooper and Mo Jongryn wrote in 2012, is that it "stands out . . . as the first authentically 'high table' forum that is global in composition."[64]

A more specific theoretical ambition informing this study, as discussed previously, relates to the character of institutional arrangements in this field. Several contributions to the literature in recent years have sought to describe the relationship between formal and informal governance across a variety of institutional arrangements, but also through in-depth studies devoted to specific international organizations, issues areas, or instances of institutional transformation.[65] The findings in such contributions suggest that major actors are often well aware of the opportunities and limitations of pursuing either formal or informal governance when working with counterparts and that they, on a case-by-case basis, seek to appropriately balance solutions for the purpose at hand. In formal governance actors have incentives to create collective oversight procedures and joint control over information and to enter into binding commitments, features that increase transaction costs but at the same time open up opportunities for repeated action and effective enforcement. In informal governance, conversely, actors are encouraged to maintain state autonomy, political flexibility, control over information, and thereby to limit transaction costs and bureaucratic complexity and to prefer nonbinding agreements.[66]

The potential for binding commitments, and the implications stemming from that potential, thus critically differentiates formal from informal governance. Notably, however, an acclaimed study examining formal and informal governance found hybrid institutional forms to be the norm in some of the most influential institutional arrangements of today. Randall Stone, the study's author, argued that hybridity was attractive to such arrangements "because they make it possible to accommodate the interests of both strong and weak powers."[67] Having juxtaposed the International Monetary Fund (IMF) against the World Trade Organization (WTO) and the EU, Stone derived his conclusion from the theoretically grounded notion that the interests of weaker powers are generally protected through formal governance mechanisms. He also noted that past students had tended to overlook the significance of informal governance mechanisms in formalized international organizations, writing them off as aberrations or contingent on specific factors or personalities affecting the process.[68] Within formal organizations that regularly delegate authority to diplomats or civil servants, Stone was able to demonstrate that informal governance mechanisms are in fact quite prominent, providing rich illustrations from case studies of the IMF, WTO, and EU.[69]

Stone's observations regarding the significance of informal governance lodged within formal institutional arrangements represent a critical assumption in this study. Yet the author's view on hybridity, reconciling formal governance with informal institutions, will nevertheless be treated as one of two rival propositions in this study, called the "hybridity proposition." The rival

Hybridity   Differentiation

<——>

Figure 1.2. Formality versus Informality

proposition is inspired by the work of Philip Selznick in the mid-twentieth century and emphasizes the tension inherent in the formality-informality nexus that continually reproduces the differentiation of institutional status. Selznick, in his pathbreaking work on local social and political organization in Tennessee, clearly viewed this nexus and the reproduction of differentiation as central to our understanding of institutions and as more complex and difficult to manage than organizational charts in manuals and textbooks are able to convey. According to Selznick the informal structures of institutions are easily overlooked but always at a cost, since those informal structures are "at once indispensable to and consequential for the formal system of delegation and control itself."[70] Hence this will be referred to as the "differentiation proposition."

Building on the insights of Stone and of Selznick, this study therefore aims to take us inside the formality-informality nexus and to examine how predominantly formal and informal governance settings are related to the form and content of security-related diplomacy. I will explore nested informality at the "political level" of actors who seek to creatively exploit the opportunities and ambiguities within a predominantly formal setting of high-table diplomacy (such as unofficial consultations between political leaders or trusted top-level officials and senior diplomats seeking to manage internal rules or membership issues or to de-escalate a crisis while formal deliberations are ongoing) and at the "technical level" of governance in formal settings (for instance, when members of a specialized unit within a particular institutional arrangement try to establish common ground on a procedure or a contested legal passage).[71]

The opposite side of the formality-informality nexus is represented by predominantly informal settings of high-table diplomacy. This dimension of the study will thus pay equal attention to the analysis of nested formality at the corresponding levels of governance in informal settings. This pertains in part to the wider set of legal and political principles and agreements in which informal governance takes place (such as the norm of national sovereignty or the 1949 Geneva Conventions) and in part to highly routinized practices established for handling certain issues within informal settings of high-table diplomacy (for instance, the holding of regular, agenda-based working group meetings among national government officials specializing in antiterrorist financing).

A second specific theoretical ambition of this study concerns the relationship between nontraditional and traditional concepts of security. Contributions to the literature on planning, decision making, and implementation of public policy in adjacent issue areas suggest that the impact of practices may be bolstered through mutually reinforcing measures.[72] This is especially the case when institutional arrangements are patchy and need to be supplemented by networks of professionals and reference groups that share an outlook and perception of problems and solutions.[73] In areas that are contentious or highly complicated, as Keohane and Victor point out, states are typically "highly uncertain about the gains they will accrue and their exposure to risks from regulation."[74] In the realm of international security, where there is little room or appetite for horizontal policy coordination based on hierarchy or markets, networks involving government officials and experts who seek parallel or joint solutions to problems using their common professional outlook are often the most promising approach.[75]

As in the case of the formality-informality nexus, I will contrast two rival propositions, one of which says that a separation of roles has evolved by which the UNSC caters to traditional security that involves the management of conflicts involving military violence and the GX summitry to a range of nontraditional challenges. Following a contemporary functionalist understanding of international institutions, I therefore propose to call this the "complementarity proposition."[76] With the G20 taking over several of the tasks previously performed by the G7/G8, it could be argued that separation of roles should be enhanced so as to make the informal summitry add value to international security institutions by handling issues that otherwise may not be dealt with. The inherent flexibility, adaptability, and non-transparency of GX activities would from this vantage point constitute competitive advantages.

The rival proposition regarding nontraditional and traditional security is the "contestation proposition." This proposition posits that the boundary between the two is constantly being contested or undermined by stakeholders in a particular institutional arrangement seeking to shift the ground so that maximum credit goes to them and maximum blame to the other side.[77] Within the framework of existing international security institutions, it is a well-established notion that the UNSC is criticized for doing too much and too little at the same time, while the major countries capable of unblocking its potential accept virtually no part of the criticism for its malfunctioning. The GX summitry, meanwhile, is often a clearinghouse for major political initiatives both within and outside the UN.

Complementarity

Contestation

Figure 1.3. Traditional versus Nontraditional Security

The basic logic of the rival propositions of complementarity and contestation resides in the stark contrast in collective legitimation available to the principal two high tables. The GX summitry has no basis of legitimacy in a founding act or universal membership but has to gain collective legitimation through practical and concrete accomplishments. The UNSC, by virtue of its strong formal standing at the center of international relations, sustains a high level of collective legitimation regardless of any particular instance of accomplishment. Needless to say, this does not make the council immune to criticism of poor performance or wasteful use of resources.

The existence or absence of a tendency to move issues, or entire sets of issues, between the two high tables is expected to help us settle the matter. If what the literature has called "forum shopping" or "forum shifting" is a phenomenon that great powers engage in over international security matters—as they typically possess the necessary leverage to mold the diplomatic process—then the contestation proposition appears to be the more plausible one.[78] Contestation would, in other words, be affirmed by a government's recurrent search for a suitable venue at which its own preferences are likely to be realized in an international agreement or set of rules. But if great and middle powers allow for a gradual separation of roles between the GX summitry and the UNSC, avoiding overt or tacit disputes over the proper arena for addressing security challenges, then the complementarity proposition is validated.

In this study several research objectives are thus pursued in parallel. Introducing concepts that have the potential to recalibrate our viewpoint, above all what is referred to as "high-table diplomacy," is one such objective. Another is to contribute to theoretical advancement, especially by adjudicating between rival propositions: hybridity versus differentiation regarding the formality-informality nexus and complementarity versus contestation pertaining to nontraditional and traditional concepts of security. A third research objective is normative in character, potentially transcending factual circumstances and geared toward a broader question: namely, does high-table diplomacy provide a promising solution to complex governance issues beyond the realm of international security? As a corollary, is the theory of a "stakeholdership of the few" plausible?

Subordinated to the objective of exploring high-table diplomacy, finally, the study draws on the analytical themes of polarity, prestige, and process, which will be comprehensively outlined in chapter 2. Each of the concepts represents an individual premise of the broader argument, as well as an analytical theme to be deployed at different stages of the analysis, and will help examine ways in which the relevant policy areas are organized in international arrangements that address international security challenges. Whereas polarity is conventionally to be found in general arguments about the distribution of power in a region or in the entire international system, here it is employed to gauge how high-table platforms are affected by changing relations among great powers. Prestige is intended to capture the intensity of ambition on the part of actors involved in such changing power relations, with real implications for how institutional arrangements associated with international security are shaped. The term "process," finally, turns our focus toward specific administrative, political, and diplomatic practices in the realm of international security, as well as to the problem-solving capacity of such institutional arrangements.

Put differently, if there is real purchase in the concept of high-table diplomacy, the institutional arrangements and the most consequential decisions made by great powers should be mutually related in more than one way. As outlined previously, the expectation is to find considerable correspondence between the nature of great-power politics and constantly evolving institutional arrangements. Changes in the underlying global power configuration (polarity) of international relations need to resonate with the political sensitivities associated with influential institutional arrangements (prestige), which in turn influence the incentive structure for addressing and resolving major transnational problems (process) for the benefit of stakeholders and the world community at large. In other words, polarity, prestige, and process need to be aligned with institutional arrangements in international security if they are to be sufficiently robust.

Organization of the Book

The rest of the book is organized as follows. Chapter 2, "Great-Power Diplomacy and International Security in Historical Context," revisits the history of diplomacy in order to sketch a background to great-power bargaining at the high tables of nineteenth-century Europe and the creation of the UNSC and the GX summitry in the twentieth century. It goes on to discuss the resurgence of high-table diplomacy at the time of a sharp downturn in the world economy as a means to coordinate the crisis management efforts of major powers seeking to affect demand and supply, monetary policy, and trade flows. In paving the way for subsequent chapters, it introduces polarity, prestige, and process as heuristically justified analytical themes. This introduction purposefully draws on recent scholarship but also on fruitful and undeservedly neglected theoretical contributions from the 1950s and early 1960s. The latter, many of which grapple with the doubling of UN member states between 1950 and 1965, were penned at the cusp of decolonization and the debate over UN Charter revisions pertaining to the regulatory framework of the UNSC. The chapter ends with methodological remarks on case selection, empirical evidence, and the analytical techniques by which high-table diplomacy is examined, including a belated justification of the plausibility probe reported in the introduction.

Chapter 3 is the first of three addressing high-table diplomacy in 2009–14 in the realm of international security and is titled "Conflict Management." This chapter primarily deals with the central role of the UNSC in responding to threats to international peace and security, in accordance with the UN Charter and the general rules and principles that apply to diplomacy and international law. The investigation takes us through a series of international conflicts that became the subject of UNSC deliberations in one way or another, some being handled in formal meetings and others via informal groups set up in conjunction with a particular set of problems or a geographic region. In the latter type of format, the institutional arrangements of the GX summitry played into the diplomatic process at the UNSC, for instance, by paving the way for the NATO-led military action in Libya of 2011 but blocking a similar intervention in Syria. For high-table-level decisions that set aside national sovereignty in order to pursue the loftier goal of international peace and security to carry weight, it would appear, the formal legitimacy of the UNSC is difficult to substitute with another type of arrangement.

Chapter 4 examines another policy area of international security, namely, "Counterterrorism Cooperation," in 2009–14. This chapter analyzes the recent reinforcement of financial controls initially advanced by the G7, expanded by the UNSC following the 9/11 attacks against the United States, and then made part of the broad agenda of GX summits. Whereas the G7 and the UNSC had set up a system geared toward thwarting transnational money laundering and terrorist financing, the arrangements put in place successively encouraged the integration of financial controls into the regular procedures conducted by national and international supervisory organs, creating an arrangement equally effective for addressing large-scale tax evasion as for combating organized crime. It is striking how well the council arrangement, with a Counter-Terrorism Committee (CTC) under its auspices regularly interacting with national governments at its core, was grafted onto a transnational arrangement that originally combatted money laundering through enhanced transparency in the financial sector.

Chapter 5 is called "Climate Change Mitigation" and examines the daunting challenge of climate change and the way it intersects with a broad understanding of international security, also in 2009–14. While UN conferences on climate change and the environment over several decades helped raise awareness of the problem, it took the UNSC until July 20, 2011, to expressly recognize the existence of climate change as a potential threat to international peace and security. The GX summitry, meanwhile, engaged in a series of programs aimed at mitigating the effects of ongoing climate change, as well as transitioning to energy production that relies on renewable and carbon-free energy sources. If formalized procedures, established practices, and veto rights exert a constraining effect on the council in this policy area, the very absence of such strictures helped generate political impulses in the context of GX summits. The question remains whether formal or informal settings and governance, or a combination of both, will be useful to prepare for, and respond to, rising challenges in this policy area.

The last section, "Conclusions," returns to the theoretical and empirical questions asked at the outset, in this chapter, paying particular attention to the two sets of rival propositions. It does so by interpreting the findings from the preceding three chapters containing analyses of separate policy areas, including the overall pattern of attention to international security issues raised at the annual general debates at the UN. The emphasis of the section is nevertheless on eliciting theoretical implications from findings regarding high-table diplomacy and the juxtaposition of institutional settings and diplomatic practices prevalent at the UNSC and the GX summitry, respectively. The chapter ends by teasing out lessons from using polarity, prestige, and process as the overarching analytical themes of the volume and by responding to the normative question whether high-table diplomacy and minilateralism represent the solution, or at least a significant part of the solution, to complex governance challenges that the world is confronting today.

NOTES

1. Berridge, *Diplomacy*, 43–44.

2. Ibid., 167–69.

3. Naim, "Minilateralism," 135–36. Another term in the same vein is "plurilateralism."

4. Graber, *Crisis Diplomacy*; Richardson, *Great Powers*.

5. Agha et al., *Track-II Diplomacy*.

6. Risse-Kappen, "Long-Term Future"; MacFarlane and Weiss, "United Nations, Regional Organisations," 277–95.

7. Prantl, *UN Security Council*.

8. C. Smith, *Politics and Process*, especially 223–46.

9. The term "nested" is derived from Tsebelis, *Nested Games*, and the adaptation by Karen Alter and Sophie Meunier, "Nested and Competing Regimes."

10. "Interview with: Sergio de Mello," United Nations Oral History, Dag Hammarskjold Library, May 5, 1998, http://www.unmultimedia.org/oralhistory/2013/03/mello-sergio-vieira-de.

11. Dewar Viscarra, "Exercising Responsibility."

12. Franck and Nolte, "Good Offices Function," 143–82.

13. Crocker, Hampson, and Aall, *Managing Global Chaos*; Whitfield, *Friends Indeed?*; Iji, "Contact Group Diplomacy."

14. McLaughlin Mitchell and Hensel, "International Institutions and Compliance."

15. Adibe, "The Liberian Conflict"; Williams and Bellamy, "Who's Keeping the Peace?"

16. Gartner and Bercovitch, "Overcoming Obstacles to Peace."

17. Touval, "Mediator's Flexibility"; Manning and Malbrough, "Bilateral Donors and Aid Conditionality."

18. Sievers and Daws, *Procedure of the UN Security Council*, 94–97.

19. Author's interviews, 2010–14; interlocutors listed in the appendix. The interviews were conducted with senior national diplomats who had experience with the work of the UN Security Council, along with a handful of UN Secretariat officials and scholars specializing on council affairs, between 2010 and 2014. For details see "Methodological Remarks" in chapter 2.

20. Paul, "Arria Formula."

21. Ekpe, "Intelligence Assets," 379–80.

22. Weitz, *War and Governance*.

23. Derviş and Drysdale, "G-20 Summit at Five," 10.

24. Hameiri and Jones, "Politics and Governance," 462.

25. Ibid., 462–63.

26. Ibid., 465.

27. Drezner, "Power and Perils."

28. Hale, Held, and Young, *Gridlock*, 4.

29. Keohane, *Neorealism and Its Critics*, 3.

30. Ruggie, "Anatomy of an Institution," 11.

31. Keohane, "Contingent Legitimacy of Multilateralism."

32. Brummer, *Minilateralism*, 1–2.

33. Oye, "Explaining Cooperation under Anarchy," 21. On group size and effectiveness in general, see Olson, *Collective Action*, 36–42, 53–56.

34. For a critical use of the concept, see Prantl, *UN Security Council*, 221. Prantl, whose pathbreaking work will be cited repeatedly in this study, used minilateralism in 2005 to mean "*ad hoc* groupings appear[ing] as a multilateral gathering with small numbers." Kenneth Oye, Miles Kahler, and Lisa Martin, who discussed the term in the

1980s and 1990s, did not evoke temporality or permanency as a defining feature of mini- or multilateralism. I will follow the latter line of reasoning.

35. Martin, "Rational State Choice of Multilateralism," 99.

36. O'Connor and Griffiths, *Rise of Anti-Americanism*.

37. Murray and Brown, *Multipolarity in the 21st Century*.

38. Gorodetsky, *Russia between East and West*, 3–11; M. A. Smith, *Power in the Changing Global Order*.

39. Zagorski, "Russian Approaches to Global Governance."

40. Morgan, "Multilateralism and Security."

41. The Contact Group created to help resolve the conflicts arising from the dissolution of the former Yugoslavia was composed of six countries, namely, the P5 countries minus China, plus Germany and Italy.

42. Tucker and Hendrickson, "Sources of American Legitimacy."

43. Zarate, *Treasury's War*.

44. Drezner, *System Worked*, 17–33.

45. This is consistent with Stone's prediction that the United States, the preeminent power facing relative decline over time, is compelled to act with greater constraint in order to maintain the legitimacy of international organizations. See Stone, *Controlling Institutions*, 8.

46. Claude, *Changing United Nations*, 73ff; Hurd, *After Anarchy*.

47. Heinbecker, "United Nations and the G20," 243.

48. The "club-like" character of the G20 is highlighted in Badie, *La diplomatie de connivence*.

49. Shorr and Wright, "G20 and Global Governance," 188.

50. Larionova, Hajnal, and Kirton, *G-X Summitry*.

51. Malone, *UN Security Council*; Doyle and Sambanis, *Making War and Building Peace*.

52. Martin, "Rational State Choice," 99.

53. Author's interviews.

54. Mahbubani, "Permanent and Elected Council Members," 256.

55. Simma, *Charter of the United Nations*, 404.

56. Some 130 UN member states have served, and around sixty have not, in the non-permanent member category.

57. Peterson, *UN General Assembly*, 2–5, 78–85; Baturo, Dasandi, and Mikhaylov, "Analysis of State Preferences."

58. Putnam and Bayne, *Hanging Together*; Hajnal, *G8 System and the G20*; Yamashita, "Group of 8."

59. Prantl, *UN Security Council*.

60. For an overview of "diplomacy without diplomatic relations," see Berridge, *Diplomacy*, 207–52.

61. For authors who view informal rules as deeply problematic and disruptive of legitimate institutions, see Helmke and Levitsky, "Informal Institutions and Comparative Politics"; Cooper and Farooq, "BRICS"; Kleine, "Informal Governance."

62. Putnam, "Diplomacy and Domestic Politics."

63. Claude, *Swords into Ploughshares*, 24.

64. Cooper and Jongryn, "Middle 7," 107.

65. The theoretical reasoning underlying these claims will be further developed in chapter 2.

66. Vabulas and Snidal, "Organization without Delegation," 216–17. For ongoing research in this vein, see papers presented by Charles Barclay Roger and Daniel Odinius presented at the Annual Convention of the International Studies Association (ISA) in New Orleans, February 18–21, 2015, respectively titled "Varieties of Networks: Agents and Agency in Transnational Cooperation" and "Between Forum Shopping and Forum Shifting: The Relationship of Institutionalized Summits and Formal International Intergovernmental Organizations."

67. Stone, *Controlling Institutions*, 33.

68. Ibid., 207.

69. Ibid., 32.

70. Selznick, *TVA and the Grass Roots*, 251.

71. For "complex nesting" approaches, see Slobodchikoff, *Strategic Cooperation*, 20–26.

72. Peters, "Concepts and Theories"; Bernstein and Hannah, "Coherence."

73. Houseman and Zaelke, "Making Trade"; Soda, Usai, and Zaheer, "Network Memory."

74. Keohane and Victor, "Regime Complex for Climate Change," 9.

75. Eistrup-Sangiovanni, "Network Theory and Security Governance."

76. The "complementarity proposition" is loosely based on Vabulas and Snidal, "Organization without Delegation."

77. Sabatier, "Advocacy Coalition Framework."

78. "Forum shopping" denotes the selection of a decision-making forum likely to produce the optimal outcome on an international issue. "Forum shifting" refers to the practice of altering earlier decisions on a particular meeting or deliberation format after major stakeholders agree that another venue is likely to produce a more beneficial (or less damaging) outcome, from their vantage point. For an influential account, see Drezner, *All Politics Is Global*, 63–64.

Great-Power Diplomacy and International Security in Historical Context

The concept of diplomacy has spawned a vast, rich literature penned by scholars, diplomats, and individuals who combine the latter two professional identities. This heterogeneity of literature encompasses several competing approaches to the study of diplomacy, each highlighting a different set of properties and characteristics of the phenomenon at hand. At the same time there is relatively little controversy about what constitutes modern diplomatic practice, which emerged out of a standard created by European practitioners of the profession over the past four to five centuries.[1]

The tendency to treat as universally valid the practices of asset-rich modern powers is well documented, as is the bias toward the Western Hemisphere inherent in this scholarship. A related trait of the literature is to draw almost exclusively, when providing examples and illustrations of diplomatic practice, on the nineteenth- and twentieth-century diplomatic history of Europe and North America. To be sure, over the past two centuries the leaders and representatives of Western powers were the preeminent diplomatic actors, whereas many developing countries sought to emulate the former in style as well as in substance.[2] But, as an evolving genre of diplomatic history is beginning to demonstrate, there are certainly older non-European precedents worth taking into account.[3] One reason for exploring the latter is that the Western bias of the literature, no longer perceived as generic and universally valid, can be relativized by including other experiences. Another reason is that the rising great powers of non-Western origin are likely to utilize more of their distinctive legacies as repertoire while moving forward to make their mark on twenty-first-century political developments.[4]

Only a very modest attempt to include that broader heritage is made in the following pages. As a conceptual starting point, it is assumed that the established academic discourse on diplomacy, though clearly perpetuating its European legacy, will serve us sufficiently well. Three partly diverging, though mostly overlapping, concepts of diplomacy are employed to capture the variety of practices of professional diplomats in general and of great powers in particular. The three concepts emphasize diplomacy as negotiation, as representation, and lastly, as the employment of leverage. With regard to the latter dimension, which is closely associated with the narrower notion of great-power diplomacy, it is important to not fully accept the recurring claim of many scholar-practitioners that diplomacy is wholly divorced from the use of force.

A consistent and eloquent advocate of the notion that the core of diplomatic activity constitutes negotiation is Geoff Berridge, the author of *Diplomacy: Theory and Practice.* In the fourth edition of this standard work of reference, published in 2010, Berridge explains that diplomacy "consists of communication between officials designed to promote foreign policy either by formal agreement or tacit adjustment."[5] As an intellectual lineage of this concept, he approvingly cites the seventeenth-century French cardinal Richelieu's dictum that diplomacy is best described as a process of "continuous negotiation" (*négociation continuelle*).[6] Unlike several other authors, though, Berridge does not hold that this activity is restricted to the diplomatic profession or to conventional channels of communication.

In the view of Paul Sharp, another astute observer of the field, diplomacy primarily denotes representation. This does not exclusively mean representation of an official, formally adopted government position but, more broadly, the representation of interests, power, ideas, and less tangibly, acts that express political symbolism.[7] The concept of diplomacy as representation allows for perceiving international institutions as stages or arenas of national diplomatic initiatives, but also for accepting that institutions, in turn, empower national governments. In this respect Sharp, like Berridge, is skeptical of defining diplomatic thought and practice too narrowly, precisely since the activities associated with the profession constantly undergo change. Whereas some scholars profess that diplomacy is "whatever diplomats do," Sharp insists that this view simply turns an important and unavoidable conceptual disagreement into a dispute about who belongs to that professional community, without producing more clarity.[8]

Diplomacy as the employment of leverage is a concept that, contrary to the previous two, lacks support in the 1961 Vienna Convention on Diplomatic Relations, the document which for the last half century provided an authoritative terminology on the subject. This concept runs counter to the principles of sovereignty and equality of states, but without it the study of diplomatic practice would make much less sense. Attempts have been made in academic literature to try to capture the "raw power" element of diplomatic practice, such as in the terms "coercive diplomacy," "gunboat diplomacy," or "big stick diplomacy." Some scholars have resorted to the metaphors of magnetic poles or a scale/balance to pin down the systemic ramifications of a diplomacy that chiefly utilizes leverage, a feature that tends to be accentuated in situations of great asymmetry of power or antagonistic sentiments among political actors. Also, Berridge, who considers diplomacy the most important institution underpinning the society of states, clearly accepts such insights when he acknowledges that the latter only holds when its impact is considered "together with the balance of power."[9]

Great-Power Diplomacy

Leverage is what sets one category of political entities apart from the others in the society of states and by the same token what creates prerequisites for a diplomacy that takes this differentiation into account. The basic analytical rationale of the term "great power" is that it denotes a category of prominent and asset-rich political entities that in decisive ways shape their own environment and in relation to which small powers may need to act with caution, or even deference. The term "great power," in other words, cannot operate without an implicit typology that entails at least two components, the second representing the category of small (or lesser) powers.

In international relations scholarship of the second half of the twentieth century, the typology was frequently three or four tiered, including superpower at the top of the hierarchy and middle power as an intermediate category.[10] Although superpower is a category that in several dimensions of leverage still applies to the United States, it will be argued later that the use of this term today—in contrast to during the Cold War and early post–Cold War period—warrants qualification. For the purposes of this study, the original straightforward dichotomy distinguishing great and small powers provides the overwhelmingly important distinction between platforms that form an integral part of institutional arrangements here referred to as high tables and those that do not. When taking current and anticipated changes in polarity into account, though, a more differentiated view is justified from an analytical standpoint.

Certainly, the concept of great power stands out as the most frequently employed element of any such typology, today as well as in the past. Great power is a concept that students of international relations have used ever since that discipline was established in the early twentieth century, as it resonates with a terminology that some say existed as far back as in ancient antiquity. *The Peloponnesian War* by Thucydides, dated to 413 BC, famously deployed an analytical distinction between great and small powers. If great powers in this conventional sense are a constant in diplomatic history, the interplay among them has not always dominated the nature of international relations. Historical periods in which great powers are said to have thrived are those characterized by "regional multipolarity" and absence of dominant empires, such as the Greek Mediterranean world of the fifth and fourth centuries BC, India of the seventeenth century, and Europe of the seventeenth, eighteenth, and nineteenth centuries.[11]

In the context of diplomacy, great powers' abundant assets build on the level and type of leverage that they are able to wield, which in turn enhances their prospects of succeeding in terms of effective negotiation and representation.[12] That is not to say that diplomatic activities cannot have an impact without such leverage, as in such circumstances they largely rely on powers of persuasion, bargaining skills, and ideas and symbols of what national leaders and professional diplomats can bring to bear on a political process.[13] But most observers would likely agree that plentiful resources in an aggregate sense constitute the major asset in many circumstances and therefore an indispensable prerequisite for a diplomatic outcome that political principals will find acceptable.

In international relations scholarship more widely, diplomacy is surprisingly often not expressly listed as an important variable or institutional arrangement with significant impact on world affairs. In this respect Hedley Bull and followers of the "English school" he helped establish were among the few who awarded considerable weight to diplomacy as a generic phenomenon. But Bull was also adamant that diplomacy and international law are only two of several system-wide features that maintain the international order. Two additional such institutions are war and the balance of power. Beyond those phenomena he highlighted the role played by the special position of great powers "by maintaining local systems of hegemony within which order is imposed from above, and by collaborating to manage the global balance of power and, from time to time, impose their joint will on others."[14]

Great-power diplomacy, in this view, is not primarily about acting in accordance with an abstract balance of power but about great powers paying attention to systemic stability and minimizing unnecessary friction between political actors, large and small. Unlike many accounts suggesting that it will be sufficient for the maintenance of international order if great powers largely conduct their business in a reactive, or "defensive," manner, Bull seemed to prescribe a proactive engagement derived from a sense of responsibility or duty. In managing relations among great powers in particular, he argued, decision makers and diplomats cannot stand back but must actively pursue stability and security in world affairs.[15]

Needless to say, not every great power will consistently heed this somewhat abstract sense of responsibility. Historically speaking, though, examples of an informal type of "concert diplomacy" can be found at the regional level. Archetypical is the post-Napoleonic arrangement on the European continent, which with few exceptions helped sustain peace between great powers from 1805 to the mid-nineteenth century with residual influence lasting to 1914.[16] If a more commercially oriented arrangement is accepted as an instance of "concert diplomacy," the fifteenth-century Islamic diplomacy that underpinned the durable trading network connecting the Persian Gulf to the eastern part of the Indian Ocean deserves mention. In this case Persian merchants organized customs houses from Basra to the coast of Indonesia and operated as agents of a sophisticated diplomacy that helped sustain a vast commercial system, with trade routes extending from the Atlantic Ocean, by way of Portugal, to eastern China.[17]

Another example of a loose arrangement with similarities to "concert diplomacy" is that of East Asia from the thirteenth to the eighteenth centuries, almost consistently characterized by peaceful trade and cultural exchange. Although its stability often is attributed to China's regional influence during much of this period, scholars have more recently pointed out that there was neither a balance-of-power system nor a full-blown hegemony in which peripheral political entities in a real sense were subordinated to the desires of Beijing emperors. In the view of David Kang, China issued official documents that demanded deference to the empire but the system "did not involve much loss of independence, as these states were largely free to run their internal affairs as they saw fit, and these nations could also conduct foreign policy independently from China."[18] The assertion that China maintained a hierarchical system in East Asia for six centuries is also misleading when it comes to territorial integrity, Kang argues, since "boundaries and borders were relatively fixed, and nations did not significantly change during the time period under review."[19]

From that vantage point the main differences between the post-Napoleonic Vienna arrangement and that of East Asia consisted in the European great powers' explicitly agreeing not to alter borders against the will of their "peers" and communicating on points of actual or potential controversy with some regularity, whereas their Asian counterparts operated on an implicit agreement to restrain their activities and not upset the regional political system. In either case, however, great-power diplomacy gave rise to institutional arrangements that served to enhance commercial relations and preserve the status quo. No doubt this resonates with Bull's understanding of great-power responsibility.

It is probably fair to say that the preoccupation with status quo and regional stability is a characteristic trait of much, though not all, great-power diplomacy. Arguably, in regional contexts middle powers should also have significant leverage. What much classical theorizing about great powers neglects is the leverage that derives from incumbency in such platforms, together with the practical benefits it yields in intelligence and political clout. In this study incumbency in high-table platforms will be treated as an asset and property of leverage and a justification for applying generous operational definitions of great- and middle-power status. Membership in either of the two main high tables examined here is thus a necessary, as well as sufficient, requirement to be classified as a great or middle power.

Distinguishing great powers from small states and, to a lesser extent, from middle powers does not necessarily mean ignoring a host of issues relating to political autonomy, legitimacy, and participation that any categorization implies. Nor does it deny the considerable contributions that small countries and their representatives have made to the establishment of international institutions in the realm of public and private law, technical standardization, and dissemination of norms. But a longer historical gaze suggests that the formal equality of sovereign states may in fact have peaked during the twentieth century, following the deep self-doubt of leaders of major countries brought about by devastating wars in the first half of that century. Indeed, as Inis Claude noted in the mid-1960s, it was the international conferences devoted to peace and humanitarian causes in the early twentieth century that first "ushered in the heyday of the small states."[20]

For the purposes of this research, in other words, the term "great powers" will in a straightforward fashion refer to nine of the countries included in the G20.[21] These are countries that, roughly speaking, belong to the top 5 percent of the most asset-rich nations on Earth. This is a significantly more generous operational definition than that used in some international relations research, here justified by the analytical focus on minilateralist institutional arrangements and the position that countries occupy within them. Within that category, as mentioned previously, there is nevertheless a need to differentiate between two tiers: there are the incumbent great powers of the first tier, corresponding to the P5 member states in the UNSC, and a second tier made up of the countries viewed as serious candidates to be added to that exclusive group. In light of their large populations and considerable economic and political clout, as well as acknowledgment that they are top contenders for permanent seats on the UNSC (widely recognized by many UN member states), India, Japan, Brazil, and Germany will be viewed as second-tier great powers. The

Table 2.1 Great and Middle Powers

1st-tier great powers	United States, United Kingdom, France, China, Russia
2nd-tier great powers	Germany, Japan, India, Brazil
Middle powers	Indonesia, South Africa, South Korea, Argentina, Italy, Canada, Australia, Turkey, Mexico, Saudi Arabia

rest of the "G-powers" consequently belong to a third tier of actors involved in high-table diplomacy: the middle powers.

Middle powers is a category that remains theoretically less developed and that during the Cold War period often became submerged under what Buzan referred to as the "overlay" generated by bipolar antagonism, including in the work of international relations scholars. One important exception to this rule is Keohane's useful conceptualization of middle powers as political entities whose leadership recognizes they cannot act effectively alone but may exert systemic influence when closely collaborating with another sizable state or operating via international institutions.[22] In the past few years, several scholars have sought to reestablish the term in the context of a global power shift in the making. Some authors have focused on the political dynamics associated with the inclusion of emerging powers in the GX summitry,[23] whereas others have tried to identify a suitable level at which middle and small powers can be differentiated on the basis of their capacities.[24]

At the other end of the spectrum, China is today unequivocally a first-tier great power. This is certainly due to its P5 incumbency, though it is also because nonparticipation in the G7/G8 is less consequential following the upgrade of the G20 to the main forum for coordinating macroeconomic policies. In staying true to the analytical focus on international security institutions, I have also resisted the temptation to elevate the United States to a separate category above the others. Although the informal clout wielded by Washington in and of itself would justify such a modification of the framework, the concept of high-table diplomacy highlights the power that grows not out of the barrel of a gun but out of political resources that are magnified—yet also reined in—by a deep commitment to international institutions. That commitment is, quite clearly, not seriously questioned by any of the here enumerated great powers, including the United States.

But before turning to the analysis of the 2009–14 period, a final component of the framework needs to be introduced. International relations theory provides a rich menu from which useful concepts and theories can be selected and heuristically employed in relation to a research problem. For the purposes of this book, I will draw on three theoretically grounded notions that resonate with well-established expectations of how international relations change as the influence of second-tier great powers and middle powers grows as well as how the leverage of the second most asset-rich first-tier country, China, begins to close in on that of the United States. According to a fairly substantial body of literature, a leveling of the playing field in terms of power relations ought to have a number of implications, among which three are here singled out as particularly important analytical themes: polarity, prestige, and process.

Polarity

The first and straightforward implication is that there will be a shift in polarity as the relative power of emerging great powers becomes closer to that of the preeminent, first-tier great power. Even if the epistemological status of the concept of polarity is deeply problematic, the term belongs to one of the most enduring terminologies in the study of international relations.[25] Together with "hegemony" and the "balance of power," "polarity" has accompanied the study of international relations from antiquity to the Italian Renaissance, and further to the emergence of modern political ideologies in the era of postrevolutionary France, and subsequently to the incorporation of natural scientific terminology into the social sciences in the twentieth century. In its contemporary understanding, moreover, the concept of polarity cannot easily be disentangled from that of a balance of power or from the magnetism metaphor that many associate with the concept.[26]

"Polarity," "balance of power," and "hegemony" are all terms that can be applied regionally as well as globally. If hegemony presupposes global reach as well as ubiquitous and pervasive influence on politics on the part of a preeminent great power, this is an unusual state of affairs that extends beyond a simple hierarchy. It is a condition that, at least temporarily or partially, must be understood to suspend the workings of the balance of power.[27] A balance of power, on the other hand, is according to a wide variety of international relations scholars virtually always present, as it describes a situation of rivaling interests and mutual projection of power, quite regardless of whether such tensions ever precipitate all-out conflict. Polarity, finally, denotes power relations between the most asset-rich political entities within the system (which can be either regional or global in scope) and the prominence of those entities within it. By the same token, polarity may or may not encompass a condition of hegemony.[28]

Polarity as such is therefore a rather crude analytical instrument, and any theorizing that draws on it needs to take this into consideration.[29] The basic forms that scholars have explored are unipolarity, bipolarity, and multipolarity. Sometimes tripolarity has been added. A highly unusual, early contribution was that of Richard Rosecrance, who in 1966 criticized a number of scholars— and Kenneth Waltz in particular—for unequivocally crediting bipolarity with having a stabilizing influence on world affairs. After he had critically examined the characteristics of both "parent forms," as he put it, Rosecrance advocated a more complex system called "bipolarity-multipolarity," according to which the excesses of either could be avoided. He wrote, "The two major states would act as regulators for conflicts in the external areas; but multipolar states would act as mediators and buffers for conflicts between the bipolar powers. In neither case would conflict be eliminated, but it might be held in check."[30]

Nearly forty years later, Barry Buzan described a very similar notion as one of his two scenarios for a world in which US preeminence is waning. Although the scenario "No superpowers and several great powers" corresponds to symmetrically organized multipolarity, Buzan outlined another possibility that he labeled "Two or three superpowers and few great powers."[31] According to the latter, either the two superpowers would be the United States plus the EU, in an all-liberal constellation of first-tier entities, or they could turn out to be the United States plus China.[32]

More than ten years have passed since Buzan analyzed the top tier of political entities in international relations, and the likelihood of the EU approaching parity with the United States in any power dimension except the size of its economy has in the meantime evolved little, or even diminished, despite a host of efforts to strengthen its foreign, security, and defense arm.[33] The opposite can be said for China. The past decade has thus rendered Buzan's diagnosis of unipolarity somewhat less accurate, while his scenarios seem more plausible. Writing in 2004, notably, Buzan described superpower status in the twenty-first century as a property that relies more on an "ability to create and sustain international societies than on war fighting ability."[34] This was an area in which the United States excelled during the Cold War, and an ability accentuated through the period of dismantling the Soviet-led communist alternative to that leadership, especially the 1990s.

The "ability to sustain" that forms part of this concept of superpower status still appears to be largely intact, as John Ikenberry has explained with respect to the formidable challenge that China would face in the event that—sometime later in the twenty-first century—Beijing might want to refashion the institutional arrangements according to its own preferences.[35] The plethora of international institutions, intergovernmental accords, and arrangements are simply staggering compared with those of previous historical junctures at which major powers in ascent aspired to supremacy in the world order. But the question remains whether even the United States today also finds itself in a position of strength so preeminent that it could, at will, fundamentally redesign the world order. Does the United States still qualify as a superpower in that it wields the "ability to create" another, hypothetical set of institutional arrangements and foist them onto the world?

The question is indeed hypothetical in that Pax Americana was designed to suit US interests in the first place.[36] Yet, today, some observers consider this proposition to be tenuous, suggesting that the United States no longer lives up to Buzan's full criteria for superpower status. Such an assessment further relates to the distinction between two types of unipolarity to which I alluded previously. One is a demanding type of unipolarity, requiring some features of hegemony and an active (or "offensive realist") stance to world affairs. The second type is what David Wilkinson has referred to as "unipolarity without hegemony,"[37] a stance that derives from a set of capabilities that ensure preeminence but not dominance. He writes, "If hegemony is understood as a unipolar configuration of politico-military capability with a structure of influence that matches capability, unipolarity without hegemony is a configuration where the preponderant capability of a single state is not matched by a predominant influence. Such a structure embodies the distinction drawn by Jean-Jacques Rousseau between 'strength' and 'mastery' in *The Social Contract*, where 'the strongest is never strong enough to be always the master.'"[38] Unipolarity without hegemony is a rare historical phenomenon, writes Wilkinson, but not necessarily short-lived in the modern era. Compared with the bipolar system, unipolarity does not encourage escalation to a global "deadly quarrel" and allows for "managing, mediating, settling, localizing, restraining, and containing such wars," as there are no major risks involved in doing so for great powers including the preeminent power.[39] Apparently, this notion resonates closely with describing the United States as the "indispensable nation," a term coined by then–US Secretary of State Madeleine Albright in 1998.

But if there is a slow slide from unipolarity toward multipolarity, under the current conditions of "nuclear peace" and market interdependence as mitigating factors, what would motivate an ascending power to aspire to eclipse the preeminent standing of the non-hegemonic unipolar political unit? In eschewing the functional determinism of the eighteenth- and nineteenth-century versions of balance-of-power theories, as well as of the power transition theory paradigm developed in the late 1950s, what would drive great-power rivalry in the twenty-first century? Energy and trade interests are certainly significant factors, but which social dynamics are implied in, accompany, and possibly even reinforce the "multipolarization" of world affairs?

In Rosecrance's original 1966 article discussing the various properties of bi- and multipolarity, the author argues that the latter potentially provides "the basis for a stable social system" by virtue of its capacity to produce positive as well as negative feedback and that the availability of alternative partners makes it possible to respond in ways other than by military means.[40] At the time Rosecrance did not himself expand the argument to one of social theory, and in this context he deferred to the work of Karl Deutsch and Isaac Singer. In an article published a year earlier, cited by Rosecrance, Deutsch and Singer had noted that multipolarity "affords a greater number of interaction opportunities" and therefore "diminishes the attention paid to other states."[41]

In foreshadowing the constructivist insights that today are rather commonplace,[42] Rosecrance deftly pointed out that polarity shifts profoundly affect the social dimension of international relations. Yet his summary of the argument of Deutsch and Singer misrepresented their theoretical claims in one important respect. Deutsch and Singer specifically asserted that multipolarity reduces the attention that "any nation can devote to any other nation,"[43] which is markedly different from insisting that "other states" do not figure as much in states' considerations and calculations. General insights from the fields of sociology and psychology would instead suggest that a social system without a clear hierarchical structure, that is, one in which a whole category of peers emerge as the socially most prominent, is not less but more likely to produce serious concerns about standing and prestige within relevant social groups.[44]

Prestige

Since prestige concerns are undoubtedly part of the human condition, there is little point in criticizing them or seeking their elimination. Hans Morgenthau, the German émigré who helped establish the modern study of international politics in the mid-twentieth century, viewed prestige as an instrumental end, but one that at times could be pursued for its own sake.[45] Morgenthau also provided a cue to what was to become so-called power transition theory, asserting that a sharp discrepancy between the prevailing prestige hierarchy and the real distribution of power might precipitate war.[46] The latter prediction helped spawn a substantial literature that examines the likelihood that a great power aspiring to preeminence, such as China, purposively seeks to acquire sufficient capabilities so as to displace the preeminent power, currently the United States.[47]

Amitai Etzioni, the sociologist and social philosopher, had in the early 1960s already advanced a set of related claims revolving around prestige as a theoretical concept. In the 1962 article "International Prestige, Competition and Peaceful Coexistence," Etzioni drew on standard insights from individual psychology to suggest that a reasonable measure of concern with the image one creates in the eyes of others "is both unavoidable and desirable. It makes for responsiveness to the public opinion of other countries and, in a sense, to world public opinion." But Etzioni then went on to issue a note of caution, directed at the political leadership of any given polity. That leadership should be wary, wrote Etzioni, of giving rise to "excessive concern with one's standing in the eyes of others [as it] heightens frustration generated by minute prestige fluctuations [and might induce members of that community to] express themselves in various irrational responses including aggression."[48]

Some authors who do not share the analytical focus of power transition theorists on military confrontation, war, and competing ambitions of global hegemony still maintain that we should not neglect social concerns as key factors in international relations. In his unpublished thesis explicitly devoted to "the prestige motive in international relations," Daniel Seth Markey recommends that prestige should not be as easily discarded as it has been in the modern era of international relations theorizing but be acknowledged as an intrinsic motive behind conflict.[49] Richard Ned Lebow essentially makes the same point in his magisterial 2009 *A Cultural Theory of International Politics.* A similar idea has been expressed by William Wohlforth, who instead of harking back to classical texts introduces the status differentiation theory of Henri Tajfel in this context. According to Wohlforth, great powers are often acutely preoccupied with their status among their peers, a feature typically overlooked in neorealist and neoliberal literature.[50]

To highlight the social dimension of international relations means to affirm the lack of political and social self-reliance of nation-state actors, each of whom can choose to either facilitate or impede the functioning of high-table diplomacy. Because the pursuit of prestige is a social phenomenon and prestige levels are relative to those of others, it makes sense to expect that the logic of the game fundamentally changes in a world where no power is able to sustain "superpower," let alone hegemonic, capabilities. Uninterrupted collaboration with others is no longer merely a possibility but an indispensable necessity if international security (and a global order) is to be maintained. And when material factors alone cannot tell us which political entity is undisputedly the most influential power in the world, social considerations—such as prestige and status concerns—come to the fore.

This insight is inevitably neglected if one fully subscribes to positivist social science practices established in the middle of the previous century and similarly ignores the constructivist insight that anarchy is "what states make of it."[51] As Lebow and Wohlforth appear to agree, the "struggle for recognition," lucidly portrayed already in the nineteenth-century philosophy of Georg Friedrich Hegel, is nevertheless an analytically important aspect of prestige. More recently, the significance of mutual recognition in many types of social interaction and conflict situations has been elaborated further in international relations research conducted by Alexander Wendt, Erik Ringmar, and Lene Hansen.

In fact, to most scholars who acknowledge that nonmaterial factors matter and that socially induced considerations are significant in international relations, prestige seems to feature prominently in great-power bargaining in general and top-level diplomacy in particular. It has even been described as "a valuable currency in international relations."[52] A world that in the foreseeable future will be made up of great powers of more equal material strength might hold the promise of "a more stable social system," in Rosecrance's phrase, and a collaborative approach on the part of that category of political entities. By the same token, though, a social system of roughly equal great powers might for the reasons cited previously also accentuate socially induced risks. Overall, reputational sensibilities are easily hurt among peers who jockey to improve their relative position vis-à-vis others.

Larson and Shevchenko, who like Wohlforth have turned to Tajfel's theory of social differentiation (although they refer to it as social identity theory), in 2010 examined the challenges of forging cooperation between the United States, on the one hand, and China and Russia, on the other, given the social aspirations of the latter two. When governments with great-power aspirations no longer regard the social standing of their country as favorable, Larson and Shevchenko point out, Tajfel's theory predicts that social agents will engage in social mobility, social competition, or social creativity. In the field of international relations and international security, as in other contexts in which groups compare their standing with that of other groups, social mobility involves emulation of the behavior of members of the peer (group) toward which they aspire, social competition corresponds to mastering a direct challenge of the authority of a (peer) group leader, and social creativity constitutes the search for preeminence in an area other than the one in which the preeminent power predominates.[53]

In line with such contemporary and more nuanced theorizing, there is little doubt that prestige concerns have been at the center of much behavior in high-table diplomacy in recent years, in Asia as well as in Eastern Europe.[54] During the past two decades, both main high tables examined here were not just arenas within which considerations of pride and prestige were common but coveted objects of desire on the part of middle- and second-tier great powers that most assertively pursued membership.[55] In the case of the G7/

G8 summitry, a primary motive on the part of midsize economic powers was an obvious fear of being excluded. That anxiety presumably had something to do with concerns that important decisions might be made in their disfavor in a forum to which they did not belong. But part of the evidence suggests that the fear of how it would look to *others* if exclusion was accepted was itself a powerful incentive to pursue membership, or at least indirect representation. Those others would be the domestic electorate as well as neighboring countries and peer states.

Still, the choice of prestige as one of the thematic emphases of this study should not be understood as a reductionist commitment to the application of sociological and psychological theory to aggregate actors like states and institutional arrangements. A vast array of other motives plays directly into the considerations of governments and diplomats in the field of international security, as in others. For instance, the P5 has for over sixty years engaged in conflict mitigation and distinctly assumed a sense of responsibility for maintaining global political stability.[56] The same can be said for the members of the G7/G8 summitry, now partially overtaken by the G20, in that concerns about "systemic stability" of the world's political and economic order were frequently reflected. Prestige concerns, in other words, do not exclude the significance of contravening motives and considerations associated with substantive issues facing nations and humanity as a whole.

Process

Thus the third implication of leveling the playing field among great powers relates to process as an analytical theme, and to specific political and social practices in the realm of international security as well as the problem-solving capacity of such institutional arrangements. Process as an unqualified, multifaceted philosophical concept will not be dealt with here.[57] For the sake of clarity, that is, it is the narrower term "diplomatic process" that will be employed in this study. This analytical theme organizes a set of concerns at the forefront of scholarship since the founding of the first generation of international organizations aimed at contributing to world peace and security in the late nineteenth and early twentieth century.

Diplomacy as continuous negotiation was introduced in the beginning of this chapter and represents a process-oriented notion of the concept. Diplomatic process was in 1958 defined by Claude as a phenomenon "most clearly in operation when states are negotiating with each other to achieve peaceful settlement of a dispute or agreement on a matter of mutual concern, and when such negotiations have the fundamental quality of a *bargaining* session, involving the necessity of reciprocal concession to produce an agreed result."[58] Claude's preoccupation in the late 1950s was with multilateral organizations, as he sought to illuminate the real and potential contributions that often remained invisible to national decision makers and public opinion. But he also noted that multilateral bodies should not be understood as useful for all types and all stages of conflict resolution, as their misuse might unleash "the bull in the diplomatic china shop."[59]

Claude, like many of his generation, was all too conscious of diplomatic history to ascribe overly ambitious expectations to international organizations. The diplomatic process of the Congress of Vienna of the 1800s had been limited to direct communication among the political leaders of the Habsburg Empire, Russia, Great Britain, France, and Prussia. For the most part the joint commitment went little beyond the original agreement from the 1804–5 deliberations, which concerned the preservation of territorial integrity as long as at least one of the European great powers so desired.[60] It was a great-power condominium only so far as it respected the Vienna agreements and kept diplomatic channels open in an effort to handle issues that emerged in spite of efforts to avoid a clash of interests. In the latter respect problems were resolved, or at least set aside, in an ad hoc manner by the countries involved.

The UN and its Security Council, as is widely accepted, were intended to address all major threats to peace and security, and to do so more transparently and less arbitrarily than nineteenth-century conferences and top diplomats exchanging eloquently phrased letters. In particular, the UN system was born out of the experience of a dismal failure with the League of Nations, its predecessor. Although the League of Nations setup made a lot of sense from the vantage point of international law and the value of preserving national sovereignty, the logic of great-power politics and of the social dynamics that drive international affairs was sorely neglected. So were the opportunities associated with informal governance, in the sense applied here, a deficit that soon facilitated the emergence of competing political processes and the undoing of the League of Nations.

The creation of a high-table platform at which a select group of great powers would wield overwhelming power on the basis of a formal agreement, yet in the presence of a numerically larger but much less influential category of elected member states that would hold their seats for two years at a time, was therefore a radical invention in the mid-1940s. The framers of the UN Charter created a solution to the conundrum of international security that married great-power bargaining to a central structure in international law, the UNSC, as an authoritative source of interpretation and of innovation.[61] Through the UN Charter, the council's provisional rules of procedure, and the working methods, the organization found a way forward that promised to sustain the overall framework within which it operates, while giving rise to several formal and informal processes to serve as focal points for problem solving in the relevant domains of activity.[62]

The functional logic introduced into the UN system had the considerable advantage of moving the evolution of institutional arrangements beyond the ad hoc approach of the Congress of Vienna and evoking questions about means and ends, budgets and administrative procedures that committed all stakeholders to invest in the overall diplomatic process. As Morawiecki put it in another early analysis of the political and administrative challenges confronting the main UN bodies, "In a general way the functional approach to the structural problems of international organizations seems to be the most reasonable one. It means that the character of functions entrusted to definite organs determines or should determine their structure and principles of action. Thus an important question arises: How should the institutional arrangements be shaped and what should be their principles of action to assure the proper exercise of different functions."[63] Many institutional arrangements had not been at hand in the original formula, in the sense of being inherent to the UN Charter and the provisional rules of procedure. During the mid-1960s political crisis at the UN, issues such as the eventual influence of the General Assembly over matters of peace and security, the implications of decolonization on the institutional balance, the expansion of non-permanent members in the UNSC, and the procedural handling of peacekeeping missions loomed large.[64] But the UN survived the crisis and the expansion from 51 to 114 member states over its first two decades and made significant adjustments also to the composition and working methods of the council.

The understanding that multilateral arenas such as the UN General Assembly, but also "minilateralist" bodies such as the UNSC's P5 caucus, can reinforce tensions in international relations and aggravate threats to peace and security dawned early on observers of UN politics. In an article published at the height of the political crisis of the mid-1960s, Thompson quoted Secretary General Dag Hammarskjöld's open admission that "the best results of negotiation between two parties cannot be achieved in international life, any more than in our private worlds, in the full glare of publicity with current public debate of all moves, unavoidable misunderstandings, inescapable freezing of position due to considerations of prestige, and the temptation to utilize public opinion as an element integrated in the negotiation itself."[65] Following the expansion of the UNSC to fifteen member states, and the increased practice of informal deliberations that resulted from the reform, the "full glare" dimension was radically cut back. Other bodies within the UN system, such as the

Economic and Social Council (ECOSOC) and General Agreement on Tariffs and Trade (GATT), were affected by politicization during the Cold War in that they either became gridlocked by East-West conflict or bogged down with technicalities as a method to limit the diplomatic damage.

It took another crisis, in the early 1970s, to produce momentum for the idea of creating a second principal high table, at which the privacy of conversation would be ensured. The G7 (originally G5) platform was forged around the response of major oil-consuming countries with regard to acting as a powerful counterpart to the Organization of Petroleum Exporting Countries (OPEC). Within a few years, as discussed previously, the G7 had begun to tackle broader issues relating to the global financial system, currency fluctuation, levels of taxation, trade issues beyond the rather technically oriented GATT system, as well as individual, high-profile challenges in foreign and security policy.

The diplomatic process at the G7 (and later the G8) was never laden with the formalism of the working methods and prescriptive international law provisions prevalent at the UN. Because of the summitry mode of operation, it was not continuously influenced by the mind-set of cautiously treading professional diplomats either. The nonpublic nature of summit preparations and meetings allowed for exploring and pursuing common ends without individual statements and initiatives constantly being put to close scrutiny by national constituencies. There is little doubt that informal governance facilitated a more flexible approach to the rise of new issues and solution formulas than formal diplomatic venues and contexts.

Some but not all of the advantages of the informal setting elaborated at the G7/G8 are also available to the G20. But it should be recognized that the rise of the latter, combined with the increased institutionalization of its work, also diminishes the suitability of GX summitry for fast-paced crisis management and problem solving, compared with a predecessor with narrower membership. Because of its size and heterogeneity alone, the G20 will never be able to draw on the "fireside chat" format that the G7/G8 put to good use in the past.

The UN General Assembly: Inclusive and Universal

Notwithstanding the inclusiveness of this platform, commentators tend to be dismissive of the annual opening session of the UN General Assembly, especially when it comes to the policy content of statements made by small countries. In an institutional setting far removed from "fireside chats," most capitals continue to be represented by a political leader or top-level diplomat at this annual event. In 2009–14 a total of 115 speeches were made by representatives of G20 members. Thirty-seven of those speeches were given by foreign ministers, thirty-five by heads of state, nineteen by heads of government, and merely four by ambassadors (permanent representatives) to the UN. While there is no conclusive evidence that General Assembly speeches are more carefully scrutinized than others given by top-ranking politicians and civil servants, the level of diplomatic reporting on, and media coverage from, this august forum creates strong incentives for speakers to be mindful of the broader implications of how they express themselves and whether they touch (or do not touch) on topical and sensitive themes, values, and loyalties.

As the results concerning individual policy areas reported in chapters 3–5 (and table 2.2) suggest, there were clearly significant differences among the priority levels awarded by individual G20 government representatives addressing the UN General Assembly in 2009–14. In particular, the theory of a stakeholdership of the few receives only qualified support from the analysis of contributions to the opening session general debate, extending to the first-tier great powers but not to the second tier, let alone to middle powers. In accordance with what one might have expected to be the stance of incumbents, countries that themselves are members of the exclusive P5 and G7/G8 categories rated high on all three policy areas, with only a couple of deviations. Notably, Germany made no mention of terrorism as a threat to international security during any of the first five years examined, and Italy only one throughout the full six years. Moreover, Russia was the single country in the entire G20 community that never addressed climate change.

In the annual statements at the UN General Assembly, there was little to support that middle powers sensed they belonged to a group of exclusive stakeholders with special responsibilities for international security. Most non-P5 member states either scored low on international conflict, terrorism, and climate change or fluctuated in their priorities from one year to another.[66] In that broader community of G20 members, Saudi Arabia scored low on international conflicts but was in fact represented only three times at the opening session of the General Assembly. This makes Saudi Arabia unique not only in the category of great powers but also in the entire UN membership.[67] Another political entity that deviated substantially from the general pattern was the EU, which was allowed to address the assembly for the first time in 2011. The EU representative, as will be shown in chapter 4, in the course of the four years that he participated in the opening debates, never once raised the issue of terrorism and similarly scored low on climate change.

Some of the most unambiguous aggregate trends in 2009–14 were those demonstrating the relative attention paid to policy areas in the realm of international security when juxtaposed against the other two. International con-

Table 2.2 International Security Issues at the UN General Assembly Opening Session, 2009–14, Breakdown by G20 Members and Policy Areas

	UNGA Speaker						International conflicts	Terrorism	Climate change
	09	10	11	12	13	14			
United States	HS	HS	HS	HS	HS	HS	14	13	5
China	HS	HG	FM	FM	FM	FM	11	6	4
Japan	HG	HG	HG	HG	HG	HG	7	2	6
Germany	PR	FM	FM	FM	FM	FM	12	2	9
France	HS	FM	HS	HS	HS	HS	7	7	7
United Kingdom	HG	FM	HG	HG	HG	HG	12	11	5
Brazil	HS	PR	HS	HS	HS	HS	7	5	9
Russia	HS	PR	FM	FM	FM	FM	9	5	0
Italy	HG	FM	FM	HG	HG	HG	8	1	4
India	FM	FM	HG	FM	HG	HG	7	14	10
Canada	FM	HG	FM	FM	FM	PR	9	9	4
Australia	HG	FM	FM	HG	FM	HG	9	5	9
Mexico	FM	PR	HS	HS	HS	HS	7	6	11
Rep. of Korea	HS	FM	HS	FM	FM	HS	10	8	15
Indonesia	FM	FM	FM	HS	FM	HS	5	4	9
Turkey	HG	HS	HG	FM	HS	HS	11	9	5
Saudi Arabia[1]	FM	X	X	FM	X	FM	4	7	4
Argentina	HS	HS	HS	HS	HS	HS	7	8	4
South Africa	HS	FM	HS	HS	HS	HS	7	4	9
European Union[2]	X	X	HS	HS	HS	HS	7	1	4

Note: In the UN General Assembly speaker column, HS stands for head of state, HG for head of government, FM for foreign minister, and PR for permanent representative (UN ambassador). The US president qualifies as head of government as well as head of state and is referred to as the latter since head of state is a higher ranking in diplomatic protocol. The scores in the issue columns (international conflicts, terrorism, and climate change) are correlated first to the share of the speech awarded to the issue, second to its prominence in the speech, and third to the emphasis given to the message. Three score levels were used: (1) brief mention, (2) elaborated topic, and (3) key priority.

[1]Saudi Arabia was the only country without a speaker at the UN General Assembly opening session during three out of the six years examined. As a result, the score is lower for Saudi Arabia.

[2]The European Union was granted the right to address the General Assembly in 2011. That right has been bestowed on the president of the European Council, the EU's closest equivalent to a head of state.

flicts, which is the policy area closely associated with the primary mandate of the UN and its Security Council—not least through the practice of peacekeeping and humanitarian missions—received a steady level of attention from most G20 members. By contrast, the corresponding score for terrorism fluctuated markedly over the six years, with the year 2011 reaching twice as high as 2010 and then receding before reaching its peak in 2014. A straightforward interpretation of the near doubling of the interest government representatives had in terrorism between 2010 and 2011 is that the political and social upheavals of North Africa and the wider Middle East during the so-called Arab Spring reinvigorated the attention paid to this topic, and the 2014 peak was precipitated by the sudden emergence of the Islamic State in Iraq and the Levant (ISIL).[68]

No other trend, however, was as pronounced as the extraordinary drop in relative attention given to climate change as a policy area during the first five of the six years covered here. The priority that government representatives awarded this issue in the beginning of the period, in 2009, was more than five times higher than in 2013. We know from the account in chapter 5 that virtually every UN member state helped mobilize political momentum before the Copenhagen conference in December 2009, and we can from that observation deduce that this explains most of the spike in relative attention.

An extended interpretation might be that 2009 at the same time represented an unsuccessful attempt to attach climate change mitigation to an institutional arrangement characterized by a multilateral, formal setting and a governance mechanism associated with such an institutional arrangement. Instead, the minilateral Copenhagen Accord, struck between the United States, China, India, Brazil, and South Africa, gave rise to only a rudimentary informal setting, one lacking a proper governance mechanism. As a result, climate change remained an "immature," not yet institutionalized, international security issue, seemingly in search of a proper venue. The modest resurgence of the theme in 2014 would in this interpretation be related to growing expectations that the 2015 Paris Climate Change Conference might produce a universal, binding agreement after all.

The UNSC: Predominantly Formal

It is not surprising that the relatively robust post-Napoleonic institutional arrangement aligned with the global power configuration of the nineteenth century, epitomized in the "Concert of Europe," would be one that political leaders thought worth replicating and developing further. Scholars of diplomacy have described, in considerable detail, how a number of nineteenth-

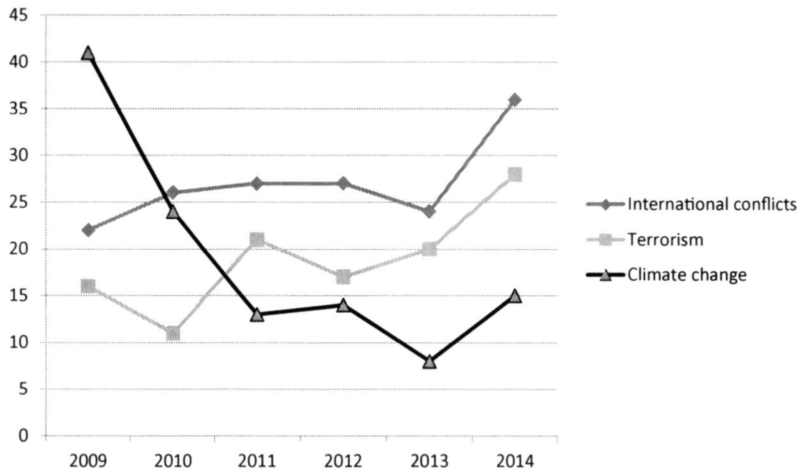

Figure 2.1. International Security Issues at the UN General Assembly Opening Session, 2009–14, Trend

Note: The missing data with regard to Saudi Arabia and the EU (see table 2.1) have in this graph been filled in by extrapolating the scores for the years for which data was available.

century international conferences held in the European context paved the way for latter-day multilateralism, international organizations, and a set of practices that we associate with modern diplomacy.[69] Attempts to create a governance mechanism superior to one based on the balance of power failed miserably in the late 1910s and early 1920s, as the advent of the Second World War demonstrated with horrifying clarity.[70] The experiment of the League of Nations, constructed around the idealist notion of collective security, was replaced by an institutional arrangement largely premised on realist insights. This was the UN, with a condominium of great powers in the shape of the UNSC at its core.[71]

Not unlike in the heydays of nineteenth-century great-power bargaining, a series of summits and conferences convened at critical junctures just before and after the end of the Second World War placed the first-tier great powers in the driving seat through institutional arrangements they subsequently revised and extended. The deal struck at the 1944 Dumbarton Oaks Conference by the major political leaders of the day reflected the winning side of the Second World War in that it married convenience with necessity and a desire to build an institutional arrangement that would—in contrast to the League of Nations—stand the test of time. Participants at the 1945 San Francisco Conference questioned various elements of the arrangement, but not its basic properties. Nor was anybody prepared to probe the commitment of the first-tier great powers to erecting a body that would be charged with international peace and security, jeopardizing what some feared were fickle pledges that might be undone through wrong-footed diplomacy.[72]

Once established, there was nothing fickle about the UNSC. The institution played a significant—and sometimes a central—role in the vast majority of major international conflicts during the Cold War period, ranging from the Middle East to Central Africa and further to East Asia. The defining conflicts were the 1950–53 Korean War, the 1956 Suez Crisis, and the 1960–63 Congo Crisis, the management of which gave rise to UN peacekeeping and the elaborate de-escalation techniques of UN and national diplomats working at the UN Headquarters in New York.[73] Later on direct lines of communication were established between US and Soviet leaders, and great-power bargaining assumed more predictable forms. The latter also meant that conflict management more frequently bypassed the council, especially when it came to problems in the geographic proximity of the two main protagonists in the Cold War.

Indeed, the UNSC was able to adjust to major changes in world affairs, in part by creating parallel, unofficial channels that constrained formal diplomatic practices associated with the council. In essence, the decolonization movement and the doubling of UN member states over less than two decades also necessitated revising the UN Charter in order to sway newly independent states to seriously commit to the UN system. The 1965 enlargement of the non-permanent members from six to ten contributed substantially to putting an end to the pervasive domination by Western states of this fundamental international security institution and, by the same token, bringing about a major advance in representativeness. Less than twenty years after it had been established as the world's premier institutionalized arrangement in the field of international peace and security, the council had been enlarged and the grip of first-tier great powers over its decision-making process somewhat lessened.[74]

The 1965 reform may not have significantly transformed the US-Soviet relationship, but it did affect the UNSC's overall mode of operation through consequences insufficiently explained in much of the standard literature.[75] Because the council was made more heterogeneous as a decision-making body, its proceedings necessarily reflected a broader set of values and viewpoints, rendering negotiations more complex. And to maintain effectiveness in terms of its outcome, formal deliberations were increasingly substituted with informal talks, away from the eyes of the public, in the adjacent consultation rooms. Ever since the 1965 enlargement of the council, criticism that a culture of secrecy pervades the institution has been a recurrent theme among small and middle powers, and great powers have taken to chastising "propaganda alliances" that form amid countries without direct recourse to the council.[76]

Over the next couple of years, the UNSC only gradually found a new modus operandi based on a recalibrated equilibrium between permanent and non-permanent member states, drawing on legal mechanisms in conjunction with widely accepted customs and diplomatic practices. One example of a balanced compromise was the pragmatic solution concerning regional representation among non-permanent council member states that emerged at an early stage and was then adjusted to fit the enlarged body, with candidates drawn from five geographically organized groups. If the post–Cold War push toward UNSC reform were to eventually bring about further expansion, analogous adjustments would be required. Political momentum for institutional reform first peaked in 1997 as Ambassador Razali Ismail's well-crafted reform proposal was tabled and again in 2005, when a high-level panel put together by Secretary General Kofi Annan offered a revised proposal. Formal intergovernmental negotiations on council reform were launched under Ambassador Zahir Tanin in 2008 but had—as we shall see later—by the mid-2010s yet to produce tangible results.[77]

Today there is broad understanding of the importance of sustaining and consolidating the role of the UNSC, as well as increased appreciation for the more subtle assets by which it has been able to help carry out its main functions. One important such asset is the legitimacy that has accrued in most countries regarding the institution's significance as a security guarantor of last resort.[78] Another important resource is the multiplicity of informal groups, networks, and other arrangements that over decades evolved in close cooperation with the council and its P5, allowing for stakeholder governments to contribute to international conflict management when it comes to individual countries, missions, and security challenges. Many such informal groups are temporary and reflect priorities set by individual governments and ministries of defense and foreign affairs, whereas others are long lasting and stem from geographic proximity or other strategic considerations.[79]

The G7/G8: Predominantly Informal

The UNSC had from the very outset experienced frequent contestation concerning the conditions under which its decisions are allowed to infringe on political and territorial sovereignty, as well as the precise scope of issues that should fall within its mandate. But if informal groups, by assisting the council, had enhanced its efficacy, nonbinding commitments constituted the defining feature of a second set of international security institutions created in the mid-1970s.

The context for forming the G7 as an institutional arrangement consisting of summits between Western great-power leaders was the 1971 collapse of the exchange rate, the energy crisis, and financial turmoil and recession in the world economy as the likely ramifications. As a response to these systemic challenges, the first meetings of top-level leaders of the world's largest economies at the time were held in Rambouillet, France, and San Juan, Puerto Rico, in 1975–76. The G7 was originally set up primarily as a counterweight to OPEC and sought to mitigate the economic and political leverage of the world's biggest producers of fossil fuels. Later, though, its member states found it useful for other purposes as well.[80] Indeed, there were important political motives behind the establishment of the G8 and G20 formats in 1998 and 2008, respectively, including long-term concerns about international security.[81]

The different formats of GX summitry have persisted over the years, even as the respective mandates of the G7, G8, and G20 underwent substantial change. A consistent achievement of this predominantly informal high table is its contribution to the avoidance of grave instability and uncertainty in the global financial system and the world economy at large. This achievement grew out of a long-standing effort to coordinate the response to the financial shocks and crises, loosely related to the then ongoing energy crisis, of the early 1970s. By providing indicative and, over time, increasingly comprehensive and detailed guidance for the operation of capital markets, currency exchange, and banking in general, GX member states were instrumental in helping to sustain a long period of economic growth in the Western Hemisphere.[82] The most recent financial crisis, in 2008–9, necessitated a broadening of stakeholders, but macroeconomic coordination remains the key function of that institutional arrangement.

The GX summitry may have started as a group of self-regarding, large economies. But the relative stability of growth and the price of energy resources have, in the long run, proved beneficial not just for industrialized and oil-exporting economies. Transnational monetary and trade flows similarly found their way to a growing number of developing countries. The macroeconomic stability beginning in the late 1970s coincided with an era of deregulation of capital markets that greatly facilitated foreign direct investment outside the area of the OECD. In Southeast Asia in particular, a number of forward-looking governments created a favorable environment for foreign investments and were able to attract sufficient capital to build new industries in, for example, the textile and home electronics sectors. In the late 1980s and early 1990s, the rapid industrialization path produced substantive results in terms of high economic growth and investment in many developing countries.[83]

That economic impetus extended to trade as well. In the 1970s and 1980s, the GATT was the most palpable instrument for sustaining a reliable regime that benefited investors and emerging economies alike. After 1995 the WTO assumed a more consequential role, as an arbiter between governments that disagreed on whether their trade policies were compatible with global trade norms. This important shift, however, would hardly have occurred without the support of GX (the G7 in this case) member states, which consistently promoted a set of economic priorities that served to underwrite the global trade regime. In fact, free trade had been a key priority from the outset, as evidenced in the original summit declarations.[84]

The GX summitry provided similar systemic support to other international organizations charged with the supervision, monitoring, and regulation of global markets. This is true for the IMF, the World Bank, and the Bank for International Settlements (BIS), which in the late 1990s all became crucial to staving off financial volatility in Asia and Latin America. Even though these organizations differ in terms of mandates and accountability structures, the governments of the leading Western economies—and the United States in particular—effectively control their respective agendas and have ever since they were set up after the Second World War.[85] Whenever the deliberations of the GX summitry overlapped with the work of international regulatory or supervisory bodies, the conclusions reached in such meetings exerted considerable indirect influence on their activities. This leverage was reflected as early as in the 1976–77 summit communiqués.[86]

The end of the Cold War not only vindicated the GX summitry but bolstered its status and influence. Apart from Russia—the inclusion of which in 1998 broadened and (partially) transformed the G7 into the G8—no other candidacies were seriously considered.[87] After 1998 the G8 label was exclusively used to denote the summit of heads of state and government that included Russia, whereas "technical issues" related to currency fluctuation, financial, and budgetary issues were left to the G7 finance ministers meeting. The latter had a much lower profile but continued to serve as a body that could calibrate and coordinate specific policy provisions among the major economies of the Western Hemisphere.[88] In most years the G7 finance ministers would convene between two and four times, sometimes in augmented delegations that included central bank governors and other top government officials, to discuss regional or global economic affairs. An annually recurring pretext for the latter type of gathering was the IMF–World Bank spring meeting in Washington, DC.

By and large, the fundamental confidence experienced by market actors remained intact for over three decades. But the sharp financial turbulence of 2008–9 suddenly rendered G7/G8 efforts too narrow and insufficient, or so it seemed. In September 2008 the United States' financial crisis suddenly worsened with the collapse of the Lehman Brothers investment bank and the ensuing worldwide repercussions. In November 2008 US president George W. Bush convened the first ever G20 meeting of heads of state and government, in Washington, DC, seeking to achieve a coordinated response among major emerging economies and the largest industrialized countries. The action plan adopted at this first summit was primarily oriented toward strengthening regulatory, supervisory, and accounting practices.[89] A follow-up meeting of top political leaders was held in London in April 2009, at which a further set of joint commitments were agreed to. Most important among the latter was a joint pledge to make $850 billion available for bank recapitalization, countercyclical spending, balance of payments support, and the funding of infrastructure and social support.[90]

In essence the G7/G8 at this point acknowledged that it was politically and financially overstretched to deal with the fallout from the financial crisis. At the 2009 summit of the G20, held September 24–25 in Pittsburgh, the hitherto largely technical cooperation of G20 finance ministers and central bankers was officially upgraded to the summit format.[91] The Pittsburgh summit document was given a distinctly programmatic character that entailed as many as fifty separate items, plus two annexes. A key formulation appeared in item 19, stating that the heads of state and government had now "designated the G20 to be the premier forum for our international economic cooperation." It depicted the situation at the London summit held in April the same year as "the greatest challenge to the world economy in our generation," asserting that the group's "forceful response [already] helped stop the dangerous, sharp decline in global activity and stabilize financial markets."[92]

The G20: Shaping the Mandate

Early on member states were in agreement to let the G20 operate within a fairly narrow frame of activity, devoted to providing guidance for the global economy by way of agreements on monetary policy, supervision, and regulation of the financial sector and a limited number of questions concerning banking and accounting practices. The G20 has since its inception in fact proved to be even less of a decider than the G7/G8, but rather a mechanism providing strategic guidance for the world economy and operating informally in the sense of lacking statutes and procedures other than those of regular summit diplomacy. So the G20 attends to crisis response functions when needed, as in the aftermath of the 2008–9 global financial crisis, and at other times acts as a steering committee. In the immediate aftermath of the financial crisis, the G20, in the latter capacity, helped review and reform regulatory systems in an unexpectedly comprehensive way.[93]

Indeed, the G20 is uniquely placed to orchestrate financial regulation via the Financial Stability Board (FSB), the BIS, the IMF, the World Bank, the European financial institutions, the International Standard Classification of Occupations (ISCO), and the International Accounting Standards Board (IASB).[94] Its members include the powerful G7/G8 countries from North America and Europe, in favor of which international financial institutions—owing to their economic clout—remain skewed. When reforming the overall setup, voting rules, and other regulations, this group needs to make substantive concessions. In other words, the expansion and growing maturity of capital markets and associated institutions in Asia and elsewhere create demands for a swift inclusion of emerging economies in key decision-making bodies. Arguably, most if not all G20 countries have legitimate claims on representation in such regulatory bodies.

Following the crisis-response measures adopted at the 2008–9 summits of the G20, the overall regulatory framework of global finance remained at the center of attention. No major breakthrough was achieved on controversial topics such as a global financial transactions (Tobin) tax, primarily because of strong resistance from the financial industry and governments that are reliant on revenues from that industry, the United States, Canada, and the United Kingdom in particular. On other regulatory issues associated with the financial sector, some progress was registered. For instance, all G20 member states committed to implementing the Basel II and III Accords regarding bank capital adequacy, stress testing, and market liquidity risk.

Three economic policy areas closely connected to the core tasks of the G20 agenda deserve to be highlighted. First, a major focus of G20 deliberations has been efforts to sustain a mutually beneficial trade and commerce regime at the global level. Whereas the Doha round of negotiations aimed at deepening and extending the framework for global trade has gradually wound down, this failure was not allowed to precipitate an across-the-board breakdown in existing tariffs and domestic regulations, which in turn would have a dampening effect on export and import levels.[95] Currency fluctuation has been a bigger problem in recent years, with some countries (such as the United States and Japan) effectively depreciating their currencies and others (mainly China) being reluctant to appreciate theirs. But again, most commentators agree that these problems would most likely have been more severe without the (fragile and incomplete) commitment to currency stability within the G20.[96]

Second, a well-functioning regulatory financial framework upholds key norms underwriting global trade and commerce yet at the same time creates conditions for a roughly equitable distribution of responsibilities and duties among member states. The voting rights of G20 countries in the IMF and the World Bank are ever so slowly shifting toward the emerging markets and especially expanding the quotas of China, India, and Brazil. There have been increasingly detailed discussions about whether the Chinese currency should be included in the Special Drawing Rights (SDR), as an acknowledgment of the increasingly important role that China plays in global finance, even though the yuan still does not rise to the standard of a "freely usable currency." The EU position was that integration of the yuan needs to be explored, and a G20 working group was formed in November 2011 to study the implications of this option. By mid-2015 US objections to admitting the Chinese currency into the SDR had also faded.

Third, the phenomenon of tax havens has received considerable attention, almost exclusively from a critical perspective. Following up on the London summit of 2009, the identification and blacklisting of "noncooperative jurisdictions" that are widely believed to facilitate the financing of organized crime and terrorist activities has moved ahead. At subsequent summits the Convention on Mutual Administrative Assistance in Tax Matters, drafted by the OECD and the Council of Europe, was signed by representatives of most G20 countries.[97] Detailed information sharing on financial and fiscal policies represents another step in the same direction. The Mutual Assessment Process (MAP), by which countries can review other measures to enhance global growth, is in and of itself a significant novelty.[98]

Especially the crackdown on tax havens, with significant connotations in the global struggle against terrorist financing, would appear to render moot the debate about whether the G20 should concern itself with "soft," nontraditional security issues that has accompanied the summits following the Pittsburgh 2009 upgrade of that body. Owing to its potential as a group of countries that represents 85 percent of the gross world product and 80 percent of world trade—along with some two-thirds of the total world population—the G20 is clearly in a stronger position than the narrower G7/G8 constellation when it comes to mobilizing a greater amount of economic and political resources for nontraditional security purposes. As it includes the countries that by far wield the most military firepower (only two of the world's nuclear powers, Pakistan and Israel, are missing), moreover, the resources it can bring to bear on a military, civil, or humanitarian crisis outstrip, hypothetically at least, those of any other institution.

Because of the combined resources that the G20 countries possess, along with the potential agility and flexibility of decision making in an informal institutional arrangement, attempts have been made to persuade its leaders to take ownership of matters of general and acute concern. Emerging great powers in the Southern Hemisphere have insisted on the G20's accepting, in return for their endorsement of attempts to prop up the financial system mainly located in Western capitals, a long-term strategy for economic development. Attempts to persuade North Americans and Europeans to engage in large-scale developmental assistance have not been successful.[99] But when a "soft security" dimension has been identified, primarily through an initiative expressly aimed at preventing or reducing social and political conflict over time, progress has at times been made. Examples of issues that have been directly addressed by the G20 are food price volatility in agricultural markets, the lack of economic infrastructure in conflict-ridden parts of Africa, and climate financing programs. As will be elaborated in chapter 4, G20 countries have assumed at least partial responsibility concerning transparency of transnational financial transactions, an area that in recent years has been central to counterterrorism and the combat against organized crime.

The Resurgence of High-Table Diplomacy

If institutionalized arrangements for great-power management of world affairs and security matters were common in the past—not least at the regional level—but then submerged during several decades of pervasive multilateralism, why are they reappearing today? What is the appeal of minilateralism and high-table diplomacy in the era of democracy, human rights, globalized commerce, transnational media, and cultural interaction on a massive scale?

This book is designed to provide a tentative, though not an exhaustive, answer to these broader questions and in this respect build on the widely accepted empirical observation that the underlying global power configuration is changing in the beginning of the twenty-first century.[100] This is to be seen in bilateral relations as well as in the reinvigoration of minilateral bodies at the expense of multilateral institutions, as chapter 1 explained. As the most elaborate expression of a multilateral orientation in international relations during almost seven decades, the UN is today suffering from a variety of ills that great and middle powers are either unable, or unwilling, to remedy.[101] The failure to negotiate a new set of rules for global trade in the Doha round, which was halted in mid-2008, and the weak outcome of the Copenhagen environmental summit in 2009 clearly reflect and may have temporarily accentuated this trend.[102]

In the realm of international security, both the UNSC and the GX summitry have had problems projecting an image of being effective in devising and delivering solutions. Whereas the existence of the UNSC as such may not be in question, the G7/G8 many times came under scrutiny as demands were raised that it be dismantled and persuaded to hand over most, or all, of its tasks to the wider G20 constellation.[103] After Russia in March 2014 was expelled from the G8 (now G7) meetings, such sentiments could very well be reinforced. Given that most observers agree that the underlying global power configuration is broadening rather than narrowing, the G20 may be perceived as a potentially stronger candidate to fill the space left by the presently defunct G8.[104]

Stone, who in theoretical terms is liberally inclined, has suggested that "international governance improves when the distribution of power becomes more egalitarian."[105] From a different theoretical vantage point, some realist scholars also subscribe to the view that the transfer of tasks from a narrower constellation of great powers to a broader one may help recalibrate the global power configuration and thereby ensure access to shared public goods and the suppression of nontraditional threats. In late 2011 the journalist Nathan Gardels asked veteran security observer and former US secretary of state Henry Kissinger if the G20 ought to be in a position to provide such public goods and thereby to help ease in a new world order. Kissinger responded in the affirmative and without reservations about the significance of the project: "Yes, the G20 is the forum for this adjustment. But it will be a big and difficult effort for it to do so. There is no certainty of success, but the effort is critical if we want a stable world."[106] Although the deeper trend was long in the offing, the "adjustment" that Kissinger refers to here hit home quite abruptly at the time of the recent financial crisis. "What has been revealed for all to see," Bradford and Lim wrote in 2011, "is there is a crisis of confidence in the markets, a crisis of capacity of the international system to cope with the global dimensions of the crisis, and a crisis of trust in political leadership."[107] The immediate problems of the 2008–9 financial crisis may have stemmed from regulatory inadequacies in the US markets, but similar norms and rules existed in Europe and elsewhere, raising questions about the role of the G7/G8 governments in a massive failure of anticipation. According to Bradford and Lim, the void revealed by the inability of the G7/G8 to cope with the financial crisis posed fundamental questions about global public goods, and the tentative responses were unsatisfactory: "The answer in the case of the financial crisis seems to be that no one 'was minding the store,' especially when it came to oversight, supervision, and regulation of financial institutions and markets."[108]

G7/G8 complacency was probably a significant part of the problem.[109] On several levels the sharp 2008–9 crisis can be seen as a consequence of the unusually long period of sustained, cumulative growth that the Western Hemisphere experienced for more than twenty years before the crisis. The World Bank estimates that from 1985 to 2007 the world economy grew by between 2.9 and 4.3 percent per year, before falling to 1.6 percent in 2008 and to negative growth, –1.9 percent, in 2009.[110] Among G8 members only Russia had in the early 1990s suffered negative growth as a result of the breakdown of the planning system of the communist era and the slow emergence of a market-based system. All other G7/G8 countries, that is, had previously experienced continuous growth for over two decades.

Complacency may also be related to the fact the G7/G8 membership gradually became too narrow for governments to pay sufficient attention to the extraordinarily dynamic transformation of economies and societies in the emerging countries in the past two decades, gradually shifting economic power from the OECD countries east- and southward.[111] The expansion of the financial services sector in the United States and several European countries evidently helped fund the growth of production and innovation in emerging countries, while securing high levels of return for institutional and individual investors. But growth levels in the industrialized states remained low, comparatively speaking, as emerging capital markets in Asia, Latin America, and Central and Eastern Europe gained a larger share of the global economy by virtue of their general economic growth, with levels at 5–10 percent.[112]

The broadening of the base of asset-rich states that can assume responsibility for the stewardship of the global economy was from this viewpoint long overdue. The integration of the Russian Federation into the G8 summitry for the first time violated the in-house "club rule" of not accepting members beyond the seven incumbents, albeit further expansion was tacitly resisted. In the late 1990s member states of the informal group were becoming more inclined to consult with nonmember states in conjunction with top-level meetings, an approach that Japan extended to official consultations with regional powers at the 2000 Okinawa summit. In the early twenty-first century, the United Kingdom and France went about cautiously promoting the notion of expanding the membership base, an aspiration demonstrated during the preparations for the 2003 and 2005 summits in Évian-les-Bains and Gleneagles, respectively. Two years later, in 2007, British finance minister Gordon Brown and French president Nicolas Sarkozy expressly endorsed an expansion of the G8 to the G13.[113]

Metaphorically speaking, in 2008 representatives of the most asset-rich emerging economies were no longer roaming the lobby looking for an opportunity to persuade individual club members to recognize their credentials and support their candidacies for membership. Instead, the president of the club, in a manner of speaking, suddenly stepped outside to invite eleven prospective member states plus the EU (which already attended G7/G8 meetings informally) to sign up. Immediately thereafter those eleven new members (hitherto not part of the G8) were invited inside and presented with a massive debt that the old member states could not foot on their own. In essence, the latter asked the former to help pay a bill run up under "club statutes" over which the newcomers had had little or no influence.

The global power configuration, in other words, was in the process of expanding its base to second-tier great powers and middle powers as the economic clout of such asset-rich countries grew. The symbolic 2009 upgrade of the G20 from a meeting of finance ministers and central bankers to a summit of heads of state and government was an overt acknowledgment of this underlying power shift. The direct involvement of heads of state and government was meant to commit emerging great powers to far-reaching implementation of the agreements made in terms of an acute crisis response. In this sense the reinvigorated, summit-based G20 was able to help avoid backsliding and keep issues like reforming IMF quotas high on the agenda.[114] There were also signs that several of the eleven member states with no prior experience of the G7/G8—most notably China—subsequently "internalized" the G20 in domestic politics.[115]

When united, the G20 can indeed argue that it speaks for the overwhelming majority of the world's population and that it controls, as mentioned previously, some 85 percent of all economic resources. To a lesser extent the G20 can draw on numerical authority but at least point out that its broader membership constitutes a major improvement on the G7, with only Japan (and between 1998 and 2013, Russia) not wholly belonging to the traditional Western countries located in North America and Western Europe. An elaborate consultation mechanism, like that employed by Japan in 2000, could in part also compensate for the noninclusion of small and medium-size states. What it cannot compensate for is the loss of democratic legitimacy that the G7 (though less the G8, which of course included "semi-democratic" Russia) wielded in the sense that each member state was governed by elected politicians.[116] On this particular point it is clear that the inclusion of China and Saudi Arabia diluted the credibility of the broader group.[117]

Similar criticisms have long been waged against the UNSC and the veto rights of P5 member state incumbents. While France and the United Kingdom typically work hard to make themselves useful in the eyes of the world, they are fully aware that their position in the institution is a consequence of mid-twentieth-century political history and not reflective of the current global power configuration. Russia, during its protracted economic woes of the 1990s and 2000s, apparently suffered from the same inferiority complex vis-à-vis rising giants such as India and Brazil. Moreover, France and the UK are aware that this insight is shared by the large emerging powers as well as by long-standing economic powerhouses such as Japan and Germany. Hence, the five veto member states lack convincing normative arguments for seeking to preserve the status quo. Thus, the P5 plays for time while the council operates as effectively as possible and individual member states portray their own contributions as constructive with regard to council reform.

International Security: A Still-Evolving Division of Labor

The UNSC began responding to threats to international peace and security in January 1946, holding its first session just months after the end of the Second World War. Although the UN system ever since its creation has attracted criticism for its handling of individual issues and for being unresponsive to the needs of certain groups of countries, the council is indisputably the core of a formal, rich institutional arrangement in the realm of international security. As is well-known, the veto rights of the P5 render it impossible for any government to reach decisions that run counter to the fundamental interests of the United States, China, Russia, France, and the United Kingdom. The "hidden" or "informal" veto of the incumbent permanent member states can further prevent a variety of pressing international security issues from being placed on the council agenda.[118] That being said, the P5 states cannot fully control the agenda-setting mechanism that is influenced by the majority rule governing procedural matters and by non-permanent member states taking turns to hold the rotating council presidency. There is also the opportunity to raise issues under "other business."

Besides, the UNSC does not constitute an entirely static institutional arrangement, a fact that is sometimes overlooked by casual observers. First, the informal dimension of council deliberation and implementation grew in importance in the 1970s and onward.[119] Second, the need for wider legitimacy in order for the council to stay effective as a political arena, a source of international law, and a decision-making body providing directions for implementation forces all stakeholders to consider that body's standing in the mind of public opinion. The latter makes it difficult for P5 governments to ignore the expectations of the public in general, and the electorate of important states in particular, concerning the performance of the council with regard to any security challenge that might be construed as one that the council should address.[120]

After nearly seventy years of handling threats to international peace and security, the UNSC has a well-established remit of activities. Thematic debates on various cross-cutting topics aside, the main task is stemming large-scale military conflicts between independent states and using diplomatic means to do so. Only when diplomatic options of negotiation and bargaining have been exhausted may the council move to consider binding resolutions that create peacekeeping operations, punitive sanctions, or observer missions. The authorization of "all necessary measures," potentially unleashing military force, only occurs in those rare cases when political and military intervention is considered warranted by all P5 countries plus at least four E10 member states.[121]

The GX summitry, as was mentioned previously, was originally forged out of a modest consultation forum between finance ministers and central bankers among the five biggest Western economies. But the 1973 oil crisis and its financial repercussions soon propelled it into a full-fledged high-table platform gathering heads of state and government. In the context of this crisis, the G7 became a clearinghouse for measures aimed at quelling unrest in the financial markets, facilitating economic recovery, and, in a broad sense, creating stable conditions for investment and foreign trade in the entire Western Hemisphere. To this day a key feature of the GX summitry, if conceptualized as an aggregate institutional arrangement meeting in a variety of different formats, is the regular gathering of finance ministers at least twice a year.[122]

Foreign affairs evolved to become an integral component of this broader endeavor, so much so that the G7 foreign ministers met separately at each summit from 1975 to 1997. Trade ministers met from 1978 to 1999 as "the Quad," with the United States, Canada, Japan, and the EU as the four parties in the talks, but this constellation in fact wound down their meetings after Russia joined in 1998. The ministers of science, health, and the environment have nevertheless continued holding regular meetings since the 1990s, either at regular G8 summits or other venues convenient for the affected government officials.[123]

A nontraditional security agenda grew out of the G7 institutional arrangement, combining crisis management procedures with administrative, political, and diplomatic practices exercised in the course of the 1970s, 1980s, and 1990s.[124] A major innovation was the 1989 creation of the Financial Action Task Force (FATF) at the G7 Paris summit, unique in that it was set up as a separate entity aimed at fighting money laundering. The FATF formulated forty recommendations for stemming the growth of money laundering by organized crime syndicates, especially those engaged in illicit arms and drug trade. In revised form the recommendations a quarter century later remain the most authoritative regime regulating the global financial services sector, with regional offshoot institutions in virtually all parts of the world. The latter, so-called FATF-style regional bodies, are what turned FATF recommendations into a world-encompassing regime enhancing transparency of financial transactions.[125]

A decade later, the transformation of the G7 into the G8 in 1997–98 allowed Russia to enter the summitry and relegated the former to a (still influential) meeting of finance ministers. The G8 was somewhat successful in reining in the damage caused by the failure of the Contact Group to peacefully resolve the 1998–99 Kosovo Crisis.[126] But this experience, and NATO's intervention in former Yugoslavia to end the attacks of Serbian forces against Albanian insurgents in the Kosovo province, precipitated an acrimonious debate about the division of labor between relevant high-table platforms. The great powers eventually reaffirmed the view that it would be inappropriate to take measures and institute reforms that undermine the UNSC. Most EU and NATO countries, but also Russia, agreed that the unrivaled legitimacy of the UNSC is a major asset to the world community at large.[127]

A clearer division of tasks between the G8 and the UNSC was elaborated in the aftermath of the 9/11 attacks, as nontraditional security concerns loomed large in the face of large-scale transnational terrorism. From this point onward a number of institutional arrangements grew out of the G8 to deal with counterterrorism, counterintelligence, peace building, and regional stabilization. Over the years the G8 became associated with a number of long-standing working groups, including the Counter-Terrorism Action Group (CTAG), the Peacekeeping/Peace-Building Experts' Meeting, the Africa Clearing House, the Roma-Lyon Group, and the Global Partnership Working Group.[128]

An infrastructure of nontraditional security arrangements was thus in place when, as a result of the 2008–9 financial crisis, the G7/G8 abdicated to the G20 in the realm of global financial and macroeconomic policymaking. Some expected that the G7/G8 would be disbanded as a result of this handover of the primary functions, but in 2014 both the G7 finance ministers meeting and the G8 summit remained operational, yet with a sentiment in some countries that G7/G8 "precooking" were shaping G20 decisions.[129] This criticism aside, the broader question is whether the G20 will persist, in the long run, as "the premier economic forum" or whether its members will have it expand, as suggested by Australia's foreign minister, Kevin Rudd, to issues of development, trade, and climate change.[130] Other commentators, such Bradford and Lim, have specifically singled out truly universal challenges as appropriate for the G20 format, above all "climate change and energy security, in which the rest of the world also has an enormous stake."[131]

Were the G20 to go down this route and seek a broadened agenda, there is the obvious precedent of the G7/G8. The G7/G8 has addressed a wide variety of global problems over four decades of existence, even coming up with a rudimentary regime for climate change as early as 1979. In 2005 the G8 famously decided to eliminate debt for a number of heavily indebted poor countries.[132] John Kirton, who has researched G8 and G20 affairs for many years, goes as far as to assert that "the G8's legacy and limitations suggest that the G20 will succeed if it becomes a club with a comprehensive agenda."[133] Kirton thinks that the G20 currently embraces "the first-order, functionally linked, political-security dimensions of its existing agenda on finance, economics, trade, development, food security, disaster relief, climate change/energy, corruption, and terrorist finance."[134] Another eminent Canadian scholar and former top diplomat, Paul Heinbecker, believes that it is likely that "the G20 ultimately will absorb the G8."[135]

When it comes to institutional arrangements pertaining to softer security issues than counterterrorism and peace building, such as health, migration, and the environment, neither the UNSC nor the GX summitry has so far exercised much leadership. As a result, global governance on these matters remains underdeveloped. In many cases this may not be a problem, as the measures required to thwart or mitigate specific threats are only marginally helped by intervention by a corporate body that acts on behalf of the world community. But the broader challenges of mass migration and climate change, which increasingly warrant the large-scale coordination of resources and a concerted effort by the governments of great and middle powers, may be exceptions to the rule.[136] If worst-case scenarios outlined by scholars who extrapolate data on extreme weather induced by climate change come to pass in terms of massive ecological disaster and species extinction, the existence of a legitimate corporate body capable of taking charge of decision making and resource allocation might even be of critical importance.[137] For the time being, only the UNSC and the GX summitry are in a position to assume such tasks.

To summarize this chapter's analysis of the current state of affairs regarding the separation of roles, the parallel existence of a formal and an informal institutional arrangement at the apex of international relations is historically unprecedented. At no point in history has high-table diplomacy pertaining to international security been routed through two world-encompassing sets of institutional arrangements, one constituting a standing body staffed with senior diplomats who are ready to meet and respond to security contingencies that arise in any part of the world and another based on serial summits in which the top leaders meet in person. Each arrangement has its own specific background, justification, and function in today's international relations. But in the next three chapters, I hope to be able to demonstrate that they are not

Table 2.3 High-Table Diplomacy: Platforms and (Ideal) Division of Labor

	UNGA	UNSC	G7/G8	G20
Policy area in international security	Debate framing across policy areas	Conflict management	Counterterrorism cooperation	Climate change mitigation
Primary objective	To sensitize great and middle powers	To avert war among great powers	To avert WMD and large-scale terrorism	To avert ecological disaster and "sixth extinction"
Secondary objective	To mobilize political and economic resources	To prevent or mitigate interstate war and genocide, mass atrocities, and crimes against humanity	To thwart non-WMD and small-scale terrorism	To mitigate and adapt to severe climate change

as independent of each other as we might be led to think and that the way in which both arrangements have evolved is predicated on the existence (and mode of operation) of the other.

Methodological Remarks

It should be obvious by now that in terms of distinctions among levels of analysis, approaches that are agency- or structure-oriented, rationalist or reflectivist, or indeed, realist, liberal, or constructivist, a relaxed view is taken here.[138] Instead of fully siding with one school of thought or methodological stance, the aim is to deploy methodological distinctions where they can be the most productive, as heuristic devices that help order social and political phenomena.[139] This study can even be seen to straddle the Realpolitik and liberal-institutionalist perspectives in that it explores the interplay between great-power politics and the opportunities and constraints created by high-table diplomacy. In that sense it is assumed that neither perspective can be reduced to the other.

The empirical units of analysis in the rest of the study are high-table diplomacy and the institutional arrangements that operate at the apex of international security, with the twin nexuses of formality-informality and traditional-nontraditional security representing the foremost theoretical concerns. The overarching research objective is to contrast the two sets of rival propositions outlined in chapter 1 and to examine diplomatic practice at the world's two most exclusive high tables, or "clubs," of international relations, namely, the UNSC with its P5 veto powers and the GX summitry. The results of an examination of speeches made at the opening session of the UN General Assembly will be briefly revisited when the results are reported of the three policy area analyses in chapters 3–5, which represent the core of the study and cover the years 2009–14.

Most of the sources used in chapters 3–5 and in the plausibility probe summarily reported in the introduction are conveniently available online. The official website of the UNSC has been expanded and made more transparent over the past decade and still includes the useful database maintained by the Dag Hammarskjöld Library, in many instances offering more than one route to finding the meeting records, resolutions, letters, and statements made on the behalf of the UNSC. Regarding the GX summitry, the most complete analogous trove of information is that maintained by the University of Toronto, where a research group devoted to the study of the G7, G8, and G20 has accumulated a complete set of summit declarations and a wealth of related documents. Alongside this database are numerous analyses written by associated scholars and students trying to make sense of the deliberations as well as the outcomes.

In addition to these readily available records, I have, as mentioned at the outset, conducted a series of interviews between 2010 and 2014 with diplomats serving at the UN Headquarters in New York, all of whom had insights into the work of the UNSC. The majority of these diplomats agreed to speak to me off the record about the work of the council, its procedures and working methods, and the ways in which non-P5 countries may or may not influence the outcome of its deliberations. The prospects of an expansion of the council to what in this book are called second-tier great powers were explored, as were the broader prerequisites for, and possible implications of, such a development. Although many of my interlocutors were prepared to have their names listed (in the appendix) and some did not mind being cited, I eventually decided not to explicitly attribute any specific statement or assessment to an individual interviewee. I must therefore take full responsibility for my own evaluation of this valuable input, without which this book could not have been written at all.

Because the analysis of 2009–14, as laid out in chapters 3–5, constitutes the main empirical contribution of this book, the account in the introduction of how minilateral diplomacy evolved over twenty years merely served to provide us with an analytical access point.[140] A much more comprehensive historical overview was offered in this chapter, in an effort to render subsequent chapters more pertinent and informative. Here three understandings of diplomacy were combined, acknowledging that the term may mean negotiation, representation, or the employment of leverage. I explained that I agree with theorists of diplomacy that the latter notion is especially critical to the practice of great and middle powers. Further, leverage can be either blunted, or accentuated, through institutional arrangements within which actors have made long-term commitments. This chapter also introduced three analytical themes, all put to heuristic use in the analysis. Polarity, prestige, and process are concepts directly pertinent to a study of great-power diplomacy and its conduct within key institutions of international security. All three themes help refine the conceptual dimension of the research and justify the analytical focus on international security as a fruitful field of theoretical inquiry into the formality-informality and traditional-nontraditional security nexuses.

That being said, a narrower set of delimitations, methodological tools, and analytical techniques have been outlined in chapter 1. To capture the formality-informality nexus at work in international arrangements devoted to international security, the years 2009–14 will now be examined in the three chapters that review substantive security challenges. This enables us not only to analyze the rather subtle changes taking place in the UNSC and its sub-sidiary bodies but also to incorporate the evolution of the G20 as a summit of heads of state and government in the analysis, as the latter absorbed some of the tasks previously performed by the G7/G8. The period 2009–14 is also promising in that quite a variety of traditional and nontraditional security issues needed close attention in high-table diplomacy. Although chapters 3–5 for the most part conform to a chronological time line and describe the successive unfolding of events in considerable detail, the analytical themes and rival propositions structure the narrative in ways that help elicit insights regarding the two principal high tables and the cross-cutting dynamics of formality-informality and traditional-nontraditional security.[141]

The analysis in chapters 3–5 aims to adjudicate between two pairs of rival propositions, as explained in chapter 1. Is high-table diplomacy characterized by the growing hybridity of the formal and informal spheres of institutional life? Or is differentiation reproduced in formal institutions, such as the UNSC, and in serial summits attended by great and middle powers? And to what extent is the boundary between nontraditional and traditional security upheld? Are these concepts complementary in terms of high-table diplomacy or contested, for instance, by political leaders resorting to forum shopping or forum shifting in international security? Merely asking these questions underscores the view of high-table diplomacy as a form of governance that, by virtue of its regularity, relative permanency, and scope of institutional arrangements, constitutes an entanglement that exceeds its historical precedents.

In an effort to examine different institutional arrangements associated with high-table diplomacy and adjudicate between rival propositions, the first policy area investigated is conflict management. This is, quite clearly, the traditional domain of the UNSC and makes up the subject of chapter 3. This is what methodologists refer to as a hard case for the differentiation proposition, given that the P5 states constitute the authorized stakeholders in this issue area and that their views determine the parameters of international law by virtue of their elevated status in that institutional arrangement. Both realism and liberal-institutionalist theoretical approaches accept that the council as a whole, and the P5 states as the individual "guardians" of that system, lack peer institutions and are in a position to neglect the interests and desires of informal groups that include second-tier great powers and middle powers.

The second attempt to substantiate claims derived from rival propositions concerns counterterrorism cooperation, including antiterrorist financing measures. This case is easier to make because a range of elaborate arrangements now have existed for more than a decade and would not have been successful without the combined measures undertaken by the GX summitry and the UNSC. While the G7 first put a set of anti-money-laundering practices in place in the late 1980s and early 1990s, the council created a legal framework for reinforcing and extending the regime. Following this precedent, the G8 was in the early 2000s able to consolidate working groups, initiate projects, and expand networks in the realm of nontraditional security. This case, as one would expect, ought to be characterized by institutional hybridity in at least some areas of international security, and similarly by complementarity of policies conducted in adjacent areas.

The third case examines climate change mitigation, an area in which the UNSC and the GX summitry so far have established only a rudimentary role, but in which the potential for institutional complementarity is likely to grow in the years to come. Climate change mitigation was initially a UN concern, raised at the environmental summits held in Stockholm in 1972 and, more prominently, in Rio de Janeiro in 1992 and Johannesburg in 2002. Owing to entrenched opposition to raising climate change as an issue at the UNSC, the security ramifications of global warming long appeared to have better prospects of being taken seriously by the GX summitry. The narrow membership of predominantly Western, industrialized countries nevertheless rendered the G8 an ineffective venue for probing the complexities of climate change. Today some observers believe that the G20, which encompasses more societies that soon may be adversely affected by climate change repercussions, could be a more promising avenue for moving the issue forward. Differentiation between formal and informal institutional arrangements is expected to be sustained.

NOTES

1. Anderson, *Rise of Modern Diplomacy*; Berridge, Keens-Soper, and Otte, *Diplomatic Theory*. In a characteristic comment that praises New Delhi's increasingly effective foreign policy in the early 1960s but at the same time reflects an underappreciation of the rich diplomatic history of the subcontinent, William Hayter wrote that India had "meanwhile taken to diplomacy as a swan to water" (Hayter, *Diplomacy of the Great Powers*, 65).

2. Watson, *Evolution of International Society*.

3. Jönsson and Hall, *Essence of Diplomacy*; Kerr and Wiseman, *Diplomacy in a Globalizing World*.

4. See, for instance, Suetong, *Ancient Chinese Political Thought*.

5. Berridge, *Diplomacy*, 1.

6. Ibid.

7. Sharp, *Diplomatic Theory of International Relations*, 612–18.

8. Ibid., 75.

9. Berridge, *Diplomacy*, 1.

10. Keohane, "Lilliputians' Dilemmas"; Cooper and Higgot, *Relocating Middle Powers.*

11. Sheehan, *Balance of Power*; Knutsen, *History of International Relations Theory.*

12. Acknowledging the complexity of the concept, I will short-circuit the problem of the nature and properties of power by referring to the "assets" of great powers that manifest themselves in a variety of ways. Being "asset-rich," in other words, is treated as a statement of fact when it comes to great powers; without an abundance of assets they would cease to be "great."

13. On purposeful "value creation" in security diplomacy, see Rathbun, *Diplomacy's Value,* 22–57.

14. Bull, *Anarchical Society,* 92–93.

15. Ibid., 16–22, 97–98.

16. Hobsbawm, *Age of Revolution*; Kissinger, *World Restored*; Clark, *Hierarchy of States.*

17. Vosoughi, "Kings of Hormuz."

18. Kang, "Stability and Hierarchy," 221.

19. Ibid., 218.

20. Claude, *Swords into Ploughshares,* 24–25.

21. This is the concept implied, if not explicitly adhered to, in Jongryn, *Middle Powers and G20 Governance,* especially chapter 4 by Andrew F. Cooper and Mo Jongryn, "The Middle 7," 63–126.

22. Keohane, "Lilliputians' Dilemmas," 295, 298.

23. A. Cooper, "Squeezed or Revitalized?"

24. Cooper and Jongryn, "Middle 7"; D. Cooper, "Between Great and Small."

25. Sheehan, *Balance of Power.*

26. Gaddis, *We Now Know,* 26.

27. Gilpin, *War and Change.*

28. Wilkinson, "Unipolarity without Hegemony."

29. G. John Ikenberry, Michael Mastanduno and William C. Wohlforth, "Introduction: Unipolarity, State Behavior, and Systemic Consequences," in Ikenberry, Mastanduno, and Wohlforth, *International Relations Theory,* 6.

30. Rosecrance, "Bipolarity, Multipolarity," 322.

31. Buzan, *United States and the Great Powers,* chaps. 7 and 8.

32. Ibid., 121–26.

33. Cameron, *Introduction to European Foreign Policy*; Engelbrekt and Hallenberg, *European Union and Strategy*; Biscop and Fiott, *State of Defence in Europe.*

34. Buzan, *United States and the Great Powers,* 139. One must readily agree with Buzan, as well as with Joseph Nye and Geir Lundestad, that the United States throughout the second half of the twentieth century successfully cultivated this "ability" in the Western Hemisphere. See Nye, *Bound to Lead*; and Lundestad, "Empire by Invitation."

35. Ikenberry, *Liberal Leviathan.*

36. Brooks, Ikenberry, and Wohlforth, "Don't Come Home."

37. Wilkinson, "Unipolarity without Hegemony."

38. Ibid., 143, citing Rousseau, *Social Contract and Discourses*, 8.

39. Wilkinson, "Unipolarity without Hegemony,"167.

40. Rosecrance, "Bipolarity, Multipolarity," 317.

41. Ibid., 317.

42. Wendt, *Social Theory of International Politics*.

43. Deutsch and Singer, "Multipolar Power Systems," 396.

44. Tajfel, *Social Identity and Intergroup Relations*.

45. Markey, "Prestige Motive in International Relations," 15.

46. Organski and Kugler, *War Ledger*; Markey, "Prestige Motive in International Relations," 15–16.

47. Tammen et al., *Power Transitions*.

48. Etzioni, "International Prestige, Competition," 23.

49. Markey, "Prestige Motive in International Relations," 31.

50. Wohlforth, "Unipolarity, Status Competition."

51. Wendt, *Social Theory of International Politics*.

52. Berridge, *Diplomacy*, 105.

53. Larson and Shevchenko, "Status Seekers," 66–67.

54. As Friedberg put it regarding long-standing points of friction among Asian neighbors, in some cases "the issues are almost entirely symbolic and have everything to do with national pride" (Friedberg, "Ripe for Rivalry," 18). Although the actions of the Russian Federation in early 2014 with regard to Ukrainian territory no doubt are related to military-strategic rivalry and the political economy of regional integration, numerous observers agreed that a key aim was tied to the restoration of prestige and honor to the Russian nation (Nicole Gaouette, "Putin's Motives Rooted in History Remain a Mystery Abroad," *Bloomberg News*, March 18, 2014, http://www.bloomberg .com/news/articles/2014-03-17/putin-s-motives-rooted-in-history-remain-a-mystery -abroad).

55. This is the subject of Paul, Larson, and Wohlforth, *Status in World Politics*, especially chap. 7 by T. V. Paul and Manesh Shankar, "Status Accommodation through Institutional Means: India's Rise and the Global Order," 165–91, and chap. 8 by Vincent Pouliot, "Setting Status in Stone: The Negotiation of International Institutional Privileges," 192–218.

56. Westra, "Cumulative Legitimation, Prudential Restraint."

57. See, for instance, the rich and ambitious examination by Whitehead, *Process and Reality*.

58. Claude, "Multilateralism,"44.

59. Ibid., 52.

60. Clark, *Hierarchy of States*, 121.

61. Cronin and Hurd, *UN Security Council*.

62. Prantl, *UN Security Council*.

63. Morawiecki, "Problems Connected," 915.

64. Finkelstein, "United Nations."

65. Secretary General Dag Hammarskjöld, cited in Thompson, "New Diplomacy," 403.

66. The detailed scores for each G20 member state are available in table 2.2.

67. Saudi Arabia treats its membership in the UN differently than almost any other country does; it is seemingly more reliant on informal diplomatic practices and shies away from taking an active, high-profile role. Against this background, Riyadh's decision not to make use of the UN Security Council seat it was awarded for 2014–15 should perhaps be less of a surprise, as it would have required abandoning this stance in favor of speaking up in diplomatic arenas.

68. Two alternative terms exist for ISIL, one being Islamic State (IS) and the other Islamic State in Iraq and Syria (ISIS). Each of the three is contested on the grounds of apparently ascribing or denying political legitimacy to this organizational entity, which lays claim to religious authority as a "caliphate" as well as to a territory based in the Middle East. ISIL is employed here primarily because it is the term used in UNSC resolutions.

69. Kissinger, *World Restored*; Berridge, *Diplomacy*.

70. Gathorne-Hardy, *Short History of International Affairs*; Clark, *Hierarchy of States*, 145–66.

71. Bosco, *Five to Rule Them All*.

72. "Interview with: Lawrence S. Finkelstein," United Nations Oral History, Dag Hammarskjöld Library, November 23, 1990, 30–33, 40–42, http://s3.amazonaws .com/downloads2.unmultimedia.org/public/dhl_oral_history/transcripts/Finkelstein 23Nov90TRANS.pdf; Hilderbrand, *Dumbarton Oaks*.

73. Bosco, *Five to Rule Them All*, 39–111.

74. Claude, *Changing United Nations*, 49ff.

75. A significant exception is Hiscocks, *Security Council*.

76. Berridge, "'Old Diplomacy' in New York."

77. Hassler, *Reforming the UN Security Council*, 199–201.

78. Hurd, *After Anarchy*.

79. Prantl, *UN Security Council*.

80. Putnam and Bayne, *Hanging Together*, 11–14, 44–58.

81. Apl, *Die sicherheitspolitischen Dimensionen der G20*.

82. Bayne, *Staying Together*, 213–35.

83. World Bank, *The East Asian Miracle: Economic Growth and Public Policy* (Washington, DC: World Bank, 1993).

84. "Declaration of Rambouillet," Rambouillet, France, November 17, 1975, ac-

cessed May 21, 2015, item 9, http://www.g8.utoronto.ca/summit/1975rambouillet /communique.html; "Joint Declaration of the International Conference," San Juan, Puerto Rico, June 28, 1976, accessed May 21, 2015, para. 17, http://www.g8.utoronto .ca/summit/1976sanjuan/communique.html; "Appendix to Downing Street Summit Declaration," London, May 8, 1977, accessed May 21, 2015, http://www.g8.utoronto .ca/summit/1977london/appendix.html.

85. Stone, *Controlling Institutions.*

86. "Joint Declaration of the International Conference," para. 10ff; "Declaration: Downing Street Summit Conference," London, May 8, 1977, paras. 5 and 9, http://www .g8.utoronto.ca/summit/1977london/communique.html; and "Appendix to Downing Street Summit Declaration."

87. Bayne, *Staying Together,* 5–10.

88. Stone, "Informal Governance in International Organizations," 128.

89. G20 Special Leaders Summit on the Financial Situation, Washington, DC, November 14–15, 2008, accessed May 21, 2015, annex, http://www.g20.utoronto.ca /summits/2008washington.html.

90. "Declaration on Delivering Resources through the International Financial Institutions," London, April 2, 2009, accessed May 21, 2015, http://www.g20.utoronto .ca/2009/2009delivery.html.

91. Woods, "Impact of the G20," 40–42.

92. "G20 Leaders Statement: The Pittsburgh Summit," Pittsburgh, September 24–25, 2009, accessed May 21, 2015, items 2 and 6, http://www.g20.utoronto.ca /2009/2009communique0925.html.

93. Bradford and Lim, *Global Leadership in Transition,* 4–7.

94. Woods, "Impact of the G20," 45; Gadinis, "Financial Stability Board."

95. Drezner, *System Worked,* 38–42.

96. Ibid., 59–62.

97. Eleven countries that continued to fail to meet transparency standards—Antigua, Barbados, Botswana, Brunei, Panama, Seychelles, Trinidad and Tobago, Uruguay, Vanuata, Switzerland, and Liechtenstein—were singled out for censure (Agence France-Presse, November 4, 2011).

98. Exactly what the MAP should entail has been difficult to work out, so negotiations over technicalities have proved rather painstaking. Over time, however, the list of proposed indicators for global imbalances has been narrowed down. Among the commonly agreed-on indicators are current account balance, exchange rate levels, size of foreign exchange reserves, public debt, and private savings.

99. For instance, in early 2010 Brazil and Argentina proposed a reform of the Inter-American Development Bank (IADB) for consideration by the G20. The idea was that the group's aims in terms of financial regulation would be advanced through a better functioning IADB. Since the November 2010 summit, the High Level Panel on In-

frastructure Investment, attached to the G20, has been charged with outlining plans and identifying sponsors for large-scale infrastructure projects, mainly in Africa, the Middle East, Asia, and Latin America.

100. Layne, *Peace of Illusions*; Zakaria, *Post-American World*; Fontaine and Lord, *America's Path*; Alexandroff and Cooper, *Rising States, Rising Institutions*.

101. Hale, Held, and Young, *Gridlock*.

102. Brenton, "Great Powers in Climate Politics"; Brummer, *Minilateralism*.

103. Cooper and Thakur, *Group of Twenty*, 133.

104. Engelbrekt, "Mission Creep?"

105. Stone, *Controlling Institutions*, 224. On page 8 Stone nonetheless predicts that the preeminent power will continue to be tempted to rely on informal power.

106. Nathan Gardels, "Henry Kissinger: G20 Work Is 'Essential.' Alternative Is 'Dangerous Outcome,'" *Christian Science Monitor*, November 3, 2011, accessed July 10, 2014, http://www.csmonitor.com/Commentary/Global-Viewpoint/2011/1103/Henry-Kissinger-G20-work-is-essential.-Alternative-is-dangerous-outcome.

107. Bradford and Lim, *Global Leadership in Transition*, 5.

108. Ibid.

109. Robert Samuelson, "The World According to Geithner," *Washington Post*, May 18, 2014; Geithner, *Stress Test*.

110. World Bank, *World Development Indicators 2012* (Washington, DC: World Bank, 2012), accessed July 10, 2014, http://data.worldbank.org/data-catalog/world-development-indicators/wdi-2012.

111. International Monetary Fund, *Regional Economic Outlook: Asia and Pacific. Sustaining the Momentum: Vigilance and Reforms* (Washington, DC: International Monetary Fund, 2014), accessed July 24, 2014, http://www.imf.org/external/pubs/ft/reo/2014/apd/eng/areo0414.htm.

112. Sharma, *Breakout Nations*.

113. Smith and Heap, "Canada, the G8, and the G20."

114. Woods, "Impact of the G20," 43.

115. In March 2010 even Chinese prime minister Wen Jiabao cited, in an official government report, the G20 as an important arena for Chinese foreign economic policy. See Xue and Zhang, "Turning the G20," 55.

116. White, *Russia's Authoritarian Elections*.

117. From a representativeness perspective, meanwhile, a lingering weakness is the continued European emphasis of membership. While the G20 is more inclusive and diverse than the G7/G8, sizable non-European countries are likely to remain critical of the fact that this body also has, in all, seven EU representatives when we add joint institutional leaders to heads of state and government of individual member states. At the March 2010 summit, it was eventually Pascal Lamy, a former EU commissioner and then head of the WTO, who spoke bluntly about the imbalance. At the very least,

Lamy argued, Europeans needed to carefully coordinate their interventions ahead in order to keep the rest of the G20 listening to them. Agence France-Presse (London), March 28, 2010.

118. Nahory, "Hidden Veto."

119. Prantl, *UN Security Council*, 106–11.

120. Voeten, "Outside Options."

121. Malone, *UN Security Council*.

122. On the basis of this quasi-permanent regularity, I believe it is wrong to object to the G7/G8 being labeled an "institution." For the opposite view, see Hodges, "G8 and the New Political Economy," 69.

123. Hajnal, *G8 System and the G20*, 67–71.

124. Pentillä, *Role of the G8*; Heinbecker, "United Nations and the G20," 237.

125. Gardner, "Fighting Terrorism the FATF Way."

126. Heinbecker, "Kosovo," 544; Pentillä, *Role of the G8*, 27–29; Crawford, "Pivotal Deterrence."

127. See Heinbecker, "Kosovo," 549; Prantl, *UN Security Council*, 217–21. The latter describes how a special negotiating device, a "Consultative and Co-ordination Process in New York relating to the work of the Contact Group," had to be created to carefully transfer the agreement of the informal group to the UN Security Council without undermining the latter's authority.

128. G. Smith, "G8 and the G20."

129. This sentiment is not unreasonable, given the history and accumulated cohesion of what can be described as "the G7 caucus." On the other hand, it could be argued that it is incumbent on other member states within the G20 to present viable and elaborate policy proposals that constitute politically realistic alternatives to those promoted by the G7 caucus. The forming of a "BRICS [Brazil, Russia, India, China, and South Africa] caucus" is one step in that direction, though so far one that tends to impede rather than enable coordination on international security affairs.

130. "Kevin Rudd Sounds Alarm over Need to Aim Higher at G20 Summit," *Australian*, October 8, 2011.

131. Bradford and Lim, "Introduction."

132. Kirton, "G8," 17.

133. Ibid., 18–19.

134. Ibid., 32.

135. Heinbecker, "United Nations and the G20," 237.

136. Hale, Held, and Young, "Gridlock," 229.

137. One of several recent worst-case predictions uses the term "the sixth extinction" for the demise of the Anthropocene, an ecological environment in which humans can live and thrive. Kolbert, *Sixth Extinction*.

138. Sil and Katzenstein, "Analytical Eclecticism."

139. This implies a commitment to the soft line on theory generation described in Eckstein, "Case Study and Theory," 125–31.

140. Ibid., 147–52.

141. Bates et al., *Analytic Narratives*; George and Bennett, *Case Studies and Theory Development*, 92–94, 210–11. For a good example of blending analytical and chronological accounts in international relations, see Walt, *Origins of Alliances*.

Chapter 3

Conflict Management

Given the clear mandate of the UNSC in the realm of conflict management, one would not expect much hybridity among institutional arrangements within high-table diplomacy overall, but rather strenuous differentiation between formality and informality. There would appear to be serious risks associated with referring part of that mandate to other bodies, risks that by extension could undermine the status and functioning of the UN system at large. For analogous reasons, one would not expect the UNSC to cede ground on traditional security issues to other organizational bodies or legal frameworks. As mentioned previously, the council and the P5 countries exert considerable influence over interpreting and monitoring those boundaries and are likely to contest what they perceive as transgressions.

Background

Conflict management can be described as the process of addressing serious differences of opinion and interest. This process typically involves domination, compromise, and integration as the three main modes of operation in the context of international relations as well as of domestic politics.[1] If sufficiently fierce, differences among political subjects and communities often evolve into overt enmity, in which case the conflict in question acquires a distinctive security dimension.[2] With or without efforts to reconcile those differences and avert an escalation of the situation, the outbreak of violent acts may ensue. The management of "violence and insecurity," which in international relations could be tantamount to war or the threat of war, constitutes an essential part of such activities.[3] Conflict management, as here understood, would be substantively and qualitatively different without international security institutions.

There is no doubt that the UNSC has been at the core of international conflict management ever since the 1946 foundation of the UN. Charged with

maintaining peace and security by way of the UN Charter, the council established itself in that capacity in the course of the following two decades. The
rapid decolonization process and subsequent rise in the number of UN member states from fifty-one to over one hundred in the early 1960s nevertheless
posed an enormous challenge to the young institution. The UN had to accommodate the growing heterogeneity of international diplomacy by altering
the deliberation format applied at many levels, and it had to make room for
hundreds of civil servants from the new member states. All of these changes
presented the UN and its associated agencies and programs with substantial
legal, political, and social difficulties that needed to be overcome.[4]

Most important, the decolonization process and the spawning of new
UN member states required a reform of the council, which had to take place
through an amendment of the charter that also brought about adjustments in
the council's size as well as in its mode of operation.[5] Although an increase
in the number of permanent member states was categorically rejected by the
P5 governments, they readily acknowledged that an expansion was justified
from the vantage point of representation. The council members under the
leadership of the P5 countries decided on the reform expeditiously, and the
1965 charter amendment increased the number of member states from eleven
to fifteen and the majority for action from seven to nine votes. As alluded to in
chapter 1, the repercussions of the reform were felt within a few months. The
number of meetings open to the public decreased, and the council expanded
the practice of informally deliberating in its entirety ("informal consultations
of the whole"), in alternative constellations ("informal consultations of other
than the whole"), in "private meetings" (after which a single copy of a protocol
is kept by the secretary general),[6] and in unofficial consultations among council members or with member states credited with the desire and capability of
helping to move a particular issue forward.[7]

In the late 1960s and the 1970s, the diplomatic process accompanying international conflict management by the UNSC slowly stabilized, with several
caucus groups helping to solidify loyalties. Outside the P5 and E10 groups
of countries that are directly derived from charter rules, the Non-Alignment
Movement (NAM), the Group of Seventy-Seven (G77) developing states, and
the EU caucus have demonstrated longevity. A number of "contact groups"
and "friends" of a particular country exposed to conflict have also emerged,
leaning on the UN Secretariat or P5 permanent missions for support and
inspiration. Although newspaper reports from time to time cited initiatives
by representatives of such caucus groups, much of the diplomatic activity was
conducted unofficially and bilaterally, away from the scrutinizing gaze of the
mass media and of capitals and other diplomats.

The frequency of formal as well as informal meetings remained low during the 1970s and 1980s, rarely exceeding two per month, reflecting the intermittent character of contacts between representatives of the two "antagonistic" coalitions of UN member states during the Cold War. As has been well established in the literature, the 1989–91 transformation of Central and Eastern Europe dismantled the ideological and political constraints that antagonisms between the United States and the Soviet Union had generated almost overnight. Indeed, the immediate aftermath of the Cold War, Franck and Nolte noted at the time, "witnessed a remarkable blossoming of the United Nations."[8] The most dramatic rise was in the number of informal meetings, which went from 62 in 1988 to 273 in 1993.[9]

Above all the coalition that in 1990–91 ejected the Iraqi army from Kuwait demonstrated that the international community had a capacity to act, swiftly and decisively, in defense of smaller nations that face aggression. Even if UNSC engagement to defend the territorial integrity and political autonomy of a Persian Gulf state could not vindicate the most optimistic proponents of a "new world order," imagining the onset of a new age of collective security, it is equally true that UN conflict management never reverted back to its pre-1990s stalemate. One indication of this is that the meeting frequency has remained significantly higher than before. Bosco, in an assessment made two decades after the Gulf War, wrote that the council had moved from "an often sleepy club for high politics to a frenetic world governance body that was struggling to contain conflict, mete out punishment for crimes against humanity, and end civil strife around the world."[10]

The P5 countries, by virtue of their veto rights, to this day continue to hold the key to any resolution adopted. As a consequence the United States, the United Kingdom, France, China, and Russia need to be engaged at some stage of the diplomatic process leading to a UNSC resolution. The P5 countries are for the most part continuously involved at some level in the truly contested, high-profile international conflict situations in the Middle East, East Asia, and Africa.[11] Each of the five has a comprehensive set of diplomatic missions in areas that matter in world politics and works hard to monitor situations that are or may become subject of council deliberations. The permanent representations to the UN are centrally placed nerve centers of security-related diplomacy especially in the case of the P5, though each of the P5 countries is also served by an asset-rich foreign ministry back home and by independent (or semi-independent) research institutions and think tanks.

Despite the constant input from a vast array of information and policy brokers, for political and practical reasons the council member states, and the P5 countries in particular, drive policymaking in the institution. A large portion of the narrower consultations leading to resolutions that may make a difference on the ground are initiated by the US permanent representative to the UN, who often begins by reaching out to his or her counterpart in the diplomatic mission of the United Kingdom. This bilateral consultation practice is what long has been called the "P2" in UN jargon. The "P3" is a trilateral consultation mechanism, also employed quite frequently, that further includes France. Once all three are engaged, a common course of action is to seek out the views of the last two veto members, Russia and China, and to identify further cosponsors to a draft resolution or partners to a diplomatic effort, funding scheme, or follow-up measures. As a collective, the P5 wields almost complete power when it comes to choosing the format of deliberation.[12]

There are certainly instances in which Russia, China, or a couple of the E10 countries come up with their own initiatives. The non-permanent E10 member states are as a rule kept in the loop by diplomats from the P2, P3, or P5 constellations of countries, or by governments at a bilateral level, on upcoming resolution drafts, as the endorsement of a minimum of an additional four elected members is required for a council resolution to go through. Moreover, in the overwhelming number of cases, the cosponsors of a resolution draft work very hard to garner a unanimous vote of all fifteen UNSC members, and thereby greatly enhance the political legitimacy of a particular decision. On procedural matters a total of nine votes suffices, which helps explain the generous approach that the council takes toward UN member states that request to attend meetings at which they believe they in one way or another have a stake.

But as we have learned in recent years, the diplomatic process that revolves around formal UNSC decision making does not constitute the whole picture by far. Besides the council and its member states, there is an informal dimension of diplomatic activities that pertains to the creation of political coalitions around diplomatic initiatives, the funding of peacekeeping operations, and other ambitious programs not provided for in the UN budget and that ensures that implementation is carried through in the individual case. It has been convincingly shown that a great variety of informally agreed to, ad hoc, or more long-term arrangements helps compensate for some of the severe weaknesses suffered by the UN system in terms of mustering sufficient capacities to transform words into deeds.[13]

From the beginning of the 1990s and the vast expansion of council-induced activities, the practice of relying on informal groups for specific purposes became indispensable for the UN. The expansion of peacekeeping and mediation missions, the delivery of humanitarian relief and legal aid, and various forms of institution building require a widespread support system within and outside the UN. It has proved to be as much a burden as an opportunity to engage the broader UN community for informal purposes. In this broader development it became necessary to pragmatically include elected member states along with a minimum of two or three P5 countries in the diplomatic effort in order to secure a fair hearing in the council. Beyond mere cosponsorship of draft resolutions, there is also a growing need to integrate countries that have expertise and an economic, political, or humanitarian interest in resolving or managing an international conflict situation. Only when effective implementation is likely to follow are governments prepared to provide the bulk of the funding or substantive troop contributions, but they also want a say in the process, along with recognition of their stakeholder status.

In the late 1990s the alarm raised by a limited but intense conflict situation in Europe famously prompted the P3 and its allies to sidestep the UNSC. In the context of the unrest and subsequent NATO intervention in Kosovo, then part of former Yugoslavia, in 1998–99, NATO and the G8 briefly emerged as ad hoc venues for international conflict management.[14] Because of Russia's strong opposition to coercive Western intervention that would circumscribe Serbia's autonomy, the route to a council resolution authorizing the use of military force was blocked. But as Washington, London, and Paris would not accept being tied down in a conflict close to the heartland of Europe, they made direct reference to the UN Charter's provision of a right to self-defense on the part of regional security organizations. In terms of international law, the NATO intervention was by several prominent countries, such as Germany and the United Kingdom, interpreted as "an exceptional measure" to the established practice of requesting authorization from the council for coercive intervention.[15] When a resolution in June 1999 eventually authorized the stationing of a civilian and military presence in Kosovo, the real locus of decision making had been the G8, which left Beijing outside the diplomatic process.[16]

Over the next few years, multiple efforts were made to restore a consensual approach to political and military intervention after the controversial Kosovo intervention. But five years later, an even deeper controversy in the UNSC, precipitated by the US-led invasion of Iraq in 2003, reinvigorated the divide between the P2 on the one side and Russia and China on the other. This time France and several non-P5 heavyweights—above all "second-tier" Germany—openly sided with Russia and China to thwart Washington's request for authorization. It eventually took several years of tense deliberations, and the election of a new US president more committed to the UN than George W. Bush was, to refocus the attention of most great powers toward the joint cause of international conflict management. By early 2009, as Barack Obama assumed his office, this fraught phase in intra-council relations began to come to a close.

In the following analysis of international conflict management in 2009–14, a number of important decisions and deliberations that took place in the UNSC and its subsidiary organs are examined. I will analyze the issue of council composition and working methods in the context of a future reform of that institution, the significance of informal groups that helped pave the way for and implement council resolutions, and the relationship between conflict management at the council and consultations held in the context of GX summitry. As mentioned at the outset, the UNSC is treated as the most important high-table platform at which international conflict management takes place and legitimate decisions with great resonance around the world may be reached. That being said, this chapter also explores the impact of informal groups and of GX summitry great powers on council decision making and follow-up measures.

2008–9 Crisis as Impetus for Reform

There is no direct link between the sharp financial crisis of 2008–9 and the renewed momentum for reform of the UNSC, yet the timing of the launch of the first round of intergovernmental negotiations in 2009 augured a significant shift of thinking in many capitals. A decade earlier, the proposals of Malaysia's UN ambassador Razali Ismail had succeeded in bringing serious attention to the issue and in formulating a set of well-balanced ideas about how to go about creating a political coalition to support it. Even though the concrete proposals Razali eventually put forward never garnered sufficient support to be made reality, they still serve as basic formulas for thinking about council reform, especially when it comes to the size of the council and categories of membership.[17]

When he took charge of the intergovernmental negotiations in 2009, the permanent representative of Afghanistan, Zahir Tanin, chose a bottom-up approach. In June 2010 Ambassador Tanin and his team presented a composite text reflecting "all positions" derived from some thirty different documents and thereby blocked the introduction of new views and arguments in the diplomatic process. "We are in the middle of negotiations," Tanin commented at the time, underlining his own role as a nonpartisan arbiter by insisting that "it is not for me to guess what agreement will be reached."[18] In the General Assembly debate held in November 2010, speakers affirmed that five so-called negotiables had been identified: categories of membership, the question of regional representation, the size of an enlarged Security Council, the working methods of the council, and finally, the relationship between the council and the General Assembly.[19]

The November 2010 General Assembly debate was also an occasion when, given the momentum for reform that had been created, representatives of several key delegations articulated more comprehensive views of their preferred result. As could be expected, leading diplomats speaking on behalf of the NAM, the Small Five Group (S5) of UN member states, and the African Group reiterated their support for UNSC reform that would entail its expansion as well as enhanced representation for non-Western states. Whereas many countries took the pragmatic attitude of accepting that the council would extend its membership in both the permanent and non-permanent categories, Italy led the "Uniting for Consensus" proposal calling for an end to the former category and to the veto privilege system *tout court*.

Equally predictably, the P5 countries expressed reservations about the latter proposal and argued that it would sacrifice effectiveness for equitable representation. To accommodate the desires of some countries to take a greater responsibility for issues of peace and security, Russian ambassador Vitaly Churkin noted the new opportunities for involvement in the recently launched peace-building activities on the African continent, and China's Li Baodong praised the council's efforts to enhance transparency.[20] The French and British permanent representatives, meanwhile, reaffirmed their commitment to an "interim solution" that would bridge the concerns of P5 incumbents as well as aspiring new permanent member states through an agreement on a test run of ten to fifteen years.

UN documents released at the time, such as the statements of heads of state and government at the openings session of the General Assembly, indicate a renewed momentum for UNSC reform against the backdrop of the 2008–9 financial crisis and turmoil in international markets, along with growing concern about political stability in many parts of the world. It seems conceivable that a growing realization of a pending shift of economic weight from the industrialized West and North toward the developing countries in the East and South—especially the emerging great powers among the latter—suddenly, in indirect and intangible ways, had come to the fore and exerted influence on how international conflicts were managed by the council. As G7/G8 leaders became persuaded that the economic clout of OECD economies would not suffice to offset the financial crisis, abstract talk about emerging great powers as "stakeholders" morphed into deliberations on more substantive matters.[21]

Outside the UN and its Security Council, the combined weight of the economies of the emerging great powers was being recognized by prominent political leaders of first-tier great powers, who felt compelled to respond. As described in chapter 2, the G20 upgrade to a summit mechanism gathering heads of state and government notably turned the group into the "premier forum for international economic cooperation." This did not weaken the aspirations of the emerging great powers, whose leaders expected that the winds of change would affect politics and diplomacy at the UN and other international organizations, but seemingly reinforced them. Very quickly the conventional wisdom on the matter became that the council's membership structure was "out of sync with today's global balance of power."[22]

As the main gatekeepers at the UNSC, the P5 member states certainly had an interest in showing that an analogous makeover was unnecessary at the major institutions of international conflict management, at least in the short term. At one point the United States and the Russian Federation jointly spearheaded a significant symbolic event that demonstrated that business as usual could be conducted and that the nuclear weapons capability that united all permanent member states remained a key justification for privileged positions at the council. The event took place on September 24, 2009, in conjunction with the annual General Assembly speeches by heads of state and of government, as a UNSC summit adopted Resolution 1887, devoted to nonproliferation. Notably, the council meeting was attended by an unprecedented fifteen heads of state and government. Chairing the session was US president Barack Obama, who urged all UN member states to help ensure control of fissile material and all governments with nuclear weapons to slash existing stockpiles.

Incidentally or not, the experience of US-Russian collaboration over nuclear weapons arsenals appeared to render Moscow somewhat more flexible regarding its stance on the Iran issue. In the past Russia had consistently rejected American overtures to forge a joint position that would entail increased pressure on Tehran to abandon its nuclear enrichment program. Moreover, Russia had continued to deliver key components to the Bushehr nuclear power plant, situated along the Persian Gulf in southwestern Iran. In October and November 2009, senior Russian officials met with their Iranian counterparts in Geneva and in the Iranian capital to try to persuade the Iranians to agree to some form of compromise, but to no avail. The discovery by Moscow that the Iranian leadership had engaged in deception with regard to a previously unknown enrichment facility near Qum probably contributed to Russia's changing tack and becoming more sympathetic to Western demands to enhance the political pressure.[23]

A few months later, on June 9, 2010, the UNSC adopted Resolution 1929, which expanded and significantly reinforced the sanctions regime against Iran. It did so by introducing as many as thirty-eight different points prohibiting the import of specific products and technologies associated with missile and nuclear technology. The appendix to the resolution enumerated a considerable number of Iranian individuals and companies the international community would be banned from collaborating with, thereby creating—for the first time with Iran as the primary target—a relatively comprehensive sanctions regime.

Resolution 1929 introducing comprehensive sanctions against Iran was adopted with three dissenting votes, one being a reservation (Lebanon) and two cast against the majority. Brazil and Turkey, however, eventually opposed the resolution on the grounds that they had already negotiated a compromise formula with Iran on a fuel-swap arrangement, according to which Tehran would pledge to adhere to the safeguards regime in exchange for an explicit endorsement of its right to develop nuclear energy technology for peaceful purposes. The high-profile diplomatic moves by Ankara and Brasilia were widely interpreted as connected to the aspirations of both to play a greater role in international diplomacy.[24]

Thwarted in its attempt to interject itself in Middle East diplomacy via the latter initiative, Brazil was nevertheless able to display leadership on security matters closer to home. After the devastating hurricane in Haiti in January 2010, the UNSC assigned Brazil leadership of the UN Stabilization Mission to Haiti (MINUSTAH), its first such high-profile assignment. MINUSTAH had first been established by Resolution 1542 on April 30, 2004,[25] but was, as a result of the damage caused by the 2010 hurricane, expanded so that it could deal with a wide spectrum of disaster relief efforts.

In the meantime, in New York the intergovernmental negotiations on UNSC reform barely moved forward. A first round of intergovernmental negotiations was followed by a second and a third. Despite the careful and painstaking work of Chair Tanin to avoid alienating any coalition of countries or the P5, many governments soon appeared reluctant to become more actively engaged as they perceived no substantive advances in individual or joint positions. By mid-2011 UN parliamentary president Joseph Deiss voiced concerns that the negotiations were not making enough progress and sounded a note of caution to those deliberately or involuntarily stalling the process. "Unless we find the determination to move on this issue," he stated, "the United Nations will lose its credibility."[26]

Although many agreed with the overall assessment of Ambassador Tanin and UN General Assembly president Deiss, the credibility gap of course also had deeper origins. For instance, the readiness to at least consider institutional reforms could not be matched by an openness to broaden the range or number of issues on the council agenda. In fact, symptomatic of the 2009–10 turn of the decade was that very few new issues were allowed to enter the

Security Council agenda and that resolutions for the most part steered free from creating new political or military missions that would additionally strain the budgets of OECD countries. In what appears to contradict the claim that a reform momentum was at hand, not a single new peacekeeping mission was created in 2009 or 2010.

A prosaic and structural explanation for the UNSC's cautionary stance with regard to reform as well as agenda setting may simply point to the dire fiscal situation of national budgets in many parts of the world in the wake of the 2008–9 financial crisis. Throughout the world the financial crisis almost invariably meant cutbacks in the field of foreign, security, and defense policy, with immediate repercussions for the bottom line and the political willingness to commit to new UN missions. In other words, the era of fiscal austerity had descended on the majority of developed countries, and many governments that traditionally were easy to persuade were now reluctant to accept additional international commitments.

Diplomatic Impasse, Institutional Creativity

In the Middle East the Israeli-Palestinian peace process was at an impasse, and the diplomatic practices designed to unblock it proved unproductive and inflexible. If anything, events on the ground contributed to further cementing hardened positions. Indeed, the year 2009 began with thirteen days of open military conflict. Hamas rocket attacks were predictably met with a robust military response by Israeli defense forces in the Gaza Strip, prompting the adoption of a resolution (1890) calling for an "immediate, durable and fully respected ceasefire, leading to the withdrawal of Israeli forces from Gaza." As only the United States had abstained from voting, the message was unusually unified and might have helped sway the Israeli forces to withdraw, as they did, on January 21.

In Lebanon the 2009–11 period provided something of a lull in what otherwise was a protracted roller-coaster ride of waxing and waning domestic political tension. In June 2009 successful and peaceful parliamentary elections were held, and reasonably stable diplomatic relations were restored between Syria and Lebanon. The UN secretary general's special envoy, Terje Roed-Larsen, candidly told the council that Lebanon had just been "on the brink of civil war and back" in the preceding months.[27] Except for repeated Israeli air space infringements and political fallout from the controversial findings of the Special Tribunal for Lebanon, which pointed the finger at the Syrian regime for involvement in the murder of former prime minister Rafic Hariri, 2010 was a relatively uneventful year for a previously conflict-ridden country. As a result of the outbreak of the Arab Spring in 2011 and its destabilizing effects on Syria, however, Lebanon soon again resurfaced as a focal point of regional conflicts between religious and sectarian communities.

In Iraq, meanwhile, statements by top UN officials and American military leaders working to facilitate a smooth drawdown of US military presence struck a sober yet sometimes upbeat note. The United Nations Assistance Mission in Iraq (UNAM) was extended to help prepare for the January 2010 parliamentary elections, subsequently postponed to March 7 that year. In 2010 the UNSC held a total of ten formal meetings devoted to the situation in Iraq, adopting three consecutive resolutions (1956, 1957, and 1958) that terminated arrangements for the Development Fund of Iraq, lifted restrictions on civilian nuclear activities and trade sanctions related to weapons of mass destruction, and ended the so-called oil-for-food program created in 1991.

The onset of an age of fiscal austerity and declining defense budgets in 2009 did not mean that the UNSC's work on peace and security was curbed. Several ongoing missions were reformed, revamped, or given revised instructions so as to better fit the changing environments in which they operated during 2009 and 2010. For instance, in January 2009 the council extended the United Nations Mission in the Central African Republic and Chad (MINURCAT) to encompass objectives upheld by the European Union Force (EUFOR) regarding the protection of civilians and the distribution of humanitarian aid.[28] Similarly, during 2010 MINUSTAH was bolstered from 6,940 to 8,940 Brazilian-led military personnel and from 2,211 to 4,391 police by way of two resolutions (1908 and 1927) aimed at assisting domestic Haitian authorities in carrying out presidential and legislative elections in early 2011.

Two institutional innovations, one originating from outside the UN system and one from within, started to have a positive impact on the council's African agenda by the end of the decade. The G8 Africa Clearing House, originally set up in 2004, was forged as a reasonably simple mechanism for bringing donors and other stakeholders together in order to better coordinate and make use of funding in projects across the realm of peace and security. The UN donor heavyweights, that is, the United States, the United Kingdom, Germany, and Japan, were the first countries to host meetings geared toward strengthening peace support operations on the African continent, attended by representatives of the G8 governments. As of 2007 Washington broadened the scope of participants by launching the G8++ Africa Clearing House meetings, to which major donor and troop-providing countries also were invited.

The UN Peacebuilding Commission (PBC), created through UNSC Resolution 1645 and General Assembly Resolution 60/180 and inaugurated in 2006, is in some ways an extension of—and formalized counterpart to—the

Africa Clearing House within the UN system. According to Resolution 1645, three purposes drive the PBC, the first being to "bring together all relevant actors to marshal resources and to advise on and propose integrated strategies for post-conflict peacebuilding and recovery." The second purpose is to "focus attention on the reconstruction and institution-building efforts" that demand long-term sponsorship and patience. The third and final purpose is to "provide recommendations and information to improve the coordination of all relevant actors within and outside the United Nations, to develop best practices, to help to ensure predictable financing for early recovery activities and to extend the period of attention given by the international community to post-conflict recovery."[29]

The G8 Africa Clearing House and the PBC thus represent an effort to address some of the long-standing non-P5 countries' criticisms of the lack of opportunity for close involvement in peace processes by countries that commit troops or funding. The Africa Clearing House is a flexible and informal mechanism with a demonstrated ability to close that gap. By providing a formalized setting linked to the UNSC, the PBC has the added advantage of potentially bringing in key stakeholders that may or may not sit at the UNSC at the time at which important decision making takes place, without compromising the formal process of decision making. The PBC is run by the thirty-one-member Organizational Committee, its composition derived from a quota system under which the council, the General Assembly, and the ECOSOC each select seven countries. In addition to the Organizational Committee, the top five troop providers and the top five donor countries are admitted. The advantages attributed to the PBC are its relative flexibility, informality, and high level of interaction between major stakeholders.[30]

In early 2009 the Organizational Committee further expanded the capacity of the PBC to interact with nontraditional partners by engaging the private sector and foundations, both with a view of channeling technical expertise and financial resources as well as renewing opportunities for resource generation.[31] In 2010 meetings with top-level World Bank officials, the PBC placed a greater focus on critical funding gaps and the need to help donors leverage resources strategically. Although the PBC seeks to establish a record of inviting only NGO experts with highly relevant knowledge and skills, the need to broaden the involvement of regional and local civil society actors was also acknowledged in 2010.[32] In "informal consultations of the whole" (including all fifteen member states acting within the PBC process), these practices moreover helped the UNSC liberalize its use of video teleconferencing as a means to receive briefings directly from field missions and traveling officials.[33]

Focus on Africa

The UNSC held 171 meetings in 2009, eighty of which were devoted to developments in Africa. In 2010, 79 out of 182 meetings concerned Africa.[34] As mentioned previously, no new peacekeeping missions were created, but the council in various ways tried to adapt existing missions to the changing tasks at hand. One example is the 2008–9 attempt to respond to the uprooting of some 250,000 people in the eastern provinces of the Democratic Republic of the Congo in order to protect civilians and to prevent sexual violence and recruitment of children by the Uganda-based Lord's Resistance Army by revising the mandate for the United Nations Mission in the Democratic Republic of the Congo (MONUC). In 2011, while taking into account the desires of President Joseph Kabila and the lessening of the threat posed by the Lord's Resistance Army, the council allowed for the beginning of a drawdown of troops and a transformation of MONUC to a "stabilization force" (hence renamed UN Stabilization Mission in the Democratic Republic of the Congo [MONUSCO]).

Another dynamic conflict was in Sudan, a country stuck between a peace process and military activities continuing unabated on the ground. The 2005 Comprehensive Peace Agreement signed by the Sudanese Liberation Movement/Army (SLM/A) and the government of Sudan had not been implemented for several years, even though the United Nations Mission in the Sudan (UNMIS) worked hard to facilitate enforcement of the agreement. The Sudanese government, the SLM/A, and the international community had not demonstrated much political will in moving the process forward, and further complications arose after the International Criminal Court issued an international arrest warrant for Sudanese president Omar Hassan al-Bashir.

An AU High-Level Implementation Panel chaired by former South African president Thabo Mbeki eventually came up with a comprehensive peace plan for Sudan, which was shared with the UNSC on December 21, 2009. During 2010 the council met as many as twelve times to help pave the way for a referendum in January 2011 and to determine whether South Sudan would opt for independence or remain part of the state of Sudan. Together with Alain le Roy, undersecretary general for peacekeeping operations, UNMIS was charged with facilitating the political process in the region. In advance of the referendum, negotiations on issues relating to natural resources, borders, citizenship, currency, and other assets were held under the auspices of the AU High-Level Implementation Panel chaired by ex-president Mbeki.

In Somalia, on the coastline of the Indian Ocean, the UNSC similarly promoted the so-called Djibouti peace process for which UN Secretary General

Special Representative Ahmedou Ould-Abdallah had been appointed. The AU Mission in Somalia had its mandate extended so that it could continue to support the efforts of the transitional federal government to stabilize the security situation, especially in and around the capital Mogadishu. The UNSC met eleven times in 2009 and ten times in 2010 to discuss peace-building and reconciliation efforts, massive displacement and insurgency violence, and the issue of piracy off the Somali coast. Augustine Mahiga, who succeeded Ould-Abdallah as the special representative of the secretary general, told a council briefing in September that insurgents were growing stronger and that rapid and more comprehensive action was needed to assist the transitional federal government.

Meanwhile in western Africa, Côte d'Ivoire had been edging toward a political healing process, with presidential elections scheduled for late 2009 as a serious test case of reconciliation. After several postponements the elections were eventually held in October and November 2010, though the poll resulted in a tense military standoff. The acknowledged winner, Alassane Ouattara, was eager to enter the premises of the presidential administration, but the incumbent, Laurent Gbagbo, refused to acknowledge his defeat and leave his office. During the election preparations and the ensuing political crisis, the UNSC extended the mandate of the United Nations Operation in Côte d'Ivoire and quickly redeployed troops from the United Nations Mission in Liberia to help underpin the constitutional process in the former country.

Elsewhere in the central and western parts of Africa, the UNSC went on to monitor the situation in the Great Lakes region, Burundi, the Central African Republic, Sierra Leone, Guinea-Bissau, Liberia, and Western Africa. Most of these countries were handled under the auspices of the PBC as so-called country-specific configurations made up of various stakeholders. Burundi became the first country adopted into this framework, and in 2009–10 the focus of peace-building efforts was on socioeconomic development and preparations for the January 2011 elections. Soon thereafter country-specific configurations were established for Guinea-Bissau, Sierra Leone, and the Central African Republic in order to better orchestrate effective stabilization measures in these countries as well.

In fact, the G8-based Africa Clearing House and the UN-based PBC held their annual, parallel meetings throughout 2009–14. In an evolving partnership with the AU, both institutions substantively improved the coordination of donors and the exchange of information between G8 countries and African countries. Whereas the PBC gathered the major stakeholders with regard to a given conflict area or set of issues, the Africa Clearing House format allowed for the inclusion of a wider group of interested parties and thereby extended beyond non-G8, Western countries to all governments that sponsor significant aid and assistance programs in Africa. As an illustration of the widening community of stakeholders, as many as forty-six countries participated in the December 2012 G8++ meeting in Washington, DC, with an agenda mainly devoted to maritime security in the Gulf of Guinea in response to an increasingly challenging security situation developing there.

Exceptional Council, (Almost an) Ordinary Year

The simultaneous inclusion of all five BRICS (Brazil, Russia, India, China, and South Africa) countries in the UNSC in 2011 by some accounts helped reinforce foreign policy coordination among the council's members.[35] To at least one Russian analyst, the BRICS countries acted on the basis of common or similar positions with regard to the crises in Libya, Somalia, Côte d'Ivoire, and Sudan. All BRICS governments were agreed, Vyacheslav Nikonov wrote, that Western countries should not be allowed to instrumentalize the UNSC "to topple disagreeable regimes and impose one-sided solutions to conflict situations."[36] As two US commentators predicted when the composition of the 2011 council was settled in October the previous year, the fact that the new constellation would temporarily feature more big powers might render it "a little harder" for permanent members to be "frequently fixing deals on issues like Iran behind closed doors."[37]

In some ways 2011 was not at all an unusual year; for instance, the UNSC was mainly preoccupied with individual conflict situations and its members only rarely found time to deliberate on global or thematic, cross-cutting topics. In fact, the council was in charge of a total of seventeen UN missions across the globe, with large operations being poised to wind down in Côte d'Ivoire and Afghanistan. Among the major and particularly pressing matters before the council, three specific conflicts stood out: first, the political process in Sudan and South Sudan; second, the civil war in Libya and the international response to that conflict; and third, the continued instability in Somalia proper as well as along that country's long coastline.

As many as thirty recorded meetings of the UNSC were held on the situation in Sudan in 2011. The high frequency of meetings in part reflected the culmination of a six-year-long diplomatic process aimed at paving the way for a durable peace settlement. The basic idea was to address the profound political problems of Sudan by allowing, through the Naivasha Agreement of 2005 and the Comprehensive Peace Agreement of 2009, for public participation in reaching a compromise deal that involved dividing the country into two parts. A referendum was held on January 15 in the southern provinces, with a turnout well above the required 60 percent and an overwhelming majority voting in favor of secession. Apart from the close engagement on the part of the UN and the US State Department, an important component of diplomatic efforts keeping the 2005 and 2009 agreements in place was the AU High-Level Implementation Panel presided over by Mbeki.

Crucially, the outcome of the January referendum was not challenged by the government in Khartoum. On July 9, 2011, the Republic of South Sudan was proclaimed under the auspices of the peace process led by the UN. In particular, Resolution 1966 mandated the UN to set up the United Nations Mission in the Republic of South Sudan (UNMISS) to consolidate peace and security and help the newly instated government exercise its duties; the latter was to be accomplished with the support of up to 7,000 troops and 900 police (note that Resolution 1997 terminated the preceding UNMIS). At the July 13, 2011, meeting during which the secretary general offered his official report, nine council members were represented at the ministerial level in an effort to bolster the wider political legitimacy of the process.

Military clashes between the Sudanese Army and the Sudan People's Liberation Movement–North (SPLM-N) in South Kordofan and the Nuba Mountains nevertheless continued throughout the second half of 2011. With a significant presence in the western province of Darfur, the SPLM-N also remained openly supportive of several rebel military forces fighting the government of Omar al-Bashir and his local allies. At one point al-Bashir expressly threatened South Sudan with resuming the war if the latter did not back down from such actions.[38]

The second most frequent topic of formal UNSC deliberations in 2011—and also that which by far received the most international attention—was the rapidly escalating conflict in Libya. A total of twenty-two meetings were held in the course of the year. From the vantage point of the council, the diplomatic process was extraordinarily swift: the Libya issue was first raised in a "private meeting" on February 22 and three days later was elevated to a formal agenda item—under the inconspicuous "Peace and Security in Africa" headline—in its own right. On the same day, February 25, the UN Human Rights Council held a special session in Geneva to consider suspending Libya's membership in response to the ongoing crackdown on civilians and threats of atrocities. The latter decision then followed on March 1.[39]

On February 26 the UNSC unanimously adopted Resolution 1970. The resolution demanded "an immediate end to the violence and call[ed] for steps to fulfil the legitimate demands of the population" and included an explicit warning to the Libyan authorities to act with the utmost restraint. The resolution enacted four measures: a general referral to the International Criminal Court;

a comprehensive arms embargo, including "technical assistance"; a travel ban on Muammar Gaddafi, his family, and his closest associates; and finally, an asset freeze on Gaddafi, his family, and his closest associates.[40] In the following three weeks, the limited impact of the measures was monitored by council members while a debate ensued on the possible use of military intervention to thwart a full-scale civil war.

Mid-March 2011 was a time of preparing for political and military intervention; options were weighed and justifications articulated.[41] NATO countries met at the ministerial level on March 10 and 11 to forge a political formula under which the organization could take on a mission and to set the military planning process in motion. According to NATO secretary general Anders Fogh Rasmussen, three interconnected conditions needed to be met for the military alliance to spring into action: "Firstly, there has to be demonstrable need for Nato action. Secondly, there has to be a clear legal basis. And thirdly, there has to be firm regional support."[42] The first condition would take care of itself if the situation became sufficiently dire, one might argue. The "clear legal basis" was in this case a UNSC resolution, without which countries like Germany and Turkey would no doubt balk at authorizing NATO action. The third condition was the crucial political element that had to be addressed. To many observers the League of Arab States appeared to be the logical venue for providing formal endorsement.

The March 12 meeting of the Council of the League of Arab States in Cairo, under the chairmanship of Secretary General Amr Moussa, produced a resolution in favor of a no-fly zone after more than five hours of deliberations. Although qualifying the vote as solely focused on protecting the lives of Libyan civilians and bolstering the security and territorial integrity of neighboring countries, the unprecedented move of twenty-one Arab governments expressing support for military measures against a member state—whose membership was suspended—was perceived as virtually meeting NATO's third condition. In fact, Arab League endorsement rendered military intervention somewhat more palatable to several UNSC members that so far had stayed above the fray and helped quell the key concerns of top US decision makers.[43]

Given that a "clear legal basis" was an explicit condition for NATO, the challenge of persuading UNSC member states and in particular the two non-NATO countries, Russia and China, loomed large. An opportunity to prepare the ground and engage Moscow presented itself already at the G8 foreign ministers meeting in Paris on March 14 and 15, 2011. At this point the US secretary of state, Hillary Clinton, directly engaged her colleagues and made the case for council action. Even though the joint statement coming out of the meeting was vague, it entailed several planks that suggested a clear commitment by the UNSC might be forthcoming. The chair summary statement expressly praised the adoption of Resolution 1970 and the decision of the UN Human Rights Council to suspend Libya's membership in that body, and then went on to welcome the Arab League resolution (7360) and urgent measures by the UNSC "to ensure the protection of the Libyan population from attack by Muammar Qadhafi's forces."[44]

UNSC Resolution 1973, adopted March 17, did include the "all necessary measures" formula required to authorize military action. It was upheld by a slim margin at the council and therefore justifiably prompted an array of critical commentary. Noteworthy is first of all that a fateful decision to unleash a large-scale military operation was adopted hastily and with a bare minimum of diplomatic and political support. Given the unusual composition of the UNSC at the time, one interpretation is that key member states viewed it as a test case. For the P3 governments that favored military action, the test at hand was whether the emerging great powers were ready to accept political responsibility for military measures and further prepared to defend such action domestically. To the great powers aspiring for a permanent seat at the council, as well as Russia and China, already the "constructive abstention" that allowed for military action to go ahead entailed a test of sorts—one of political stamina. By the same token, the latter hoped that the intervention would conform closely to the constraints inherent in the resolution. In some ways, it seems, both the P3 countries and the second-tier aspiring permanent member states failed the test set up by the other.[45]

The third most frequent topic of consideration by the UNSC in 2011 was Somalia. Some half a dozen substantive resolutions on this matter were passed during the course of the year, specifying several objectives related to internal as well as external conflict management issues. Resolution 1972, for instance, calibrated the Somalia small arms embargo without overly constraining the possibility for the UN to help bolster the capacity of forces supporting the transitional federal government. While Resolution 2002 tightened the sanctions directed toward the al-Shabaab rebel militia, Resolution 2010 extended the mandate of both AU and African Mission in Somalia (AMISOM) forces and thereby enhanced their respective military role in the country, raising the ceiling on the maximum number of soldiers to 12,000.

Resolutions 2015 and 2020, meanwhile, largely addressed the worsening problem of piracy and piracy-related military actions along the Somalia coast. The former put in place measures intended to bolster the indigenous capacity of Somali authorities to deal with piracy in terms of legal process and enforcement measures. The latter was entirely geared toward rendering more effective the international response—involving the EU Operation Atalanta, NATO

Operations Allied Protector and Ocean Shield, and other maritime operations working toward the same general objective—to the growing problem of Somali piracy. Both resolutions helped clarify the ways in which domestic and international efforts, with regard to shoring up support for law enforcement, would be mutually reinforcing.

Apart from the regular activities of the UNSC involving reviewing and extending mandates of existing UN political and military missions, the 2011 council dealt with a small number of cross-cutting themes and issues. Among such themes was "the protection of civilians in armed conflict," "women and peace and security," "children and armed conflict," "post-conflict peacebuilding," "peace and security—terrorist acts," and "non-proliferation" (sometimes including "of weapons of mass destruction"). Regarding the protection of civilians, women, and children and post-conflict peace building, the meeting agenda remained heavily oriented toward the situation in conflict areas on the African continent. Especially in debates on peace building, the presence of non-Western great powers and contenders for permanent council seats, such as India, Brazil, and South Africa, affected the content and tenor of the proceedings.[46]

Organizational Tinkering

As just described, 2011 was an exceptional year for the UNSC, mostly because of the number of great powers aspiring for a permanent seat that served as elected member states. In the October 2011 elections to the council, only Pakistan was a heavyweight among the five elected member states, the others being Guatemala, Togo, Azerbaijan, and Morocco. A year later, in October 2012, the General Assembly reverted to favoring G20 countries, electing Argentina, Australia, and the Republic of Korea, along with Luxembourg and Rwanda, to serve in 2013–14. The first choice of the General Assembly in the fall of 2013 largely repeated the pattern, with the G20 being represented by Nigeria and Saudi Arabia (Chile, Lithuania, and Chad were the other three). Saudi Arabia then famously chose not to take up its seat, in what amounted to a thinly veiled protest directed at the United States and other Western states for allowing the war in Syria to drag on, as well as for lifting some sanctions against Iran, Riyadh's main rival in the region.[47] The General Assembly subsequently picked Jordan to replace the disgruntled Saudi Arabia. In 2014, however, none of the five new members belonged to the G20.[48]

By electing and reelecting asset-rich countries to the UNSC in recent years, the General Assembly has in an indirect way helped to compensate for the lack of comprehensive institutional reform. Countries such as Japan and Brazil, which have served as non-permanent member states ten times each since the establishment of the UN, clearly accumulate a considerable amount of knowledge in international affairs as a result of their UNSC experience. If the trend toward favoring asset-rich states continues, non-veto great powers will further expand their networks and knowledge of various issues, especially conflict situations, which renders them more capable actors in global diplomacy. By the same token, the opportunities for small and middle powers to gain similar expertise will be diminished as most G20 countries rotate in and out, more or less, two out of every four years.[49]

The discrepancy between the rights and privileges of permanent and non-permanent member states remains stark. The widely appreciated Hitting the Ground Running program, organized by the Finnish permanent representation, for incoming member states somewhat alleviates the information asymmetry in the initial stage by helping incoming E10 countries come to grips with current issues, and a succession of countries chairing the rotating presidency have in recent years worked to enhance transparency in the council's work. These are features that permanent member states have not actively resisted, as they only marginally impinge on council working methods.[50]

Attention to the UNSC's working methods has not been widespread among asset-rich member states, whether veto holders or elected, with the exception of Japan. Costa Rica followed up on Japan's initiative in 2008–9 and was able to pull the other S5 countries, as well as Tokyo, into the discussions.[51] Two documents referred to as Note 502 were produced at this point, and in 2011 the S5 embarked on a more ambitious project. In November 2011 an S5 proposal outlining twenty different points of improvement was ready to be put to vote. Among the points of improvement were the distribution of a tentative monthly program of work and a pledge by permanent members that in the future they would rarely use their veto. Moreover, when permanent members did use their veto, they would be obliged to expressly and without exception justify their vote. To the surprise of the S5 country diplomats, UN legal experts deemed the veto proposal to require a two-thirds majority vote in the General Assembly. Rather than bring the issue to a vote, the S5 countries withdrew the proposal.[52]

The procedural weaknesses that follow from, or are laid bare in, the UNSC's working methods are well-known. One concerns the lack of opportunities for interaction between council members and the parties involved in a particular conflict. The system of resource allocation, according to various accounts, is suboptimal because it requires a renewed vote to shift resources from one organizational entity to another. It is clear that a number of the sanctions committees created under chapter VII have much less to do today than when they were formed and that the funding could be put to better use if the work of the subsidiary organs was reviewed more frequently.[53] Another long-standing

Table 3.1 Major Permanent Seat Contenders and Elected Terms in the UNSC

	Brazil	Germany	India	Japan	South Africa
1st term	1946–47	1977–78	1950–51	1958–59	2007–8
2nd term	1951–52	1987–88	1967–68	1966–67	2011–12
3rd term	1954–55	1995–96	1972–73	1971–72	
4th term	1963–64	2003–4	1977–78	1975–76	
5th term	1967–68	2011–12	1984–85	1981–82	
6th term	1988–89		1991–92	1987–88	
7th term	1993–94		2011–12	1992–93	
8th term	1998–99			1997–98	
9th term	2004–5			2005–6	
10th term	2010–11			2009–10	

problem has been the insufficient involvement of troop-contributing states in the monitoring and management of peacekeeping operations.

But, as was mentioned previously, one institutional innovation has established a stakeholder engagement mechanism that, at least in the context of Africa, largely remedies the latter weakness. The creation of the PBC facilitated the shaping of responses to specific crises that integrate peacekeeping and peace building in ways that UNSC decision making does not.[54] The coordination between regional organizations and the council was a key topic of a debate on council working methods organized by India, an elected member state, as it held the presidency of the UNSC in November 2012. Also covered on this occasion was the issue of wider consultations when appointing chairs to subsidiary organs and ensuring that the annual council reports to the General Assembly are genuinely informative. In the annual debate on UNSC working methods in October 2013, the main suggestions discussed concerned the usefulness of so-called horizon-scanning briefings and wrap-up sessions by incoming (monthly) presidents, along with renewed efforts to improve coordination between the council and troop- and police-contributing nations. Notably, in the course of 2013, most E10 presidencies held wrap-up sessions, whereas P5 countries (with the exception of the United Kingdom) ignored the new majority practice.[55]

Meanwhile, the overall focus on Africa in UNSC-mandated activities continued in 2011–13 with 115 out of 213 (2011), 85 out of 184 (2012), and 93 out of 172 (2013) meetings dealing with that continent. In every year as many as forty resolutions addressed African problems. At the same time African institutions, above all the AU, were more frequently becoming part of the solution. The AU repeatedly demonstrated that it constituted an important partner for the UNSC when it came to maintaining peace and security, a fact that on October 26 was expressly recognized in a council press statement.[56] Anticipating that the African continent will see even more challenges in the years ahead, the council called on the AU to create a long-term road map for capacity building in consultation with other UN bodies.

If the PBC helped create a roster of stakeholders with long-term commitments, the AU contributed new instruments for addressing a wider set of regional problems. The African Peace and Security Architecture (APSA), to be administered by the Peace and Security Council of the AU, was set up at the Durban summit of 2002 and slowly gained strength in the years that followed. According to a 2010 assessment report, the core achievement of the APSA was the collaboration between the African Standby Force (ASF) and the Continental Early Warning System (CEWS). The same report recommended that the APSA framework should be further expanded through the involvement of the Regional Economic Communities (REC) to better mobilize economic, political, and military resources for specific missions. Through the management of conflicts such as those in Burundi, Sudan, Somalia, and Darfur, the AU has clearly been gaining valuable experience. In cooperating more systematically with RECs, such as the Economic Community of West African States (ECOWAS), the prospects for a broader and more integrated UN-AU framework appear to be growing.

In parts of the world where international organizations are more numerous and influential, the problem is not so much a lack of presence but one of "inter-blocking" institutional mandates. Owing to the great number of multifunctional international organizations operating on the European continent, UN missions tend to generate the need for an intricate division of labor. For instance, the United Nations Interim Administration Mission in Kosovo (UN-MIK) remains in place nearly fifteen years after the end of large-scale hostilities between Serbs and Albanians but must inevitably work closely with Western European organizations. The latter include the Kosovo Stabilization Force (KFOR) operated by NATO, along with OSCE and EU missions in the realm of security and law enforcement. In other parts of the world, individual nation-states, such as Australia in the case of East Timor, have stepped up to assume a leading and coordinating role.[57]

Conflict Management by Great-Power Summit

The final communiqués adopted at the 2009 l'Aquila and 2010 Toronto G8 summits were still characterized by the long-standing economic and financial affairs focus of that body, yet the member states this time around proved more reluctant than previously to make grand political gestures. Possibly because of the recent upgrade of the G20, the G8 largely avoided commenting on current international affairs and conflict situations. The 2010 Toronto final declaration agreed to by heads of state and government was a particularly striking example of a document practically void of contentious foreign and security policy issues. Instead, it provided a considerable amount of detail as to how the G8 should take the lead in restoring growth for both developing and developed countries.

This is to say that international conflict management by way of the GX summitry in 2009–10 took place at the separately held foreign ministers meetings, typically convened in the spring a couple of months in advance of the summit. In this context conflict management inevitably overlapped with counterterrorism (the subject of chapter 4), as it featured as a major topic at the foreign ministers meeting in Rome in 2009 and in Gatineau, Canada, in 2010. The latter meeting was mainly structured along thematic lines, listing nuclear nonproliferation and "security vulnerabilities" as the two other main issues. Under the latter, it seems, the ministers also spoke more in depth about specific challenges in various regions and individual countries, paying most attention to Latin America, the Caribbean, the Middle East, and Southeast Asia.

In the course of 2011, the G8 tentatively returned to its practice of issuing statements that would take recent international events into account, and sometimes even express loose policy guidance or a preferred direction of diplomatic efforts. An example of a reactive statement was the strong condemnation by G8 foreign ministers of the bombing of the Moscow Domodedovo Airport in late January 2011. Another example of a reactive statement was the May 27 declaration, adopted at the Deauville summit by G8 foreign ministers, which expressed support for the aspirations of people in North Africa and the Middle East during the Arab Spring events.

Precious few statements by G8 heads of state and government went beyond this reactive stance and explicitly urged political actors to try to profoundly influence a situation. At Deauville the presidents of Russia, France, and the United States issued one such statement calling on the governments of Armenia and Azerbaijan to reconcile their differences and move toward a "decisive peace settlement." Moreover, a joint declaration by the G8 and Africa, adopted at the 2011 Deauville summit, implicitly referred to G8-sponsored military training programs in saying, "We welcome efforts made by the African Union and the regional economic communities to build up the African Peace and Security Architecture (APSA), including the African Standby Force, as well as the successful implementation of the G8 Action Plan, adopted at the

Sea Island Summit in 2004, to reinforce African peacekeeping capabilities."[58] Given over four decades of G7/G8 summit history, the low profile of foreign and security policy in 2009–10 was something of an aberration. By 2011–12 the G8 appeared to have moved back toward favoring a more overtly political role in international affairs, no longer shying away from stating clear preferences when major powers were in agreement. At the 2012 Camp David summit hosted by US president Obama, the May 19 declaration reflected a few obvious American priorities in foreign and security policy but also high-priority concerns that overlap between the G8 and the UNSC. A total of nine out of thirty-nine points enumerated in the declaration dealt with "political and security issues," and another ten with the problems of Afghanistan and political upheavals in North Africa and the Middle East, inadvertently mirroring the concerns of the Security Council.

In fact, the G8 summit at Camp David dealt with only a handful of conflict situations at some length. Among those specifically addressed in the declaration were the growing humanitarian crisis in Syria, Iran's nuclear program, and the "provocative actions of the Democratic People's Republic of Korea (DPRK) that threaten regional stability," as well as the rights of women and girls and the right to practice religious faith in security and safety. But compared with the G8 statements of previous years, this was quite an extensive and precise set of commitments beyond the least-common-denominator statements often produced in connection with such meetings. According to veteran GX summitry observer John Kirton, the G8 leaders at Camp David "stood together for global peace and security in an impressively committed, comprehensive and innovative way."[59]

The absence of President Putin at Camp David in 2012 may partially explain the unusually fine-tuned phrasing on several international conflicts that in other venues gave rise to overt contention. Another explanation may be that US president Obama and British prime minister David Cameron succeeded in swaying their peers to let the G8 assume wider responsibilities in the realm of nontraditional security. Given the legacy of great-power collaboration that has accumulated over four decades, the G7/G8 would seem to have significant potential when it comes to tying security initiatives to development assistance, legal cooperation, security sector reform, et cetera. More controversial is whether the views of G7/G8 governments are sufficiently close for summits to also provide continuous guidance, through joint statements, on the main foreign and security affairs of the day.

In the course of 2013, the G8 significantly expanded the range of issues on which its leaders felt confident working toward a shared formula. In mid-January 2013 the G8 political directors made a joint statement on Mali, as a jihadist group was in the process of conquering vast territories in the north of that country. At the April meeting of foreign ministers at Aylesbury, an unusually lengthy document was adopted. The document detailed a variety of thematic problems but in particular covered the handling of several concrete conflict situations in Africa, the Middle East, and elsewhere. The ideas for further measures regarding the conflicts existing in Somalia, Mali, Sudan/South Sudan, and the Democratic Republic of Congo were quite specific, indicating that G8 governments were largely aligned when it came to working to forge durable political settlements there.

The Lough Erne summit communiqué, adopted on June 18, 2013, consisted of ninety-five individual points. While the bulk of the document was concerned with trade, taxes, transparency, counterterrorism, and climate change, points 82–94 at the end of the communiqué were wholly devoted to specific foreign policy and conflict management priorities. In this portion of the text, the heads of state and government reiterated their determination to put a stop to the "bloodshed and loss of life" in Syria, laying out a number of parameters for doing so that they agreed on. Among other things, the G8 leaders stated that they were prepared to make "exceptional contributions commensurate to the scale of the problem" and that they sought to achieve a "united, inclusive and democratic Syria."

Syria: From Nonaction to Damage Limitation

Identifying a common problem is not equivalent to reaching a diplomatic agreement on how to go about resolving it, even when the former takes on epic proportions in terms of humanitarian consequences. By the end of 2014, the war in Syria had escalated from peaceful street protests to a full-scale civil war with some 200,000 casualties and eight million displaced people, roughly two million of whom had left Syrian territory. The war had expanded into one of the greatest humanitarian emergencies in post–world war (and UN) history with manifold repercussions for neighboring states and international diplomacy.[60]

The stance of the UN secretary general and leaders of UN agencies was from the outset one of condemnation of the violence used in the conflict, which they attributed almost entirely to the government of Bashar al-Assad. The United Nations High Commissioner for Refugees (UNHCR), the International Red Cross, and other organizations were already aware of the worsening humanitarian situation by 2011 and started to engage local communities and neighboring countries. A draft resolution strongly condemning the "grave and systematic human rights violations" taking place in Syria, and explicitly warning the government of robust action were these not suspended, was nevertheless defeated by the double veto of Russia and China on October 4, 2011. As many as four non-permanent members, three of which were G20 member states, abstained from voting: Lebanon, South Africa, India, and Brazil.

While the UN Human Rights Council and other UN bodies became increasingly active with regard to the widening civil war in Syria, the UNSC failed to move beyond deliberations and renewed, yet again unsuccessfully, its attempts to adopt a resolution that would bring about an end to the armed conflict in Syria. Exactly four months after the October 4 veto, on February 4, 2012, China and Russia went through the motions anew. After having participated in the lengthy negotiating process that led up to the vote, Beijing and Moscow vetoed the draft resolution cosponsored by the P3 countries, Germany, Portugal, Colombia, Togo, and as many as a dozen Middle Eastern and North African states. Although lacking in specificity and threats of coercive measures at a later stage, a resolution supporting the protection of civilians and their right to express themselves freely and to choose their own government was seemingly unacceptable to the Chinese and Russian leaderships. In justifying its vote, Beijing said, "China maintains that under the current circumstances, to put undue emphasis on pressuring the Syrian Government for a prejudged result of the dialogue or to impose any solution will not help resolve the Syrian issue. Instead, that may further complicate the situation."[61] Moscow, for its part, similarly demonstrated its willingness to play an active part in UNSC deliberations in search of a peaceful settlement in the days leading up to the formal meeting. Ambassador Churkin cited two main reasons for rejecting the majority draft: Russia's own attempts to jump-start a dialogue between the warring parties and the perceived lack of evenhandedness, in Russia's view, inherent in a draft that failed to strongly urge that "the Syrian opposition must distance itself from extremist groups that are committing acts of violence, and calling on States and all those with any relevant opportunity to use their influence to stop those groups committing acts of violence."[62]

The next formal meeting of the UNSC that adopted a resolution (2042) was held on April 14, 2012. The resolution, which was sponsored by Colombia, France, Germany, Morocco, Portugal, the United Kingdom, and the United States, expressed strong support for implementation of the six-point plan that Joint Special Envoy Kofi Annan had worked out and put before the Syrian government during a visit a few days earlier. Although the resolution contained a passage calling on all parties to the conflict, the brunt of the responsibility for suspending military activities was placed, at least implicitly, on al-Assad's regime. Given the apparent readiness of the Syrian government to accept a widened UN role, the council was merely a week later able to pass a second resolution (2043), by which the United Nations Supervision Mission in Syria (UNSMIS) was established with 300 unarmed military observers.

In late July 2012 the council renewed the UNSMIS mandate for another thirty days. But it soon became abundantly clear that none of the attempts on the part of the international community to either bring the parties to the negotiating table or stem the escalation of military and increasingly sectarian violence had more than a marginal effect on events in Syria. As a matter of fact, reports suggested that regional and more distant governments were increasingly becoming drawn into supporting the various factions in the war. At a meeting in Doha on November 11, 2012, several rebel groups and political opposition forces united as the National Coalition for Syrian Revolutionary and Opposition Forces. But a UN Human Rights Council periodic update released only weeks later unequivocally stated that violence had "increased dramatically in and around major cities" and that mounting tensions had precipitated "armed clashes between different armed groups along a sectarian divide."[63]

The first half of 2013 saw an unprecedented deepening of the sectarian character of the conflict, and also a fragmentation of military and political loyalties beyond the Sunni-Shia divide.[64] Hezbollah veterans from neighboring Lebanon joined the fray on the side of the Syrian regime and its Shia Alawite core, which was also supported through arms deliveries from Russian manufacturers. At the same time the largely Sunni-dominated rebels were bolstered by moral, financial, and logistical means originating in Saudi Arabia and Qatar. By June 2013 the death toll was estimated at 100,000 by independent sources.[65]

The widely reported August 21 chemical weapons attack in East Ghouta, outside Damascus, temporarily injected a new dynamic into the international conflict management of the Syrian war. Even if some governments rejected claims that the attack was launched by Syrian government forces, the facts that it took place and precipitated the death of several hundred civilians and that the al-Assad regime controls dozens of chemical weapons production and storage facilities around the country are widely accepted. To be sure, the work of a UN inspection team that was present in the capital at the time of the attack greatly facilitated the collection of samples and interviews that could form the basis of a shared assessment. Direct attribution, however, was outside the mandate of the UN inspection team, and that limitation was respected in the final report.[66]

Having been divided over how to conduct conflict management in the case of Syria for several months, the UN had the opportunity after the East Ghouta chemical weapons attack to launch new political and diplomatic initiatives that would not be seen as favoring one party over another in the military conflict. Given the worldwide consensus on the illegitimacy of the use of chemical weapons, technical and factual evidence could form the basis of a new draft resolution. First there was the issue of establishing that there had been an attack that had caused a certain number of casualties. Second, there was the question of upholding international legal obligations and the prohibition of the use of chemical weapons, especially against civilians. Finally, the wider problem of promoting a peace process, by which the parties of the conflict could begin to lay the foundations for a settlement or a temporary truce, came to the fore.

The frustration of the US administration with the inaction of the UNSC, even in the face of this serious breach of an international legal norm, prompted a stern and combative message from Washington, which earlier had warned that the use of chemical weapons constituted a "red line." In late August and early September, President Obama, Secretary of State John Kerry, and Prime Minister David Cameron consequently threatened the al-Assad regime with direct military strikes. The commitment was nevertheless expressed with the condition that domestic political support was forthcoming.[67] When the UK parliament voted down Cameron's pro-war bill, the Obama administration became wrong-footed.

At this juncture the Russian foreign minister, Sergei Lavrov, invited his Syrian counterpart to Moscow, asking him to agree to a UN-sponsored scheme that would remove all chemical weapons from the territory of Syria. With key assets of the US Navy, including an aircraft carrier and several warships armed with Tomahawk cruise missiles, positioned just off the Lebanese coast and maintaining a high readiness posture, Russian diplomats worked intensely with Syrian officials and American counterparts to reach a framework agreement for ridding the Middle East country of its chemical weapons stockpiles by mid-2014. The first step would be for Damascus to produce a complete inventory of Syria's chemical weapons capabilities within a week in order for the imminent threat of US military action to be lifted. As a second step al-Assad would have to allow access to a team of UN inspectors by November 2013.[68]

With the diplomatic mechanism reinvigorated at the UNSC, other initiatives aimed at creating prerequisites for a genuine peace process were piggybacked on the chemical weapons agreement. One illustration of this was featured in the council resolution, which in Annexes I and II detailed a way forward on the parallel tracks of chemical weapons destruction and peace talks outlined by the Action Group on Syria. While Annex I clarified the sequence of actions that needed to be taken by Syrian authorities as well as by the Organization for the Prevention of Use of Chemical Weapons, charged with overseeing the former process, Annex II reaffirmed the validity of the six-point plan underlying the prospects of convening a peace conference in Geneva. All participants in the Action Group on Syria, including the secretary generals of the UN and the Arab League, along with the EU high representative and representatives of the governments of the P5 plus Turkey, Iraq, Kuwait, and Qatar, thereby reiterated their commitment to

— a sustained cessation of violence;
— release of arbitrarily detained persons;
— restored freedom of movement for journalists;
— restored freedom of association and right to peaceful protests;
— guarantees for the full respect and safety of UNSMIS;
— immediate and full access by humanitarian organizations to all
   areas affected by the fighting.[69]

Resolution 2118 did not, however, spell out any clear political conditions for the talks, as had been the case in past negotiations to end the war. For instance, the issue of the territorial integrity of the Syrian state was not reaffirmed, although several members of the Action Group on Syria behind closed doors no doubt argued vehemently to uphold this criterion. Instead, the few principles that should be considered overarching were those formulated at the 2013 Lough Erne G8 summit. Notably, the summit statement briefly stated that the signatories subscribed to the idea of holding a peace conference in Geneva, at which either side "should be fully representative of the Syrian people and committed to the implementation of the Geneva Communiqué and to the achievement of stability and reconciliation. We will engage actively with the parties in order to achieve successful outcomes."[70] Unfortunately, most of these diplomatic efforts eventually came to naught. The Geneva process yielded barely any results when it came to dampening the armed conflict raging in Syria. At best, it provided a framework within which a credible agreement on the complete disbandment of all Syrian chemical weapons stockpiles could be forged, and subsequently executed.

The Ukrainian Spoke in the Wheel

In early 2014 a conflict evolved on a continent many considered pacified, namely, Europe, directly involving a pillar of the UN-based system of conflict management, the Russian Federation, as the intervening party. It is believed that the Ukrainian war was unleashed through decisions made in the Kremlin during the last week of February 2014, as the first truly consequential orders to seize control over territory were carried out by Russian forces deployed on the Crimean Peninsula. In actions that would soon be known as characteristic of how the Russian government operated, unmarked soldiers and equipment were moved into positions in ways that failed to attract the attention of the outside world. In the following months, moreover, the Russian political leadership alternated between denying its involvement and openly sponsoring pro-Russian separatists in eastern and southern Ukraine, straining relations in the UNSC and the GX summitry.

Whether the broader context of Russian actions merely served as the pretext for occupying Crimea and the Donbass region of eastern Ukraine according to military planning completed years earlier, or whether political events in the country's capital in effect prompted President Putin to violate international law and the Budapest memorandum guaranteeing Ukraine's territorial integrity, will be for the historians to establish definitively. The so-called Maidan movement demonstrating against then Ukrainian president Viktor Yanukovych, and the latter's subsequent departure from power, at any rate provided a justification for the military intervention in Crimea and support for the nascent separatist groups in eastern Ukraine.

The issue of Russia's covert operations on the Crimean Peninsula landed on the horseshoe-shaped table on February 28, 2014, in the form of a letter from the Ukrainian permanent representative to the UN, Yuriy Sergeyev. The issue was included in the last meeting presided over by the outgoing president of the UNSC, Ambassador Raimunda Murmokaitė of Lithuania, representing a country with an understandably strong interest in regional stability along the Russian border. Owing to the contentious nature of the matter, the first meeting was a closed session after which a short communiqué was released. But because Moscow now acknowledged that Crimea had come under the control of pro-Russian armed groups whose aims Russian officials would not denounce, an open meeting presided over by the Luxembourg representative, the council president for the month of March, was held the next day. Through the public deliberations of the 7,124th meeting of the UNSC, the world for the first time saw the Ukrainian and Russian ambassadors spar over the facts, origins, and likely ramifications of what at this point still was a political and military standoff.

Only two weeks earlier, the Russian deputy permanent representative, Evgeny Zagaynov, had made a statement in a debate on the protection of civilians in armed conflict in which he stressed the importance of clear UNSC mandates those assuming responsibility for action must "unswervingly" comply with. Zagaynov went on to specifically "condemn any action under the guise of the protection of civilians that in practice pursues far-reaching geopolitical goals."[71] Merely a month later, many had already concluded that this was precisely what Moscow was doing. On March 15 the head of Russia's permanent representation in New York, Ambassador Churkin, rejected the criticism of the United States, the United Kingdom, and France and refused to declare illegal the snap Crimean referendum in support of unification with Russia, to be held the next day. Churkin affirmed the principle of territorial integrity in general but called the political, legal, and historic backdrop of developments in Ukraine "extremely complicated." The core of his defense of Russian actions in Crimea consisted of the following sentence: "With respect to Crimea, that case resulted from a legal vacuum generated by an unconstitutional armed coup d'état carried out in Kyiv by radical nationalists in February, as well as by their direct threats to impose their order throughout Ukraine."[72]

The increasingly assertive behavior of Russian authorities and Moscow-backed separatists throughout the spring of 2014 soon made clear that a land grab was in the making. On March 24 Prime Minister Cameron announced that it was "absolutely clear" that the planned G8 Sochi summit on June 4–5 would not go ahead, and other leaders suggested that Russia ought to be suspended from the group.[73] Apart from the de facto annexation of Crimea, which a majority of the UN General Assembly rejected, President Putin's request for a free hand in using Russian military forces on the territory of Ukraine from the Federation Council of the Duma, received on March 1, dispelled much doubt that observers may have harbored regarding Moscow's short- and midterm designs regarding its southeastern neighbor.[74]

Until April there was nevertheless some uncertainty as to what the Russian government might consider doing to support centrifugal tendencies in the Donbass region in eastern Ukraine. A mixture of lenient measures, such as the issuing of an amnesty to individuals who occupied administrative buildings in the Luhansk and Donetsk region in the first weeks of the conflict, and a hard-nosed "counterterrorist" approach by the Ukrainian ministry of interior, appear to have helped to rally pro-Moscow sympathizers long enough for (possibly off-duty) Russian military personnel to augment those forces. By early summer a serious fighting force was forming, most independent observers agreed, under the leadership of Russian specialist forces from the regular army and the Russian Ministry of the Interior.[75]

Regarding the matter of Ukrainian sovereignty and territorial integrity, however, Russia was not able to rely on diplomatic cover from top-level Chinese diplomats and political leaders. Illustrative is the statement made by China's deputy permanent representative to the UN, Wang Min, in a debate held on June 24, 2014. Wang Min outlined four principles Chinese foreign policy adhered to, the fourth principle saying, "China respects the sovereignty and territorial integrity of all countries, including Ukraine, and we will continue to hold a fair and objective position in actively taking part in the consideration of any proposals and initiatives for the easing of tensions and for finding a political solution."[76] Although no direct criticism was expressed against Russia's handling of the situation, the statement clearly implied that China was concerned with the disregard Moscow held for the sovereignty and territorial integrity of Ukraine, as well as the implications of its actions on international law and the conduct of international relations.

The downing of a Malaysia Airlines flight from Amsterdam to Kuala Lumpur on separatist-controlled territory some forty kilometers from the Ukrainian-Russian border on August 17 removed the last doubts about the seriousness of the fighting in eastern Ukraine. Although the origins of the missile that brought down the civilian airliner remained under investigation in mid-2015, the general view is that sophisticated Russian equipment deployed in separatist-controlled areas most likely mistook Malaysia Airlines Flight 17 for a Ukrainian military aircraft. At the UNSC the incident prompted widespread support for the civilian victims and strong and near-universal condemnation of the military and political leaders ultimately responsible.

In December 2014 a cease-fire was in place, although incidents occurred almost daily nevertheless. Meanwhile, the Ukrainian situation had caused a serious deterioration in relations among the UNSC members, including the P5. But diplomats in New York and in capitals around the world were still working hard to contain the damage so as not to jeopardize collaboration on a series of other issues. Most impressive was the passing of Resolutions 2165 and 2191 allowing for humanitarian aid to move across Syria's borders without consent from (but notification to) the al-Assad regime in Damascus.[77] It was also helpful that a number of routine issues came before the council, where mutual goodwill could be demonstrated through gestures that carried little political risk, such as the renewal of peacekeeping mandates and adoption of reports prepared by the UN Secretariat.

Beyond routine matters the UNSC continued to handle "creeping crisis" situations in parts of Africa, which similarly required virtually no political sacrifices on the part of the P5 member states. Throughout the year the slowly worsening military situation in the Central African Republic (CAR) received attention, as did the escalating political crisis in Yemen and the illicit trade in weapons and charcoal benefitting the al-Shabaab extremist militia. True to the growing commitment of the body to the stability and security of the African continent as a whole, the vast majority of statements and initiatives pertaining to countries south of Libya and west of Egypt were constructive and supportive of existing missions and programs. In the second half of 2014, the increasingly effective international response to the Ebola epidemic, orchestrated by UN agencies such as the World Health Organization (WHO), the World Food Program (WFP), and the World Bank together with numerous NGOs, signaled that the world's most asset-rich countries and governments could still set aside other issues and focus on a particularly time-sensitive health problem.

By comparison, the G20 was not deemed to have responded with agility. Australia, which in 2014 held the presidency of the group, apparently chose to concentrate almost exclusively on economic growth already at the planning stage.[78] It stuck rigorously to that priority to the extent that other issues featuring high on the international agenda were pushed aside, not least foreign and security policy. Although eleven of the countries present in St. Petersburg in September 2013 chose to adopt a "Joint Statement on Syria" to display their dissenting position on the civil war raging in this Middle Eastern country, all G20 member states stayed within the script at Brisbane in mid-November 2014. By mentioning neither the rapidly escalating military threat of ISIL (discussed at length in chapter 4) nor the Ukrainian conflagration in the concluding communiqué, analysts found that the 2014 G20 summit had taken an unprecedented stance of completely ignoring contemporary international conflicts.[79]

The Empirical Findings: Propping Up the UN System

The overall question to be answered in this part of the study is, How do contemporary great and middle powers employ existing formal and informal institutional arrangements to address challenges in conflict management, spanning traditional and nontraditional security concepts? I begin by briefly reviewing the relative priority awarded to conflict management in the speeches of G20 members at the opening sessions of the UN General Assembly in 2009–14 in order to gauge how great and middle powers tend to articulate themselves with regard to the three relevant policy areas. Although the choice of what to devote attention to during the General Assembly annual debate in part depends on whether the head of state, the head of government, the foreign minister, or the head of the permanent mission to the UN delivers the speech, the manuscript vetting process is typically quite similar from year to year.[80] Thus, it is to be expected that most speakers balance the message to reflect the priorities of the government at any given time against the expectation that countries do not frequently or abruptly alter their outlook on the world.

The three country representatives paying most attention to conflict management in 2009–14 were the United States, the United Kingdom, and Germany. All three are undoubtedly in the top category of stakeholders in international security institutions, representing three of the four leading contributors to the UN budget (Japan is in second place). The first two form the P2 duo, belong to the nuclear club of countries, are hosts to the world's two largest financial centers (New York and London), and are as a rule the two most active permanent representations when it comes to initiating UNSC action. Germany, while not belonging to that exclusive category of states, is Europe's biggest economy, the third-largest contributor to the UN budget after the United States and Japan, and one of the organization's most active member states.

Conversely, the government representatives whose statements spent the least time and emphasis on conflict management were Saudi Arabia, Indonesia, and Brazil (see table 2.2 on page 47). Saudi Arabia is in several ways a special case, as it maintains a lower profile in international diplomacy than its economic clout would suggest. Indeed, Riyadh was the only G20 capital that in three out of the six years examined here did not use the opportunity to participate in the general debate of the UN General Assembly's opening session. Representatives of Indonesia and Brazil, on the other hand, addressed the assembly each year and covered several challenges in international security, though they paid little attention to traditional intergovernmental conflicts and more to social and economic conditions under which such threats can arise.

More generally, the 2009–14 period was one in which the UNSC continued to be the high-table platform of choice in international conflict management, as mandated by the UN Charter, yet in which the strictures and routines of its mode of operation were relaxed in significant respects. As mentioned in the introductory chapter, the P5 collective of incumbent great powers in 2009–14 facilitated the participation of all G20 member states not already part of the P5 or G8 caucus in the E10 category. An example of this relaxation at the "technical level" was the permanent council members' preparedness to somewhat expand the space for nested informality with regard to appointments and certain working methods. When serving on the council, the elected member states—and in particular second-tier great powers that aspire to permanent membership—were more frequently awarded prominent roles as chairs of subcommittees or "penholders" of draft resolution texts.

Another dimension of this relaxation was the accentuated regional approach to dealing with issues of peace and security, especially with regard to the continent where most violent conflicts have occurred in recent years, namely, Africa. This dimension of the relaxation entailed a growing acceptance on the part of UN bodies, in the name of effectiveness and predictability, to allow informal coalitions and donor and troop-contributing countries to be directly involved in shaping the missions. From 2009 onward the PBC, partly inspired by the G8 Africa Clearing House established five years earlier, was able to draw more fully on the potential for pragmatic collaboration among asset-rich countries. Nested informality made inroads here also. In several cases a second-tier great power or middle power was put in charge of the PBC country-specific configuration assigned to coordinate all peace-building activities with regard to that particular country. The frequency of informal consultations, with invited speakers representing expertise or civil society, and teleconferences with field missions grew substantially in the same period.

During the six years examined, GX summits at times exercised an auxiliary function. Above all, the GX summitry acted as a legitimizing entity for international conflict management entrusted to the UNSC. It mainly did so through joint statements that were issued in conjunction with summits of heads of state and government or meetings of foreign ministers, taking place several times each year. For the most part such joint statements concerned ongoing international conflicts that the council was already involved in (or "seized by," in council terminology), with one high-table platform amplifying the message of the other. One example of a legitimizing statement was that preceding the council vote on military intervention in Libya in March 2011. In other cases G8 statements pertained to nontraditional security threats, similarly supplementing the role of the latter.

Because the G20 was charged with the former role of the G7/G8 in the sphere of financial, monetary, and regulatory affairs, the wider group stayed clear of conflict management. But as the G20 upgrade in 2008–9 meant downgrading the G8 as a summit of heads of state and government, the foreign and security policy agenda of the latter was reactivated. As of 2010 the G8 became more inclined to engage in foreign policy issues of the day and be forward-leaning on nontraditional security, apparently compensating for the more conservative stance of the UNSC.

Because G8 meetings of foreign ministers and political directors became devoted to foreign and (nontraditional) security policy matters, it can be argued that the latter acquired a nested formality dimension. In binding the group closer together on measures that indirectly reinforce projects and programs executed by international organizations, through political, financial, or logistical support, as illustrated previously, the G8 in 2009–14 helped underwrite and consolidate conflict management on the African continent and elsewhere. That being said, the narrower interests of some members of the group, and Russia in particular, constrained action in some spheres. Moscow's strong support for the Syrian leader al-Assad in 2011–14 is the clearest expression of that limitation.

The overall finding with regard to conflict management is that contemporary great and middle powers primarily utilize formal institutional arrangements to address problems in this policy area and that differentiation between formal and informal settings and diplomatic practices are upheld quite consistently. Conflict management as a policy area, in other words, proved too hard a case for the hybridity proposition advanced by Stone. A similar pattern obtains as to the traditional-nontraditional security nexus, with little overlap across that boundary. A significant exception is nevertheless the PBC, which promotes and oversees a wider range of mutually reinforcing policies and measures that encompass traditional peacekeeping as well as development and post-conflict reconstruction assistance on a large scale.

NOTES

1. Follett, *Dynamic Administration*.

2. Wolfers, *Discord or Collaboration*, 25–35; Walt, *Origins of Alliances*, 25–26, 263–66.

3. Hurrell, *Power, Values, and the Constitution*, 165.

4. Bosco, *Five to Rule Them All*, 80–111.

5. One should note that the Republic of China (Taiwan) was expelled from the UN by the General Assembly in 1971 and that the People's Republic of China subsequently assumed its permanent seat in the UN Security Council.

6. In 2009–13 only a handful of private meetings were held, on the election of judges to the International Court of Justice and a few other sensitive subjects. Author's interviews.

7. Most meeting formats and their legal and political implications are described in Bailey and Daws, *Procedure of the UN Security Council*, 45–75.

8. Franck and Nolte, "Good Offices Function," 143.

9. These statistics were collected by the Global Policy Forum and cited in Prantl, *UN Security Council*, 77.

10. Bosco, *Five to Rule Them All*, 183.

11. "The P5 have information flowing among each other much of the time," one senior diplomat told me. Author's interviews.

12. Ibid.

13. Prantl, *UN Security Council*.

14. Heinbecker, "Kosovo," 537–50.

15. Gray, *International Law*, 41-2.

16. Prantl, *UN Security Council*, 19.

17. Schrijver, "Reforming the UN Security Council"; Lee, "Feasibility of Reforming."

18. UN Department of Public Information, "Press Conference by Permanent Representative of Afghanistan on Security Council Reform," June 8, 2010.

19. UN General Assembly, "Solution to Reform of Security Council 'Is in Your Hands,'" Sixty-Fifth Plenary, 48th and 49th Meetings, GA/11022, November 11, 2010.

20. At an unofficial seminar held in Beijing in late April 2009, Russian and Chinese senior officials were open to revising article 23 of the UN Charter, permitting immediate reelection of non-permanent member states to the council (U.S. Embassy, Beijing, "PRC: Chinese Scholars Suggest Achieving Near-Term UN Security Council Reform Difficult, Unwarranted" [signed Piccuta], WikiLeaks Cable ID: #09BEIJING1572, April 30, 2009).

21. Patrick, "Irresponsible Stakeholders?"

22. Jones and Gowan, "New Members Make."

23. Spechler, "Russian Foreign Policy."

24. Ilgit and Ozkececi-Taner, "Turkey at the United Nations."

25. UN Security Council, Resolution 1542, RES/1542/2004, April 30, 2004.

26. UN News Service, "Without Security Council Reform, UN Will Lose Credibility—General Assembly Chief," May 16, 2011.

27. UN Security Council, "Security Council Advanced Thematic, Disarmament, Civilian-Protection Work Even as Conflicts in Africa, Middle East Topped 2009 Agenda," press release, January 8, 2010, accessed July 14, 2014, http://www.un.org/press/en/2010/sc9836.doc.htm.

28. Ibid.

29. UN Security Council, S/RES/1645 (2005), December 20, 2005. On the experience of peace-building activities, see Reychler and Paffenholz, *Peacebuilding*; Dayton and Kriesberg, *Conflict Transformation and Peacebuilding*; Llewellyn and Philpott, *Restorative Justice, Reconciliation*.

30. Jenkins, "UN Peacebuilding Commission," 5–6.

31. UN General Assembly / UN Security Council, "Report of the Secretary-General on the Peacebuilding Fund," A/64/217-S/2009/419, August 3, 2009.

32. Peacebuilding Commission Organizational Committee, "Report of the Peacebuilding Commission on Its Fourth Session," A/65/701-S/2011/41, January 28, 2011.

33. Once attempted in 2009, the number of teleconferences grew to eleven in 2010, twenty-eight in 2011, and forty-eight in 2012; UN Department of Political Affairs, "Highlights of Security Council Practice 2012," February 2013, accessed July 19, 2014, http://www.un.org/en/sc/repertoire/data/highlights_2012.pdf.

34. UN Security Council, "Security Council Advanced"; UN Security Council, "Importance of Protecting Civilians during Armed Conflict Grows as Security Council Remains Active in Tackling Conflict-Related Crises Worldwide," January 7, 2011, accessed July 14, 2014, http://www.un.org/press/en/2011/sc10147.doc.htm.

35. Stiftung Wissenschaft und Politik, "The 2011 GIBSA Conference on the United Nations Security Council: Positions, Demands, Shared Interests," 2011, accessed Janu-

ary 17, 2014, http://www.swp-berlin.org/fileadmin/contents/products/projekt_papiere/GIBSAPolicyReport2011_pee_tlg.pdf.

36. Nikonov, "BRICS."

37. Jones and Gowan, "New Members."

38. Alice Klein, "Sudan Warns It Is Ready to Return to War with South Sudan," *Daily Telegraph*, November 9, 2011, accessed January 17, 2014, http://www.telegraph.co.uk/news/worldnews/africaandindianocean/sudan/8879373/Sudan-warns-it-is-ready-to-return-to-war-with-South-Sudan.html.

39. Engelbrekt, "Why Libya?," 46–48.

40. Ibid., 51–52.

41. Chivvis, *Toppling Qaddafi*, 43–68.

42. Ewen MacAskill, "Libya: Nato Defence Ministers Agree on Minimal Intervention," *Guardian*, March 10, 2011, accessed January 17, 2014, http://www.theguardian.com/world/2011/mar/10/libya-gaddafi-nato-us-minimal-intervention.

43. Chivvis, *Toppling Qaddafi*, 55–56.

44. "G8 Meeting of Foreign Ministers: Chair's Summary," Paris, March 15, 2011, accessed January 17, 2014, http://www.g8.utoronto.ca/foreign/formin110315-en.html.

45. Nicole Gaouette, "U.S. 'Not Encouraged' by India, South Africa, Brazil at UN," *Bloomberg News*, September 13, 2011, accessed July 15, 2014, http://www.bloomberg.com/news/articles/2011-09-13/south-africa-brazil-india-fail-to-impress-u-s-with-their-un-performance.

46. UN Security Council, S/PV.6503, March 23, 2011.

47. Robert F. Worth, "Saudi Arabia Rejects U.N. Security Council Seat in Protest Move," *New York Times*, October 18, 2013, accessed February 20, 2014, http://www.nytimes.com/2013/10/19/world/middleeast/saudi-arabia-rejects-security-council-seat.html.

48. Spain does not formally belong to the G20, though, as was mentioned previously, it attends its sessions. The other four members-elect were Angola, Malaysia, Venezuela, and New Zealand.

49. Note that two regional middle powers critical to the prospects of Brazil and India becoming permanent member states, namely, Argentina and Pakistan, have served as many as nine and seven times, respectively. Only one more country—Colombia—has been elected seven times, presumably in part because its candidacy was strongly endorsed by Washington.

50. Author's interviews. A senior diplomat of a non-Western country was adamant that Russia and China are by far more uncomfortable with council transparency than the P3 constellation is.

51. The other four members of the S5 are Liechtenstein, Singapore, Jordan, and Switzerland.

52. Lehmann, "Reforming the Working Methods," 3–4.

53. Keating, "Reforming the Working Methods," 3–4.

54. Ibid., 4.

55. Author's interviews; "First Public Wrap-Up Session since 2005," *What's in Blue*, July 29, 2014, accessed July 29, 2014, http://www.whatsinblue.org/2014/07/first-public -wrap-up-session-since-2005.php.

56. UN Security Council, "Security Council, in Presidential Statement, Pledges to Consider All Options to Help Strengthen African Union–Led Peacekeeping Operations," press release, October 26, 2009, accessed July 15, 2014, http://www.un.org /press/en/2009/sc9776.doc.htm.

57. Trenkov-Wermuth, *United Nations Justice*.

58. "G8/Africa Joint Declaration: Shared Values, Shared Responsibilities," Deauville, May 27, 2011, accessed October 10, 2015, http://www.g8.utoronto.ca/summit /2011deauville/2011-africa-en.html.

59. Kirton, "Standing Together on Security."

60. Charlotte Alfred, "Inside the Advocacy Group That Keeps Track of Syria's War Casualties," *Huffington Post*, November 24, 2014, accessed February 24, 2015, http://www.huffingtonpost.com/2014/11/24/syrian-observatory-for-human-rights _n_6201182.html.

61. UN Security Council, S/PV.6711, February 4, 2012, 9.

62. Ibid.

63. UN High Commissioner for Human Rights, "Periodic Update," December 20, 2012, accessed January 17, 2014, http://www.ohchr.org/Documents/Countries/SY /ColSyriaDecember2012.pdf.

64. Lynch and Freelon, "Social Media and Transnational Involvement."

65. Alan Cowell, "War Deaths in Syria Said to Top 100,000," *New York Times*, June 26, 2013, accessed January 17, 2014, http://www.nytimes.com/2013/06/27/world /middleeast/syria.html.

66. United Nations Mission to Investigate Allegations of the Use of Chemical Weapons in the Syrian Arab Republic, "Report on the Alleged Use of Chemical Weapons in the Ghouta Area of Damascus on 21 August 2013," September 13, 2013, accessed January 17, 2014, http://www.un.org/disarmament/content/slideshow/Secretary_General _Report_of_CW_Investigation.pdf.

67. Ernesto Londoño, "Obama Says U.S. Will Take Military Action against Syria, Pending Congress's Approval," *Washington Post*, August 31, 2013, accessed January 17, 2014, https://www.washingtonpost.com/world/national-security/obama-set-to-speak -on-syria-in-rose-garden/2013/08/31/65aea210-125b-11e3-85b6-d27422650fd5 _story.html.

68. Shashank Bengali and Henry Chu, "U.S., Russia Reach Agreement on Syria That Avoids Military Strike," *Los Angeles Times*, September 14, 2013, accessed July 15, 2014, http://articles.latimes.com/2013/sep/14/world/la-fg-syria-chemical-deal-20130915.

69. UN Security Council, S/RES/2118, September 27, 2013, 10.

70. "G8 Lough Erne Leaders Communiqué," Lough Erne, June 18, 2013, accessed October 10, 2015, http://www.g8.utoronto.ca/summit/2013lougherne/lough-erne -communique.html.

71. UN Security Council, S/PV.7109, February 12, 2014, 15.

72. UN Security Council, S/PV.7138, March 15, 2014, 2.

73. BBC News, "G8 Summit Won't Be Held in Russia," March 24, 2014, accessed May 21, 2015, http://www.bbc.com/news/uk-politics-26722668.

74. ITAR-TASS, "Duma Says Possible Use of Russian Army in Ukraine Has Humanitarian Purpose," March 1, 2014, accessed May 21, 2015, http://itar-tass.com/en /russia/721606.

75. Franke, Norberg, and Westerlund, "Crimea Operation"; Neil MacFarquahar and Michael R. Gordon, "Ukraine Leader Says 'Huge Loads of Arms' Pour in from Russia," *New York Times*, August 28, 2014, accessed October 29, 2014, http://www.nytimes .com/2014/08/29/world/europe/ukraine-conflict.html?_r=1.

76. UN Security Council, meeting protocol, S/PV/7205, June 24, 2014.

77. UN Security Countil, "Security Council, Adopting Resolution 2191 (2014), Renews Authorization Allowing Agencies, Humanitarian Partners Continued Aid Access across Syrian Borders," December 17, 2014, accessed May 22, 2015, http://www.un.org /press/en/2014/sc11708.doc.htm.

78. Barry Sterland, "Priorities of Australia's Presidency of the G20 in 2014 and the Role of the Global Financial Safety Net," Treasury, Australian Government, December 19, 2013, accessed May 22, 2015, http://www.treasury.gov.au/publicationsand media/speeches/2013/priorities-for-australias-presidency-of-the-g20.

79. Kirton, "Summit of Small Selected Success."

80. Baturo, Dasandi, and Mikhaylov, "Analysis of State Preferences."

Chapter 4

Counterterrorism Cooperation

Considering the short history of transnational counterterrorism cooperation and the lack of a robust legal and organizational framework, the expectation is that preconditions for hybridity of institutional arrangements are present in this policy area. A legal and organizational framework for counterterrorism cooperation has evolved only in the past ten to fifteen years and appears to rely heavily on auxiliary structures provided by informal institutional arrangements. It is also likely to be characterized by complementarity when it comes to the traditional-nontraditional security nexus. Although most definitions of nontraditional security encompass terrorism, governments have since the 9/11 attacks on the United States often made recourse to traditional military means in their wider counterterrorism strategy.

Background

Counterterrorism is an activity aimed at thwarting or limiting the damaging consequences of "a political act ordinarily committed by an organized group, which involves the intentional killing of non-combatants or the threat of the same or intentional severe damage to the property of non-combatants or the threat of the same."[1] Because a good academic definition of the composite term is not available, the understanding expressed here builds on the influential definition of terrorism proffered by C. A. J. Coady thirty years ago. Most attempts to capture the phenomena at hand have moralizing overtones, whereas Coady's formulation remains concise but analytically prescient.[2] Counterterrorism cooperation, as here understood, is above all what governments via home and justice affairs ministries, finance ministries, and intelligence services, in collaboration with national counterparts abroad and international security institutions, do to prevent and preempt terrorist attacks and the damage the latter cause.

The rise of transnational counterterrorism as a set of activities and measures has been gradual and has long relied on bilateral relations between governments friendly enough to share information about terror networks and their likely targets.[3] Mutual trust tends to be a scarce commodity in relations between intelligence organizations, even within a single country.[4] Collaborative transnational arrangements are hard to establish in part because of differing legal and political traditions for addressing violence as part of a political movement and in part because of geopolitical competition between governments. Clearly, certain regimes have a history of fierce rivalries that have involved violence in one form or another. In some cases that legacy has induced contemporary governments to fund or morally support what they perceive as domestic struggles for individual liberty or cultural or material rights within another given society. For obvious reasons, this sense of solidarity can give rise to serious friction between the sponsors of "freedom struggles" and representatives of incumbent regimes.

Formal cooperation on counterterrorism was in fact long resisted by the leadership of the International Criminal Police Organization (Interpol), which perceived it as threatening the "nonpolitical" character of transnational police work.[5] Informal cooperation through liaison arrangements, on the other hand, has a history as long as that of intelligence services. Among like-minded countries, informal cooperation can even take the shape of routine meetings that lack a fixed agenda, a secretariat, and the establishment of joint protocols. The Club of Berne, which evolved among the member states of the then European Economic Community in the early 1970s, has over the years consolidated into a well-established feature of EU-wide counterterrorism activities. Today the Club of Berne has thirty member states of which only two, Switzerland and Norway, have not joined the EU. The United States has observer status.

Given the sympathies that some governments demonstrated for opposition movements in foreign lands until after the Cold War, the transnational efforts to strengthen a coordinated response against terrorism at the United Nations reflected the general state of affairs. At times a least-common-denominator formula could generate limited cooperation, or an intergovernmental convention, that coincided with short- or mid-term concerns of prominent countries. In the 1960s and early 1970s, for instance, three conventions narrowly targeted the scourge of international hijacking. In a more recent example, attention in the 1990s turned toward terrorist bombing and new technologies allowing for more intrusive inspection at airports and other security installations, producing UN conventions on the marking of plastic explosives for detection (1991) and the suppression of terrorist bombings (1997). Notably, al-Qaida became the subject of a sanctions regime in 1999, by way of Resolution 1267, and this was followed by a resolution (1269) urging all UN member states to actively participate in the fight against terrorism.[6]

Interpol had in the mid-1980s reconsidered its stance on counterterrorism and slowly begun to adopt a proactive stance, apparently in part because it feared that governments would otherwise find the body increasingly irrelevant given the challenges of the day. Fifteen years later, counterterrorism had become, according to Barnett and Coleman, "one of its calling cards."[7] By the late 1990s the governments of leading Western countries were becoming especially concerned with the suppression of terrorist financing, prompting the adoption of UN General Assembly Resolutions 49/60 in 1994 and 51/210 in 1996 and a binding UN convention in 1999. Understandably, the watershed moment was the 9/11 attacks against New York and Washington, DC, which brushed away the selective tolerance for some political movements that used terrorist tactics. But a basic set of institutional arrangements that could serve as the infrastructure for the prevention of terrorist financing was in fact already in place, courtesy of the G7, in the form of the FATF.

The FATF had been set up at the 1989 G7 Paris summit with the primary purpose of devising and promoting counter-money-laundering measures. A list of forty recommendations for the financial and banking sector was elaborated in 1990 and served as the stepping-stone of FATF activities. The impact of the FATF and its transnational activities spread quickly in the period after it had been established, and the number of member states rose to twenty-eight by 1992. Reportedly, a spontaneous debate on transnational crime occurred at the G8 Denver summit of 1997, and the topic was incorporated at the 1998 Birmingham summit as one of three core themes.[8] The FATF's original emphasis on preventing the unimpeded circulation of money generated through drug trafficking and other forms of organized crime later expanded to include vulnerable business sectors and their entanglement with financial services in free-trade zones, the real estate sector, casino and betting services, migrant remittances, international arms trade, and others.

The 9/11 attacks against New York and Washington elicited, as evidenced by the military action that ensued in the broader Middle East region, a largely unilateral military response on the part of the United States. At home the US government reacted to the 9/11 attacks not only by promptly tweaking existing institutional arrangements but also by setting up new ones.[9] For instance, to the Financial Crimes Enforcement Network, established through the 1970 Bank Secrecy Act, the US Treasury added the Executive Office for Terrorist Financing and Financial Crime. The US government also took to creatively interpreting the 1977 International Emergency Economic Powers Act. At the same time Congress passed the 2001 Patriot Act, giving the Treasury power to prohibit foreign financial institutions from conducting transactions and creating accounts in US banks.[10] The priority of the American administration was no longer to assist prosecutors in collecting evidence ex post facto but to intercept terrorist financing and large-scale money laundering before it caused harm.[11]

In the field of counterterrorism, however, some of the most effective measures to be put in place had a distinctively international and transnational character.[12] Decisive at this early stage of the unfolding counterterrorism strategy was the rapid and successful adoption of UNSC Resolution 1373, geared toward the prevention and suppression of financing of terrorist acts. As outlined in the resolution, the UNSC decided to criminalize the collection and provision of funds for the use of terrorist acts and to freeze or block funds for such use by "any persons or entities within their territories."[13] To implement Resolution 1373, the council set up the CTC. Although the political and bureaucratic clout of the United States was indispensable in this effort,[14] international security institutions, formal and informal, were critical for the struggle against terrorism to become a transnational endeavor.

Meanwhile, at the 2002 G8 summit in Kananaskis, Canada, the heads of state and government adopted a set of recommendations on counterterrorism and urged the universal ratification of Resolution 1373, along with twelve previously adopted UN counterterrorism conventions. If the first decade of FATF activities—the 1990s—had been devoted to combatting money laundering and organized crime syndicates, the second refocused efforts toward counterterrorism, effectively underpinning the implementation of Resolution 1373. The key partners in the US effort in this respect were the thirty-plus member states, plus the European Commission and the Gulf Cooperation Council. Although the number of new member states could not rise owing to the technical and administrative demands of the system, so-called FATF-style regional bodies were soon established in virtually all parts of the world. By the end of the 2000s, some level of FATF-inspired monitoring was taking place in most countries of the world, covering financial operations that ranged from fundraising to money transfers, capital management, and money disbursement.[15]

The European governments supported the establishment of this global regime but were slow to move forward with implementation in the context of EU law and politics.[16] Complex negotiations and individual liberties concerns first prevented the European institutions from taking prompt and effective action, and their legally enforceable directives never went as far as those in the United States.[17] The 2004 EU Declaration on Combatting Terrorism then introduced more flexible mutual extradition rules, biometric standards for passports, passenger name record agreements, and enhanced intelligence cooperation.[18]

Informal cooperation within the Club of Berne countries, meanwhile, produced the Counter Terrorism Group (CTG), with a clear mandate to advance transnational cooperation among European states, and major strides toward forming an effective international law regime. Combined US and EU efforts also increased the number of signatories to the International Convention for the Suppression of the Financing of Terrorism from merely 4 (pre-9/11) to 132 by late 2005, similarly aligning EU legislation with US counterterrorist aims.

As the enforcement framework of Resolution 1373 was bolstered by the mid-2000s, the UN system helped enhance the FATF financial transparency regime and vice versa.[19] But the FATF was not the only G7/G8-inspired institutional arrangement charged with tasks in the field of nontraditional security. In the mid-1990s the G8, emulating the Club of Berne in the European context, had set up working groups that facilitated cooperation on police and home affairs issues. By fusing the Roma Group, a working group devoted to counterterrorism, and the Lyon Group, charged with transnational border crime, the Roma-Lyon Group came into being in the fall of 2001. The Roma-Lyon Group is thus partly an outgrowth of the response to the 9/11 attacks and partly a structure that predates that event.[20]

The work of the Roma-Lyon Group mainly involves practical projects in transportation security, high-tech crime, criminal legal affairs, law enforcement, migration, and counterterrorism.[21] The group develops initiatives for consideration in working subgroups to ensure a shared approach among G7/G8 countries. At a later stage the group forms concrete proposals that are presented to the interior and justice ministers for approval. General status reports and overviews of the group's work in countering transnational organized crime and terrorism are regularly submitted to the meeting of G7/G8 foreign ministers.[22]

The Roma-Lyon Group received its formal name at the Evian summit of 2003. For the most part the collaboration involved is flexible and informal and gathers experts on a wide array of topics.[23] Because of its informal character, the Roma-Lyon Group typically operates by conducting inventories of best practices and disseminating ideas about transferring those experiences to other countries or to multilateral organizations that can use them as standard operating procedures. The work of the subgroups is less widely publicized. One important subgroup specializes in migration and another in high-tech crime, the latter interacting with the Internet Corporation for Assigned Names and Numbers (ICANN) and other bodies that monitor online activities. One subgroup is referred to as the Counterterrorism Practitioners Group, or the CT Group for short.

As a global counterpart to the CTG set up in Europe in late 2001, the CTAG was created and explicitly sanctioned by the 2003 Evian summit to supplement the activities of the Roma-Lyon Group. From the outset the CTAG focused on capacity building in the areas of prevention and response to terrorist activities.[24] A significant portion of the capacity-building effort was immediately directed toward document inspection, the vetting of security personnel, and threat detection in luggage screening. Apart from the G8 and the European Commission, the standing members of the CTAG are the International Civil Aviation Organization (ICAO), the International Maritime Organization (IMO), the UN Office on Drugs and Crime (UNODC), the Asian Development Bank (ADB), the OSCE, and the World Bank.

Out of the three G8-sponsored networks, CTAG from the very beginning worked most closely with units in formal international organizations. The group forged a special relationship with the UNSC's CTC to support implementation of twelve UN-sponsored international agreements on terrorism, in particular, UNSC Resolution 1373 and the 1999 International Convention for the Suppression of the Financing of Terrorism. In 2004, as the CTC was fighting "a heroic but losing battle,"[25] the council added the Counter-Terrorism Executive Directorate (CTED) to enhance implementation through regular assessments, country visits, and fund-raising for technical assistance. Also in 2004 Resolution 1540, regarding the nonproliferation of weapons of mass destruction, was adopted, complete with yet another separate committee.

The CTAG is presided over by the G8 chair country and has rigid information-sharing rules that somewhat limit its effectiveness beyond the territories of Western governments. Although influential in 2003–5, CTAG became less so later as a result of the suspension of collaboration with the FATF (which earlier provided it with considerable clout), the adoption of the ambitious UN Global Counter-Terrorism Strategy in 2006, and the rise to prominence of the G20 in 2008–9.[26] This illustrates the increasingly ambitious engagement of the UN system with counterterrorism issues as well as the pivotal position of the UNSC's CTC as an institutional entity in the global effort to prevent, delimit the effects of, and contribute to the prosecution and punishment of perpetrators of transnational terrorism. The council itself is briefed once every six months by the chairs of the subsidiary committees devoted to counterterrorism.

In the following case study, the activities in 2009–14 of not only the FATF, the Roma-Lyon Group, and CTAG but also the UN CTC and the CTED are analyzed chronologically. The objective is to explore institutional arrangements that encompass informal institutions such as the G7, G8, and G20, on the one hand, and the formal and regulated operation of the UNSC and its CTC, on the other. Since many of the instruments that make up transnational

Table 4.1 Institutional Arrangements in the Field of Counterterrorism, 1989–2004

Informal G7/G8 Networks	Formal UN Entities
Financial Action Task Force (FATF), 1989	
Roma-Lyon Group, 2001	Counter-Terrorism Committee (CTC), 2001
Global Partnership Working Group, 2002	
Counter-Terrorism Action Group (CTAG), 2003	
	Counter-Terrorism Executive Directorate (CTED), 2004

counterterrorism were already in place by late 2008, this second case study of international security devotes considerable space to implementation and follow-up measures.[27]

Transnational counterterrorism in 2009–14 is examined via the decisions and policies adopted by the GX summitry, the UNSC, and a variety of subsidiary bodies charged with fighting terrorism at the global level. Special attention is paid to institutional innovation, development, and consolidation, as the capacity to forge effective counterterrorism policies and enforcement measures clearly made considerable progress in recent years. As mentioned at the outset, the G7/G8 is considered the political source of these advances because it established several of the core institutions before, but especially after, the 9/11 attacks against the United States. At the same time, the emergence of counterterrorism networks in the informal realm has in some cases been matched by the setting up of a corresponding framework in the UN system.

Vetting Financial Transactions: A G7/G8 Framework

By 2009 counterterrorism was a well-established concept in international law and in documents governing the internal life of several international institutions. Although governments for several decades had disagreed on how to define "terrorism" in the context of the UN and other organizations, it would appear that the 9/11 attacks provided a particularly vivid illustration of the phenomenon. As a result, disputes over whether a particular organization or network prone to exercising violence to achieve political goals qualified as "terrorist" or was pursuing a legitimate cause (of liberation, democracy, or national unity) appear to have been set aside as the threat of global jihadist extremism forcefully transcended previous disagreements. With 9/11 as a catalyst, a mutually acceptable (though inevitably imperfect) compromise on the balancing of security and liberty, transparency and privacy, and organizational integrity and oversight was forged across institutional arrangements.[28]

When it came to practical measures involving delegation of authority and the scope of executive powers, genuine disagreements still arose and needed to be resolved.[29] Having suffered the 9/11 attacks and representing the primary target of al-Qaida and affiliated groups, the US government remained proactive and asked their counterparts to follow their example. Over time the remit of vetting financial transactions expanded, for instance, affecting the aid and remittances sector. Remittances originating with diaspora groups had come into sharp focus already in 2007–8, and this trend continued in 2009–14.[30] At that time leading representatives of the largest Muslim charity in the United States, the Holy Land Foundation, had been prosecuted and convicted for collecting non-designated *zakat* funds and passing them on to Hamas, which was designated a "foreign terrorist organization" by the United States and many of its allies.[31] As value-transfer services in the United States came under renewed intense scrutiny in their capacity as alternative remittance systems to banks and charities, most G8 governments began adjusting their vetting arrangements.

The World Bank estimated that the value of all global money remittances in 2009 approximated $420 billion, roughly equivalent to the GDP of Austria or South Africa. The challenge facing counterterrorism officials was one of regulatory complexity as well as of sheer size. Regulating remittances in many countries is typically done by examining accounting services and financial reports of banks, postal services, and service providers. The number of independent money remittance providers that depend on this activity as their sole or core business varies greatly. In 2010 France had only 4 legitimate independent money remittance providers, Sweden 96, and the United States 25,096. A considerable number of these providers operate as traditional financial networks, such as the *hawala*, the *hundi* (common in India), Chinese flying money, or the Philippine *padala* system.[32]

The 2009 Italian presidency readily took on the broader task of and developed several initiatives related to counterterrorism. The G8 Conference on Destabilizing Factors and Transnational Threats, held April 23–24, was a meeting of experts who discussed the "multiplier effects" that organized crime can have on terrorist activities.[33] The recurring G8 meetings of ministers of justice and home affairs, this time in Rome, provided another opportunity to broadly review efforts in counterterrorism and transnational organized crime. The three-day June 2009 meeting in the Italian capital focused on prevention of and denial of proceeds from organized criminal activities and terrorist financing, various aspects of migration and human trafficking, and urban security and quality of life in growing cities.[34]

By the time of the July 2009 G8 summit at l'Aquila, Italy, there had therefore been sufficient preparations for G8 leaders to adopt a separate declaration on counterterrorism, beyond transnational organized crime, piracy, and maritime security. The declaration had not been envisaged in the original agenda but could be seen as an attempt to sustain and develop the transnational counterterrorist agenda, not least by explicitly linking G8 initiatives to already existing UNSC arrangements:

> In constant cooperation with the competent UN bodies, the G8 plays a key role in the global fight against terrorism, primarily through the Roma/Lyon Group, which gathers our experts on counter terrorism and transnational organized crime, and the Counter-Terrorism Action Group (CTAG). We welcome CTAG's enhanced outreach initiatives and its increased emphasis on regional and local technical assistance and capacity building. Consistent with the fundamental principles embodied in all relevant UN provisions, we reiterate our commitment to respecting human rights while countering terrorism.[35]

In the l'Aquila declaration the G8 leaders further warned of converging threats that involved terrorism, drugs, and organized crime and indirectly referred to the UNSC's new focus on "the prevention of incitement to terrorism" through the notion of combatting "radicalization."[36] The text also included a ringing endorsement of the G8's own focus on soft security issues, albeit on the difficulties of reconciling counterterrorism efforts with the requirements of rule of law. At one point the G8 declaration stated that its members rejected "the idea of a trade-off between security and the founding principles of our democracies."

In placing the work of the Roma-Lyon Group in the context of UN goals to combat terrorism, the 2009 G8 declaration on counterterrorism recalled the pioneering efforts of that group in the preceding twelve to fifteen years. An early example was the introduction of biometric identity-management practices for travelers around the world; the Roma-Lyon Group had helped shape the debate in the expert community. Today the group is organized in five subgroups whose work focuses on judicial cooperation, police cooperation, law enforcement, migration issues, and cyber-crime. The technical focus of the group's deliberations appears to have helped play down legal and political ramifications in terms of privacy and human rights and thereby made enhanced security regulations associated with travel more palatable as transnational standards.

By 2009 G8 experts on counterterrorism and organized crime convened at least three times a year, with EU and OECD subgroups meeting more often.[37] But by that time a new diplomatic and political challenge had arisen for the G8 countries: how to integrate the emerging great powers—in particular China, India, Brazil, but also other G20 countries—into the process of expanding and improving the transnational counterterrorism regime.[38] According to Amandine Scherrer, the symbolic importance of the G8 counterterrorism measures should not be underestimated, as it for many years bolstered the status of its suggestions vis-à-vis the UN, the OECD, the EU, and Interpol.[39] One of the questions that the G8 countries faced in recent years was whether effectiveness might suffer if a significantly wide circle of governments became involved in the practical and technical side of transnational counterterrorism activities. After Russia was excluded from the G8 in early 2014, that problem was accentuated, since the G7 is perceived as especially biased toward the West.

The BRIC Countries' Response to Terrorism

In light of the rise to prominence of emerging non-Western great powers and a more heterogeneous set of diplomatic actors, the Italian government was keen to play down the impression that its G8 presidency would be symptomatic of the old Europe-centered international system.[40] Far in advance of the G8 summit, Rome had apparently circulated among member states a policy paper in which it made a case for extending a standing invitation to the "Outreach Five"—China, India, Brazil, Mexico, and South Africa—for the 2009 and future summits.[41] Once they had accepted, the five governments settled for the term "Group of Five" to signal equivalency of diplomatic status.

The G8 summit lasted three days, July 8–10, 2009. The Italian presidency had invited the outreach countries to attend all meetings of the second day of the l'Aquila summit, preserving the first day for internal G8 business. Working to create the impression of a more coherent constellation, the Group of Five heads of state and government held a parallel summit. Besides considering a number of common issues and preparing for the G8 sessions, leaders of China, India, Mexico, Brazil, and South Africa adopted a joint declaration.

The July 2009 Group of Five declaration consisted of a concise three-page text organized in sixteen points. Roughly half of the items concerned the economic agenda facing both the G20 and the G8. One of the issues was terrorism, about which the five political leaders wrote a brief general condemnation of "terrorism in all its forms and expressions" and an appeal for "strong, collective action" by the international community. In the last sentence on the terrorism issue, more curiously, the Group of Five urged UN member states to conclude and adopt an integral convention on international terrorism long stuck in the Ad Hoc Committee on Terrorism in the UN General Assembly owing to disagreements over the definition. This was a process over which the Group of Five countries had only marginal influence, yet their declaration indicated a common desire to bolster UN counterterrorism at the expense of closer collaboration among G8 members.

In terms of political symbolism, China, India, Brazil, and Russia had already tried to ensure that the Group of Five meeting would be a temporary phenomenon and a vehicle to speed up integration in other high-table platforms. At the June 16, 2009, summit of the BRIC countries in Yekaterinburg, Russia, a declaration had been adopted that indirectly undermined the two-tier approach promoted by some Western capitals.[42] The declaration lacked any reference to the G8 and the l'Aquila summit but fully endorsed the G20 as the legitimate forum for addressing the financial crisis:

> 1. We stress the central role played by the G20 Summits in dealing with the financial crisis. They have fostered cooperation, policy coordination and political dialogue regarding international economic and financial matters.
>
> 2. We call upon all states and relevant international bodies to act vigorously to implement the decisions adopted at the G20 Summit in London on 2 April, 2009. We shall cooperate closely among ourselves and with other partners to ensure further progress of collective action at the next G20 Summit to be held in Pittsburgh in September 2009. We look forward to a successful outcome of the United Nations Conference on the World Financial and Economic Crisis and its Impact on Development to be held in New York on 24–26 June, 2009.

While the BRIC declaration emphasized the role of the G20 as an appropriate venue for dealing with global financial and institutional problems, it made several points that served to shore up support among emerging non-Western great powers that wanted to partake fully in all major decision-making arenas and institutions. Conceptually, the text called for "a more democratic and just multi-polar world order," a turn of phrase no doubt directed at Europe and the United States:

> 12. We underline our support for a more democratic and just multi-
> polar world order based on the rule of international law, equality, mutual
> respect, cooperation, coordinated action and collective decision-making
> of all states. We reiterate our support for political and diplomatic efforts
> to peacefully resolve disputes in international relations.

Terrorism featured prominently, though vaguely, in the declaration. Like the text adopted by the Group of Five at l'Aquila weeks later, the relevant paragraph consisted of a general condemnation of terrorism, followed by an appeal to UN member states to elaborate and adopt a comprehensive convention against international terrorism.

> 13. We strongly condemn terrorism in all its forms and manifestations
> and reiterate that there can be no justification for any act of terrorism
> anywhere or for whatever reasons. We note that the draft Comprehen-
> sive Convention against International Terrorism is currently under the
> consideration of the UN General Assembly and call for its urgent adop-
> tion.[43]

In general, the rise of the G20 appears to have induced non-G8 countries to engage in global affairs and to resist accepting invitations to venues and formats proffered by transatlantic powers. The practice of keeping the G8 and G20 summits separate during 2009 might have contributed to the perception that emerging great powers were seated at one of the two main high tables, handling the effects of the financial crisis but still kept outside the other set of platforms. Here it appears that the incumbent, predominantly Western leaders underestimated the prestige concerns of their peers. The references to "a just multi-polar world order" in the June 2009 Yekaterinburg BRIC declaration, and the frustration expressed in other diplomatic circles, seem to support this notion.

Western leaders certainly had legitimate concerns about rapidly expanding their well-developed cooperation on counterterrorism to governments that might not share the underlying values of G8 cooperation or be able to deliver much additional capacity to implement the framework already in place. It is therefore not surprising that extensive cooperation between G8 countries and emerging great powers remained constrained in the field of counterterrorism. Part of the explanation appears to lie in a disbelief in the utility of rapidly and comprehensively integrating non-Western emerging great powers into the global counterterrorism regime *tout court.*

Bolstering the UNSC's Modus Operandi

If the appearance of the G20 promptly stirred up diplomatic practices within the G8 from 2009 onward, the UNSC was affected in less direct ways. Counterterrorism had been established as a top-priority task of the UNSC by virtue of Resolution 1373, adopted on September 28, 2001, only seventeen days after the 9/11 attacks. The council had at the time reaffirmed the initial "unequivocal condemnation" of September 12 and on that basis elaborated a "duty to refrain from organizing, instigating, assisting or participating in terrorist acts in another State or acquiescing in organized activities within its territory directed towards the commission of such acts."

Piece by piece, the necessary legal planks were put in place over the next few years. In mid-September 2005 UNSC Resolution 1624 called on states to prevent and prohibit by law the incitement to commit terrorist acts. A key passage in Resolution 1624 narrowed the meaning of the controversial notion of terrorism by focusing on the act and not the justification or motive behind it. The council also reiterated in the preamble of Resolution 1624 the view that terrorism falls within the remit of the council mandate: "*Condemning* in the strongest terms all acts of terrorism irrespective of their motivation, whenever and by whomsoever committed, as one of the most serious threats to peace and security, and *reaffirming* the primary responsibility of the Security Council for the maintenance of international peace and security under the Charter of the United Nations . . ."

As already mentioned, the active part of Resolution 1373 was chiefly directed at preventing and suppressing terrorist financing. It criminalized the willful provision or collection of funds to be used for that purpose and ordered the freezing of assets of people found to perpetrate or facilitate terrorist acts. It further charged government authorities with overseeing that people involved in such acts were unable to draw on the assistance of the national financial services sector in any given country. In accordance with paragraphs 6 and 7 of Resolution 1373, a committee consisting of all UNSC member states was assigned to monitor implementation. Some problems nevertheless emerged in the next several years. Since certain names on the list became contested and no procedures were in place to redress errors, a December 2009 meeting of the UNSC created an ombudsman to mediate requests by individuals, organizations, and companies for removal.[44]

Although several of the legal elements of this nascent counterterrorism regime, such as the Convention for the Suppression of the Financing of Terrorism (1999), were in place before 9/11, the organizational entities and associated procedures needed to make this ambitious agenda work were not established until 2001. Key among these was the CTC, also created through Resolution 1373. As was mentioned previously, the CTC was charged with implementation in a broad sense by Resolution 1373. In the first years of its existence, the P5 countries largely controlled the CTC and its activities. Direct influence was exerted through the chairs, which, with the exception of 2003–4 when Spain (Inocencio Arias) was at the helm, were held by the United Kingdom (Jeremy Greenstock) and Russia (Alexander V. Konuzin and Andrey I. Denisov). But in the second half of the 2000s onward, only elected member states were assigned the chair, and eight different individuals assumed the position. Providing especially active leadership were the ambassadors of Turkey and India—Ambassadors Ertuğrul Apakan and Hardeep Singh Puri—in 2010–11 and 2011–12, respectively. They contributed additional leverage as representatives of large developing nations and G20 member states.

Whereas the accomplishments of the CTC in its first couple of years were limited to putting the new ambitious counterterrorism framework enshrined in Resolution 1373 in place, developments in 2009–14 went beyond the introduction of norms and organizational procedures. As CTC chair Ambassador Arias noted in late 2003, a key task in the early days had been simply to persuade UN member states to ratify the 1997 and 1999 conventions regarding the elimination of terrorist acts using bombs and the suppression of terrorist financing in order to make the counterterrorism framework as encompassing as possible. A second challenge had been to conduct a global inventory of inadequate tools in countries that were lacking in capacity or ambition and to build contacts with regional security organizations and centers of knowledge and expertise.[45]

By 2009 the CTC was already greatly helped by the existence of the CTED, established through Resolution 1535 in March 2004 as a special political mission to assist the CTC. Although the CTED was fully staffed in late 2005 with forty legal and policy experts who reviewed the implementation reports submitted by individual countries, organizational confusion lingered over the newly created body for its first years of operation. After a reorganization in 2008–9, five "technical groups" were set up for border security, law enforcement and arms trafficking, general legal issues, terrorist financing, and issues raised in connection with Resolution 1624 (2005) on incitement to commit terrorist acts, denial of safe haven for terrorist suspects, and enhanced airline passenger security procedures.[46] Using analyses that drew on the experiences of countries and international organizations, CTED staff members were now able to produce a more useful set of policy instruments. The directorate compiled and published a directory of international best practices, a technical guide, a global implementation survey, and several thematic policy documents.

The June 2009 interim review of the work of the CTED showed that the body had made a good start in reaching out to national and regional institutions in the field of counterterrorism. It had above all sped up the collection of country reports (ninety-nine had been submitted by April 15, 2009) and, using the reports, prepared preliminary implementation assessments for 190 of 193 member states. The assessments had already been handed over to governments for feedback and updates.[47] Thus, the CTED under Ambassadors Apakan, Singh Puri, and Mohammed Loulichki (of Morocco) more than doubled the number of visits to individual countries, collecting information and sharing information and best practices with host governments and experts. More detailed technical assistance proposals resulted from this more active and dynamic interaction with various countries and donors and encouraged developing countries to create central counterterrorism entities within the government.

Furthermore, the CTED is a founding member of the Counter-Terrorism Implementation Task Force (CTITF), set up to put into practice the 2006 UN Global Counter-Terrorism Strategy. In accordance with Resolution 1805 of 2008, the CTED was also authorized to communicate regularly with the G8's CTAG. Semiannual meetings were held and produced new interest among donors. The country visits were reorganized into three categories: regional, focused, and comprehensive. For comprehensive visits representatives of several other international organizations, including Interpol, the World Customs Organization, and the FATF, were present.[48]

On September 27, 2010, the UNSC held a ministerial meeting wholly devoted to counterterrorism, noting the increasingly diffuse character of the phenomenon and the unlikelihood that military force, intelligence, and law enforcement efforts would buck this trend separately. In a presidential statement released after the meeting, the council condemned the incitement to terrorist acts and attempts at justifying terrorist acts that might incite further terrorist acts, citing as important components of a successful counterterrorism strategy the fight against organized crime, drug trafficking, kidnapping, and hostage taking; the use of sanctions; the denial of communications and financial transactions systems; and access to weapons of mass destruction and their means of delivery. It also highlighted the "importance of the support of local communities, private sector, civil society and media for increasing awareness about the threats of terrorism and more effectively tackling them."[49] A second such high-level meeting was held in May 2012, organized by council chair Azerbaijan.

UNSC Resolution 1963, adopted December 20, 2010, specifically praised the CTC and the CTED for advancing the cause of counterterrorism in the international community. It also directed the latter to step up its capacity-enhancing activities vis-à-vis member states and to contribute toward the implementation of Resolutions 1373 and 1624 by facilitating technical assistance. In addition to accounting for the 2006 UN Global Counter-Terrorism Strategy and supporting the newly established CTITF, the council encouraged CTED "to interact . . . with civil society and other relevant non-governmental actors" and "to intensify cooperation with relevant international, regional, and subregional organizations with a view to enhance Member States' capacity to fully implement resolution 1373 (2001) and resolution 1624 (2005) and to facilitate the provision of technical assistance."[50] The high-profile communications and public relations policy of the CTED were also reflected in internal documents.[51]

Reports submitted to the CTED initially tended to focus on legislative alignment, the creation of counterterrorism units within central police authorities, efforts to combat terrorist financing, and border control. But by 2011–12 CTED officials were regularly advising governments to expand their approach and to take into account Resolution 1624 on the prohibition and prevention of incitement to terrorist activities and denial of safe haven. Another challenge now addressed by the CTED concerned implementing the transnational counterterrorism agenda without compromising commitments under international law and human rights conventions. By criminalizing intent, reaching out to national and local communities, integrating terrorist victims in various programs, facilitating rehabilitation, and developing comprehensive counterterrorism strategies, efforts were made to delicately balance these values against each other.[52]

In February 2011 the UNSC received the first report of the ombudsperson office created in 2009 to oversee the listing and delisting of individuals, organizations, and companies subject to travel bans and asset freezes. The report had been prepared by former judge Kimberly Prost, the first individual to hold the office of ombudsperson. A problem that had to be overcome in the first phase of the office's existence was to ensure access to classified information so that the ombudsperson and staff members could make well-grounded assessments.

A Proactive Stance on Intolerance and Extremism

The importance of countering incitement to terrorism and enhancing intercultural dialogue was first noted in Resolution 1624, adopted in 2005. Reflecting the political sensitivity of accusing countries of providing indirect justifications for extreme and violent acts, Resolution 1624 merely formulated an appeal to governments to "continue international efforts to enhance dialogue and broaden understanding among civilizations, in an effort to prevent the indiscriminate targeting of different religions and cultures . . . and to prevent the subversion of educational, cultural and religious institutions by terrorists and their supporters" (paragraph 3). It did not, in other words, propose or describe any discreet measures by which this objective could be reached.

The long-term, proactive approach to preventing the spread of terrorism and extreme political ideologies appeared less controversial toward the end of the decade. At a meeting of foreign ministers in Gatineau, outside Ottawa, G8 representatives "emphasized the need for more systemic, proactive and comprehensive response to this challenge."[53] The ministers stressed the need not only to reinforce the activities of the G8-sponsored Roma-Lyon Group and the CTAG but also to build on the UN Global Counter-Terrorism Strategy and universal counterterrorism conventions adopted by the UN. In a related development the G8 Sherpas met with representatives of several multilateral organizations to examine how capacity-building programs in the field of non-traditional security could be rendered more effective and efficient.[54]

Two months later, the Muskoka summit of June 25–26, 2010, adopted a separate declaration on counterterrorism. This text was less specific than the 2009 document and, among other things, expressed the enduring commitment of the G8 to continue working to thwart terrorist attacks. Like UNSC Resolution 1624 of 2005, the text emphasized the act itself rather than the motives behind it. Notably, this declaration spoke about "*our* operational successes against al-Qa'ida and other terrorist groups" in a way that engaged all G8 countries and not just the United States and its NATO allies.[55] By making specific reference to one group—al-Qaida—the document above all reflected Western concerns. But the statement also reflected the spirit of the 2006 Global Counter-Terrorism Strategy by acknowledging a need for governments to "promote the rule of law, the protection of human rights and fundamental freedoms, democratic values, good governance, tolerance and inclusiveness to offer a viable alternative to those who could be susceptible to terrorist recruitment and to radicalization leading to violence."[56]

At the UNSC the new emphasis on preventing the rise of extremism and political violence in a wider social and political context was further expanded. The UN General Assembly had ever since the adoption of Resolution 3034 (XXVII) in 1972 been an advocate of this approach, in part because its members could not agree on a clear definition or a proactive stance.[57] Former secretary general Kofi Annan made statements to this effect as early as 2001.[58] A ministerial meeting held on September 27, 2010, with Secretary General Ban Ki-Moon attending, elaborated five different ways to expand counterterrorism activities. Ban began with efforts that deprive terrorists of financial resources, mobility, and access to weapons of mass destruction, as well as the need for an emboldened legal regime and shared best practices in the international expert community. The secretary general also paid attention to less tangible proactive efforts. He highlighted research on why people are drawn to violence that could be used to prevent radicalization and went on to discuss education, development, and intercultural dialogue. Ban stressed the importance of integrating the voices of terrorism victims into the counterterrorism discourse.[59]

Following the speeches of the secretary general and the CTC chair, Ambassador Apakan of Turkey, US secretary of state Hillary Clinton emphatically seconded the broad approach taken by UN entities responsible for counterterrorism and the two previous speakers: "Counter-terrorism demands a comprehensive approach. . . . It means stopping people from becoming terrorists in the first place. That requires addressing the political, economic and social conditions that make people vulnerable to exploitation. For people whose lives are characterized by frustration or desperation, and for people who believe that their Governments are unresponsive or repressive, Al-Qaida and other groups may offer an appealing view." A few years earlier, it might have been difficult for a US political leader to connect the political and social context of terrorism with membership of an extreme anti-American network, such as al-Qaida, for fear of being accused of providing an indirect justification for the horrendous acts of 9/11. But by late 2010 and early 2011, most members of the UNSC seemed to have turned a proverbial page, accepting that a portion of counterterrorism measures should be redirected toward prevention, the susceptibility of youth, and rehabilitation programs for former perpetrators. In that same debate, in fact, virtually all speakers who went on record strongly endorsed the comprehensive approach advocated in recent UN documents.

The September 2010 ministerial meeting also heard a great deal of praise for the work of the CTC and the CTED, some of which went beyond diplomatic courtesy. Japan's permanent representative, Tsuneo Nishida, spoke of the CTED's vital role "in determining the needs for support and in coordinating capacity-building activities." His Mexican colleague, Claude Heller, paid tribute to CTC chair Apakan for providing that entity with "momentum that has begun to show significant results," including streamlined working methods, frequent reporting, and a series of thematic debates devoted to counterterrorism. China joined the previous speakers in congratulating the CTC for its contribution to counterterrorism measures, saying that it would support an even larger role "in helping countries to build their capacity and in providing more counter-terrorism assistance to developing countries."[60]

In this vein, the CTED conducted country visits and assessed implementation in individual states, actively incorporating the broader counterterrorism strategy developed at the UN and within the G8. A stock-taking exercise that served as an intermediate review of implementation efforts indicated strategies that address "societal tensions and other 'conditions conducive to terrorism'" had a far better chance of being successful.[61] By concentrating on its role as a facilitator among donors, capacity-building entities, and recipient (developing) countries, the CTED was credited with successfully matching strengths with weaknesses and vice versa. By late 2010 this work was organized, as a rule, either regionally or thematically.[62] This allowed individual G8 countries to pursue different programs, according to skills and preferences, with bilateral partners.

As one example, Japan extended large grants to Uzbekistan and Indonesia to bolster border control security via a program called Grant Aid for Cooperation on Counter-Terrorism and Security Enhancement.[63] After it had consulted with Interpol, the CTED, and several EU countries, the AU adopted the Comprehensive Anti-Terrorism Model Law in July 2011.[64] In 2013 the Kingdom of Saudi Arabia, as an acknowledgment of the CTED's usefulness in the Middle East, donated $100 million to a counterterrorism center at the UN.[65]

A specific challenge associated with countering extremism was identified in connection with civil society organizations, which, on the one hand, could be subverted by terrorist networks and, on the other hand, were increasingly exposed to the suspicion of government authorities. Such suspicion, it turned out, in many cases was unjustified and used as a pretext to crack down on opposition groups. This required the CTED and international donors to pay more attention to the vulnerability of civil society groups in both directions, as recognized in UNSC Resolution 1963. In this respect CTITF contributed to an initiative involving regional consultations with Western charities and civil society in Bangkok, Auckland, Nairobi, and other cities.[66]

In the context of this broader approach, the 2011 Deauville summit provided specific impetus for the work of the High-Tech Crime Subgroup (HTCSG), a subgroup of the Roma-Lyon Group set up by the G8 in 1997, by offering mutual assistance and denying perpetrators of cyber-crimes a safe haven in a section devoted to Internet-related criminal activities in the G8 leaders' final declaration.[67] The HTCSG has, according to Scherrer, an extraordinarily broad and unwieldy mandate in that it is "keeping track of all criminal activities that are made easier or possible through the use of high technology, such as piracy, illegal content on certain internet sites and communication between criminals, which are now easier to investigate because of the increased traceability of communications."[68] To perform this function, the HTCSG early on established a G8 Network of Contact Points that is standing by twenty-four hours a day, seven days a week. Through the G8 network, Internet service providers can be asked to preserve electronic evidence related to a known or suspected crime. In recent years offers to take part in the Network of Contact Points were extended to countries willing and able to commit to creating a genuine standby capacity. By late 2007 forty-nine countries, twenty-one of which were European, had joined the network.

Partly mirroring this effort, the UN more recently set up the Group of Governmental Experts on Developments in the Field of Information and Telecommunications (UNGGE). The group held its first meeting in Washington, DC, in early August 2012 and less than a year later produced a report on the applicability of international law to the realm of cyberspace. The report summarized its findings, saying,

> International law and in particular the United Nations Charter, is applicable and is essential to maintaining peace and stability and promoting an open, secure, peaceful and accessible ICT [information and communication technologies] environment. The Group also concluded that State sovereignty and the international norms and principles that flow from it apply to States' conduct of ICT-related activities and to their jurisdiction over ICT infrastructure with their territory; States must meet their international obligations regarding internationally wrongful acts attributable to them.[69]

Notably, out of the fifteen countries that made up the government experts who penned the report, only three were non-G20 states. All G8 member states were represented, no doubt drawing on the expertise accumulated through the Roma-Lyon Group and the HTCSG in particular. The overrepresentation of European countries, analogously, is probably a result of the long-standing transnational collaboration in the Club of Berne.

The Global Counterterrorism Forum: A Platform for Enhanced Implementation

Implementation of the counterterrorism agenda among the G8 countries is difficult to assess in aggregate terms, but some attempts have been made. Researchers from the G8 Research Group at the University of Toronto's Munk School have extensive experience in monitoring GX summitry commitments and gauging compliance within a variety of issue areas, assigning scores between +1 (for full compliance) and –1 (for no compliance). In the area of terrorism, a 2013 scorecard found the United States—the target of the 9/11 attacks—at the top of the list of high-performing countries with 0.88 and Japan—with relatively few incidents and never in the sights of violent Islamic extremism—with a score of 0.38. Italy, Russia, and Canada scored almost as high as the United States (0.75–0.79), while the EU had an average of 0.64.[70]

Developing, non-G8 countries with fewer resources unsurprisingly face much greater challenges when they try to meet the demands of UN conventions and other legal instruments in the field of counterterrorism. At the mid-March 2011 Paris meeting, the G8 foreign ministers counted as positive the fact that many countries had joined the struggle against terrorism, especially with regard to Africa. Ministers expressed support for the "central role that the UN must play in the collective fight against terrorism," though they acknowledged the usefulness of a forum at which African governments could identify partners with which to advance that agenda further.[71] One example given was the comprehensive strategies for the Horn of Africa and the Sahel regions, pledged by the EU. Looking forward to the May 2011 Deauville leaders' summit, the ministers alluded to other G8 initiatives and requested that the Roma-Lyon Group prepare a comprehensive status report.[72]

The weakening of the CTAG after 2005 in combination with what reportedly has been a trend of declining interest in counterterrorism among G8 countries led the United States to launch the Global Counterterrorism Forum (GCTF) in September 2011.[73] This was part of the outcome of the G8's June 2011 Deauville summit, during which the members said that they "will consolidate progress in the fight against violent extremism, international terrorism and drug trafficking and will continue our common efforts to tackle these scourges."[74] The basic idea was to enhance the most vulnerable states' capacity to deal with terrorism and to shore up regional support in that endeavor.[75] The GCTF's founding document consisted of fourteen principles, one being to support the implementation of the UN Global Counter-Terrorism Strategy, and the forum was described as "pragmatic, action-oriented, informal and civilian-led."[76]

The GCTF provided a new type of meeting place, less cloaked in the secrecy of traditional liaison-based contacts, for senior experts and decision makers in the field of counterterrorism. The forum established itself as a means to help identify urgent needs, compare best practices, and forge new solutions and mobilize resources for addressing counterterrorism challenges. It had thirty founding member states, eleven Muslim countries among them. Top-priority areas were civilian capacity building in the realm of border management, the justice system, and efforts to counter radical violence. The focus of the senior-level meetings so far held has been the criminal justice system (Cairo and Rabat), the reintegration and rehabilitation of former extremist offenders (Rome), and the handling of kidnapping for ransom cases (Algiers).

At the G8 foreign ministers meeting in Washington, DC, on April 12, 2012, the GCTF was widely welcomed as an important vehicle for enhanced collaboration. The ministers also noted the United Arab Emirates' offer to host an international center devoted to countering radicalization, at which education, training, research, and collaboration would take place. The G8 ministers especially recognized "the cutting edge work of the Roma-Lyon Group . . . to counter the cross-cutting threats of terrorism and transnational organized crime, including drug trafficking, particularly through the development of practical tools, shared with a broad array of international stakeholders, including the United Nations and regional organizations."[77]

A few months earlier, in September 2011, the CTED had similarly praised the creation of the GCTF, with which it subsequently collaborated on regional matters. The two bodies collaborated not only on the Horn of Africa, the Sahel region, and Southeast Asia but also on thematic problems such as improving the criminal justice system, emboldening the rule of law, and countering extremism through proactive measures of various kinds.[78] The flexibility that the forum brings to transnational counterterrorism activities presents, in other words, a potentially useful asset for institutions that operate with statutes, staffs, and fixed budgets in that it helps identify vulnerabilities and then mobilize (largely government) sponsors to remedy such problems on relatively short notice.

The same can be said for UN-based deliberations on terrorism and nonproliferation that partly overlap with conflict-management measures. UNSC Resolution 1977, adopted April 20, 2011, extended the mandate of the 1540 Committee, assigned to combat the proliferation of weapons of mass destruction, and broadened its activities. The resolution thereby reaffirmed the council's commitment to stem the proliferation of nuclear, chemical, and biological weapons and their means of delivery, reiterating that they constitute a live threat to international peace and security. When it comes to applying the nonproliferation regime to the field of nuclear weapons technology and the case of Iran in particular, the council also chose to extend the mandate of the panel of experts investigating allegations that Tehran seeks to acquire such a capability. Only Lebanon abstained.[79]

Consolidating the FATF Regime

Institutional entities with an independent capacity to mobilize ad hoc coalitions and raise money do not need greater flexibility to be effective and legitimate but can rely on a sound set of enforceable rules. The FATF regime, to which nine new recommendations were added in February 2012, arguably remains a crucial part of transnational counterterrorism cooperation.[80] The 2012 recommendations, aimed at the detection, prevention, and suppression of financing terrorism, were meant to further reinforce the system and included the following:

I. Ratification and implementation of UN instruments
II. Criminalising the financing of terrorism and associated money laundering
III. Freezing and confiscating terrorist assets
IV. Reporting suspicious transactions related to terrorism
V. International co-operation
VI. Alternative remittance
VII. Wire transfers
VIII. Non-profit organisations
IX. Cash couriers[81]

The February 2012 version of the forty-plus-nine FATF recommendations was thus grouped into several sets of principles and pieces of advice. The new objectives linked anti-money-laundering measures to anti-terrorist-financing measures and the fight against sponsorship of the spread of weapons of mass destruction. About half of the recommendations dealt with division of responsibilities, transparency issues, and coordination of measures. Fifteen of the forty-nine recommendations outlined preventive measures that could be taken to stem illegitimate practices and balance them with bank secrecy, integrity, and due diligence against intrusive technological monitoring and surveillance, as well as reliance on "third parties" (meaning private corporations and financial institutions).

The revised and extended regime created the preconditions for a ten-year renewal of the FATF in late April 2012, as decided by ministers of finance. Two months later, the FATF reported on the new recommendations to the G20 heads of state and government at the Los Cabos summit. The G20 leaders endorsed the renewal of the mandate and the future implementation of the revised regime. No less significantly, they expressed their general support for the goals of the FATF in that they welcomed "the progress made by FATF in identifying and monitoring high-risk jurisdictions with strategic Anti-Money Laundering/Counter-Terrorist Financing (AML/CTF) deficiencies, using AML/CTF tools in the fight against corruption, improving transparency of corporate vehicles and increasing cooperation against tax crimes, addressing the risks posed by tax havens, as well as in increasing the reach and the effectiveness of AML/CTF measures by also considering financial inclusion efforts."[82] Indeed, by expressly incorporating the agenda of combatting money laundering and counterterrorist financing and by praising the role of the FATF in that process, the G20 leaders effectively broadened a formerly G8-driven agenda. In early November that year, at the Mexico City meeting of finance ministers and heads of central banks, another G20 communiqué went even further in affirming a commitment to the FATF objectives.

Under the presidency of Bjørn S. Aamo of Norway, the FATF also reached out to the UN and its CTC. During a special meeting of the latter on November 20, 2012, top FATF officials explained how their activities complemented and reinforced the work of the CTC. In the course of 2013 and 2014, FATF experts provided more precise guidance and examples of best practices aimed at enhancing compliance with targeted financial sanctions decided by the UNSC, as well as measures that would counter the proliferation of weapons of mass destruction, another key objective of the UNSC.

Aamo's strong focus on improving implementation and broadening the regime to encompass non-Western jurisdictions and financial services industries led the FATF to adopt "high-level principles" to guide relations with FATF-style regional bodies. Other initiatives covered the Private Sector Consultative Forum in London in late April 2013 and dialogues with nonprofit organizations. In February 2013 the FATF identified jurisdictions with "strategic deficiencies" in the area of anti–money laundering and counterterrorist financing.[83] As an example of progress in this area, the Indian financial sector could be taken off the list of high-risk countries following the eighth mutual evaluation report, completed in June 2013.

Under its first Russian president, Vladimir Nechaev, the FATF continued to emphasize implementation through FATF-style regional bodies and the development of synergies with transnational organizations charged with related tasks. In July 2013 Nechaev addressed the Egmont Group of Financial Intelligence Units, stressing the significance of its partnership with the FATF.[84] During Russia's presidency of the G20 in 2013, he was also able to secure a renewed commitment on the part of G20 financial ministers and central bank governors to the FATF at their Moscow meeting in July 2013. Critics nevertheless insist that the FATF was more successful in setting up vetting practices than in making them work, not least in asset-rich member states with sizable domestic financial corporations. Only twelve of the thirty-four FATF countries fully implement customer due diligence and record-keeping standards that the task force demands, according to an OECD report released in December 2013.[85]

Adding a Fifth Letter to BRIC(S)

The G20 thus far features rarely in the context of counterterrorism. Counterterrorism and anti–money laundering are briefly mentioned as secondary goals of financial-sector consolidation in the second annex to the June 2010 Toronto declaration, in an endorsement for the FATF regime (article 39), but not as central objectives pursued by the G20. The June 2012 Los Cabos declaration supported the strengthening of the international financial architecture and the struggle against corruption, including the "denial of safe havens." These were nonetheless goals adopted without the explicit mention of counterterrorism. They form a natural part of the original G20 formula, which circumscribed the group's mandate to shaping the global economic agenda. Fully integrating the counterterrorism agenda would be seen, at least by some, as competing with existing global security institutions, especially the UNSC, and be resented by small states that were wary that a new global "great-power concert" sought to usurp their core functions.[86]

But one group of countries, BRIC, had ambitions to set itself off from the rest of the G20. In 2011 South Africa joined the group to add a capital *S* to the acronym. As if the letter *s* also stood for "security," the political objectives of BRICS grew clearer and more pronounced at the same time. Rather modestly, at the June 2009 BRIC summit in Yekaterinburg the assembled heads of state and government stated that the member states "strongly condemn terrorism in all its forms and manifestations and reiterate that there can be no justification for any act of terrorism anywhere or for whatever reasons."[87] Another paragraph emphasized that the BRIC leaders were strongly committed to

> multilateral diplomacy with the United Nations playing the central role in dealing with global challenges and threats. In this respect, we reaffirm the need for a comprehensive reform of the UN with a view to making it more efficient so that it can deal with today's challenges more effectively. We reiterate the importance we attach to the status of India and Brazil in international affairs, and understand and support their aspirations to play a greater role in the United Nations.

In fact, at the first two BRIC summits counterterrorism was not raised by the member countries, except to indirectly hint that the issue belonged to the United Nations and its Security Council. Yet at the Sanya summit in China's Hainan province, a statement like the 2009 commitment was rephrased to expressly encompass at least part of the transnational counterterrorism agenda: "We reiterate our strong condemnation of terrorism in all its forms and manifestations and stress that there can be no justification, whatsoever, for any acts of terrorism. We believe that the United Nations has a central role in coordinating the international action against terrorism within the framework of the UN Charter and in accordance with principles and norms of international law."[88] An identical formulation was included in the 2013 Durban summit. In both cases the statement went on to urge the conclusion of General Assembly negotiations on the Comprehensive Convention on International Terrorism and to affirm the commitment to strengthen transnational information security, presumably reflective of the newly launched UNGGE network.

Meanwhile, as the aspirations of the BRICS countries started to grow, the G8 summit's attention to nontraditional security suddenly declined under the United Kingdom presidency in 2013. In the joint statement adopted at the April 2013 meeting of G8 foreign ministers, however, the chief diplomats called for further implementation of the UN's Global Counter-Terrorism Strategy, in accordance with the agreed-on comprehensive approach that included security, diplomatic, and development efforts. The group spent a significant portion of their deliberations on WMD nonproliferation, cyber security, kidnapping for ransom as a source of terrorist financing, and the renewed threat of radicalization and terrorist activities in North and West Africa. It also instructed the Roma-Lyon Group and its subgroups to examine several of the looming challenges.[89] Yet apart from a limited initiative on the prevention of kidnapping, the counterterrorist agenda did not feature as a significant priority at the foreign ministers' meeting; that is, counterterrorism was not a self-standing item at the Lough Erne summit on June 17–18, 2013.

Confronting ISIL, Stemming Recruitment

The diplomatic fallout from the annexation of Crimea and the wider Ukrainian conflagration promptly reinvigorated the bifurcation of roles between formal and informal institutional arrangements when it came to counterterrorism measures. The escalating crisis in southern and eastern Ukraine, as already mentioned, unraveled plans for a G8 Sochi summit in June 2014 and undermined the political conditions for holding talks on the sidelines of the Nuclear Security Summit in The Hague, Netherlands. As it were, the heads of state and government of all G7 countries were represented in The Hague, which became the first time Russia dispatched only its foreign minister to such an event. This did not, however, stop Sergei Lavrov from attending the BRICS meeting of foreign affairs and international relations ministers held adjacent to the Nuclear Security Summit.

The G7 foreign ministers meeting in New York, coinciding with the opening of a new session of the UN General Assembly, produced three statements on unfolding crises in the world. One statement was devoted to the handling of the outbreak of Ebola and the logistical challenge it presented to participating organizations and governments. A second statement concentrated on Ukraine, welcoming the recently signed Minsk Agreements on a cease-fire and the engagement of the OSCE in monitoring the humanitarian situation. The third statement was on an increasingly pressing matter: the rising challenge of ISIL.

In a rather extensive statement, the G7 countries expressed their commitment to UNSC Resolution 2170 regarding the widespread kidnapping of hostages, pledging to work tirelessly for the release of all individuals being held by ISIL or associated entities. Acknowledging that the struggle against ISIL requires several elements, the G7 foreign ministers expressly referred to a military component, a humanitarian component, and a political component, including support for moderate forces and dialogue with "countries willing to make a contribution" as part of the nascent strategy.

> We support this comprehensive and coordinated, long-term effort to degrade and defeat ISIL. In this context we recognize that military action as taken by the US and other countries represents an important contribution to helping Iraq to defend itself against ISIL and to deprive ISIL of safe havens. Humanitarian aid to the internally displaced persons and refugees is paramount as long as they cannot return into their homes. To make this possible we must tackle the military strength, the access to funds and fighters, and the violent radicalising and recruiting influence of ISIL. We also need to support moderate forces opposed to ISIL in both Iraq and Syria. To enhance these efforts we will seek to establish a political dialogue on security and stability within the region and platforms to enable a more structured exchange with countries willing to make constructive contributions against terrorism.[90]

The reference to "countries willing to make a contribution" can be interpreted to include the Persian Gulf states and, without much of a stretch of the imagination, even al-Assad's regime in Damascus, formerly shunned by all Western governments as partner. The statement also mentioned the GCTF's The Hague–Marrakech "Memorandum on Good Practices for a More Effective

Response to the Foreign Terrorist Fighters Phenomenon" and the assistance of the Roma-Lyon Group—now without Russia—in developing initiatives addressing the flows of foreign terrorist fighters and finance to Syria and Iraq.

The G20 Brisbane summit, to the contrary, "left out any reference to terrorism and traditional security issues," as a concise summit postmortem put it.[91] Bracht and Kulik, the authors of the assessment, found the omission of ISIL particularly blatant because the summit communiqué was issued shortly after the release of another beheading video involving Westerners. They therefore drew the conclusion that the disappearance of foreign and security policy issues in the official dimension of the G20 summit meant that deliberations on such matters presumably shifted to the unofficial portion, in reality concealing the actual content of talks held among the leaders of the world's most asset-rich countries.[92]

The only dimension of the wider counterterrorism agenda reaffirmed at the Brisbane summit was that of anti–terrorist financing. The communiqué tangentially touched on the matter of financial transparency, stating that the actions of the G20 sought "to enhance mutual legal assistance, recovery of the proceeds of corruption and denial of safe haven to corrupt officials." The 2015–16 G20 Anti-Corruption Action Plan provided more details on this objective, building on the 2010 Toronto summit agreement to launch an Anti-Corruption Working Group that should regularly review and update its recommendations. As top priorities in the combat against corruption for the coming two years, the action plan outlined practical measures to enhance beneficial ownership transparency (widely used to circumvent legal, punitive, and administrative measures against individuals), the redoubling of efforts against bribery, target measures against high-risk sectors, public-sector integrity (for instance, in public procurement), and measures to improve international cooperation.

But the growing awareness of the connections between traditional international conflict management and counterterrorism that followed from the emergence of ISIL in Iraq and Syria during 2014 should not be underestimated. A first unequivocal condemnation by the UNSC was issued as early as January 10, 2014, in a presidential statement after consultations with all fifteen member states:

> The Security Council condemns the attacks that are being perpetrated by Al-Qaida affiliate, the Islamic State in Iraq and the Levant (ISIL), against the people of Iraq in an attempt to destabilize the country and region. . . .The Security Council urges the people of Iraq, including Iraqi tribes, local leaders, and Iraqi security forces in Anbar province, to continue, expand and strengthen their cooperation against violence

and terror and it stresses the critical importance of continued national dialogue and unity.[93]

This strong language was followed up throughout 2014 in new resolutions adopted in the aftermath of military expansion by ISIL and gruesome atrocities committed against ethnic and religious minorities in Iraq and Syria or against individual hostages captured and killed by the armed groups affiliated with ISIL. Resolutions 2016 and 2161, adopted on June 17, combined measures to suppress "kidnapping and hostage-taking of terrorist groups for any purpose" directed at the Taliban of Afghanistan with an expansion of the al-Qaida sanctions committee's mandate to individuals associated with ISIL. A key point of the former resolution was to introduce a ban on travel and financial transactions for individuals and entities affiliated with the Taliban. A key point of the latter resolution was to prevent the direct or indirect supply, sale, or transfer of arms and related material of all types to individuals, groups, undertakings, and entities associated with al-Qaida.

Less than two months later, the UNSC revisited the mandate of the al-Qaida sanctions committee and expanded monitoring to members of ISIL and al-Nusra Front, both active in Iraq and Syria. Six individuals considered affiliated with the latter, and indirectly also with al-Qaida, were listed in the appendix. Resolution 2170, adopted August 15, was at the same time the first to call special attention to the growing problem of foreign fighter recruitment through the Internet and social media. It thereby urged all UN member states to suppress the flow of foreign fighters and to review and increase measures that might prevent the movement of terrorists to and from the Middle East, where they could receive weapons and training and become a bigger threat to societies around the world.

On September 24, that is, the day before the G7 foreign ministers meeting convened in New York, the UNSC extended the framework on the movement of foreign terrorist fighters through the adoption of Resolution 2178. Like the widening of the measures against networks that assist, facilitate, or tolerate terrorist financing, the resolution stepped up efforts to reduce the mobility of potential recruits to ISIL, al-Nusra Front, and al-Qaida, demanding that states prevent entry or transit of individuals when there were grounds for suspecting they might join terrorist organizations at their destination. To signal the high priority awarded to the resolution, more than a dozen heads of state and government participated in the council meeting in New York. The resolution also directed the CTC and the CTED to monitor the situation and identify gaps in the implementation of Resolutions 1373 and 1624 with regard to instruments that can be mobilized for this purpose.

The Empirical Findings: Momentum and Legitimacy of G7/G8 Pragmatism

As in chapter 3, I now turn to the empirical question: How do contemporary great and middle powers employ existing formal and informal institutional arrangements to address challenges in counterterrorism cooperation, spanning traditional and nontraditional security concepts? The four governments that most frequently raised terrorism as an issue in the opening debate of the UN General Assembly from 2009 to 2013 were India, the United States, Canada, and the United Kingdom, the last two in a tied position. As three of these countries were the objects of terrorist attacks or plots in recent years (and Canadian citizens were involved in terrorist preparations), it is hardly surprising that they would be in the lead. Conversely, the three G20 members that paid the least attention to terrorism in their statements were the EU, Germany, and Italy. Neither Germany nor Italy experienced serious terrorist attacks on their soil after 9/11, and the EU has limited authority in this field.

Perhaps to a greater extent than in conflict management, therefore, it might be reasonable to conclude that counterterrorism is a topic that reflects the recent domestic experience of the problems of violent political extremism. Although Germany, Italy, and Europe more widely grappled with terrorism in the 1970s and 1980s, at that time terrorist motives were essentially political and ideological, not intertwined with sectarian, religious, or ethnic justifications. Another distinguishing feature of countries that raise terrorism in the UN context is their tendency to treat it as a threat that warrants a coercive military or police response, not one that can be addressed primarily through prevention, preemption, and rehabilitation.

The years 2009–14 saw institutional arrangements in counterterrorism cooperation starting to displace the fragmented efforts initiated by the G8 and individual Western governments in the immediate aftermath of 9/11, thereby expanding the space for nested formality. It is still a fair assessment that today's transnational counterterrorism regime "lacks a central global body dedicated to terrorism prevention and response," as a Council on Foreign Relations overview succinctly summarized the state of affairs in mid-2013.[94] But it may be equally accurate to say that informal institutional arrangements put in place over a quarter century by G7/G8 working groups and networks continue to form the core of transnational counterterrorism cooperation. In that sense the nascent framework established at the UNSC essentially provided an extension of the informal arrangement, which had not been nearly as effective without a formal, legitimizing counterpart.

At the same time, during 2009–14 relatively few major new counterterrorism initiatives were introduced at the high-table platforms examined here, with the four countries whose membership in the P5 and the G8 overlaps being the overwhelmingly important actors and China trailing slightly behind. One reason for the new focus on making the existing institutional arrangements work is that a great variety of international legal instruments were put in place after 9/11; a decade later national authorities had become responsible for translating international law and best practices into implementation in individual countries. A combination of formal and informal settings and diplomatic practices were used by those authorities to render counterterrorist measures more effective.

Another reason for the lack of innovative policies and decisions may be that this period coincided with a time when the G8 needed to shift gears as a result of the upgrade of the G20 and the principals were still uncertain as to what to make of the narrower group's role. Nontraditional security had been one of the G8's key preoccupations since the late 1990s, presumably because it was an area in which Russia could be engaged in a constructive way. This sentiment was no doubt reinforced in the aftermath of 9/11 as Moscow and Washington, along with many other governments, agreed on the importance of coordinating counterterrorism policies and enhancing associated capacities. As the G20 became the "premier forum for international economic cooperation," moreover, the nontraditional security agenda became a key rationale for continuing with G8 summits.

The G7/G8's pragmatism in pursuing effective institutional arrangements in the realm of transnational counterterrorism was reflected in both how it made use of informal diplomatic practices and how the UNSC gradually developed its own instruments, drawing on its unique legal and political status. The nested formality of the FATF toolbox, originally created to combat money laundering, now became available for vetting financial transactions in virtually all major nerve centers of international finance in the search for schemes to fund terrorist activities. Once established and made available for transnational counterterrorism purposes, that toolbox constituted a powerful framework for targeted sanctions by individual governments, by coalitions of like-minded countries, and by the UNSC on the basis of joint resolutions.

While retaining the nontraditional security cooperation in the Roma-Lyon Group, the HTCSG, and other expert-based transnational networks, in 2009–14 the G8 made several efforts to create or bolster institutional arrangements within the UN system that would serve similar purposes on a wider scale. In repeated statements that made reference to the UN and its Security Council, such as the 2009 l'Aquila Declaration on Counter Terrorism, the G8 countries in principle deferred to the former and thereby bestowed legitimacy to a universal framework for counterterrorism. Such statements make clear that the leaders of major countries regard the legitimacy derived from the UN Charter and the status of the UNSC within it as an indispensable asset to the overall counterterrorism effort; in addition, they generally agree that sustaining a transnational regime in this field, historically associated with the jealously guarded domain of home and justice affairs, is desirable.

By 2012 the CTC, and especially the CTED, operated as a transnational network of experts and officials drawn from international organizations and national authorities. In that respect they emulated the G8-sponsored FATF, the Roma-Lyon Group, and the CTAG. Working from within the UN system, however, the CTED had the advantage of being a subsidiary organ of the UNSC and thus carried "the Council's full weight and authority."[95] By mid-2012 the CTED had adopted initial assessments of all 193 UN member states and had conducted over sixty country visits with the purpose of implementing Resolution 1373.[96] Each country visit was carefully prepared and carried out in a way that was supposed to be beneficial for the specific challenges that the country in question faced in border and airport security, terrorist financing, armed insurgency, and any other concerns that arose in the dialogue with that country.

The CTED, in others words, acquired distinct features of nested informality within the domain of the rather inflexible UNSC. Noteworthy is that the CTED has had unusually few constraints toward working closely with other counterterrorism bodies, including the Global Counterterrorism Forum, seemingly reflecting the pragmatic approach to transnational counterterrorism cooperation established by G8-induced networks. In openly acknowledging this legacy, the CTED in 2012 observed that "even though the United Nations is not formally a Forum member, the engagement of the Executive Directorate in its activities [is] similar to its engagement in those of the former Counter-Terrorism Action Group of the Group of Eight."[97] Unusual for a UN body, that is, the CTED in most contexts tried to retain an evenhanded approach toward formal and informal institutional arrangements as well as toward a range of other organizations, governmental and nongovernmental.

Equally importantly, the same period saw a growing convergence in the overall counterterrorism approach adopted by developed and developing states. Critics are correct in pointing out that individual and human rights were not always respected in this process, a problem neglected by the United States and its closest allies in transnational counterterrorism in the mid-2000s. By the same token, though, not all governments deliberately created overbroad laws but rather emulated American and Western legal documents that were counterbalanced by domestic legal or political institutions in their original versions. Such streamlining of institutional arrangements might or might not have been effective in the individual case but presumably facilitated and speeded up transnational cooperation in a field traditionally characterized by concerns over national sovereignty.

The overall finding with regard to counterterrorism cooperation is that contemporary great and middle powers draw on formal and informal institutional arrangements to address challenges in this policy area, thereby creating institutional hybridity at an aggregate level. At the same time it is important to point out that barriers between legal and political settings and diplomatic practices are not made obsolete; instead, hybridity consists of a mutual nestedness cutting across the formality-informality nexus. The integrity of both sets of institutional arrangements is not undermined as a result of these practices.

Notably, a roughly analogous pattern of complementarity obtains when it comes to the traditional-nontraditional security nexus. Even though counterterrorism cooperation is understood as a nontraditional security issue, it is a policy area involving traditional concepts as well. Following the 9/11 attacks, the trend toward sharing intelligence, planning procedures, and coercive resources has evolved rapidly in the United States, and many other governments are moving in the same direction. As a result of these developments, the level of contestation between institutions and organizational goals has gradually subsided.

NOTES

1. Coady, "Morality of Terrorism," 52.

2. A more recent, similarly analytically amoral definition is available in Shanahan, "Betraying a Certain Corruption," 177.

3. Svendsen, *Professionalization of Intelligence Cooperation.*

4. Prezelj, "Improving Inter-Organizational Cooperation," 7–9, 20–21.

5. Barnett and Coleman, "Designing Police," 609–10.

6. Oudraat, "Role of the Security Council."

7. Barnett and Coleman, "Designing Police," 613.

8. Shaw, "G8 Conclusions on Crime."

9. Clunan, "Fight against Terrorist Financing," 588–97.

10. Zarate, *Treasury's War.*

11. Hallenberg, "Anti-Money Laundering," 57–63.

12. I would in this context disagree with Phillip Bobbitt's 2008 analysis of the war on terror in as far as he asserts that every power besides the United States "is essentially regional" (487). I believe this assertion overstates the centrality of the United States and understates the contribution of other countries, in particular that of close US allies and partners.

13. UN Security Council, S/RES/1373, September 28, 2001, 1d.

14. Beyer, *Counterterrorism*, 168–72.

15. Gardner, "Fighting Terrorism the FATF Way."

16. Clunan, "Fight against Terrorist Financing," 581–82. For a recent, sophisticated approach seeking to explain the high levels of compliance with FATF rules as a result of high credibility and transparency of its institutional monitoring and blacklisting of noncooperative jurisdictions, see Morse, "International Institutions."

17. Amicelle, "Trace My Money If You Can."

18. Beyer, *Counterterrorism*, 85–86.

19. Self-reporting, mutual evaluation, and the identification of "non-cooperative countries and territories" are the three key mechanisms used by the FATF (Gardner, "Fighting Terrorism the FATF Way," 332–35). This means that although several follow-up mechanisms are available, genuine and effective implementation of the FATF regime remains the responsibility of individual states and the most demanding regulations in the field of counterterrorism are typically those of member states. That being said, the work of putting in place a broader regime was greatly facilitated by powerful observer member organizations, such as the IMF, the World Bank, Interpol, the UN-ODC, the Basel Committee on Banking Supervision, the International Organization of Securities Commissions, and the International Association of Insurance Supervisors.

20. Scherrer, *G8 against Transnational*, 113–28.

21. Ibid., 116–18.

22. "Annex to the G8 Foreign Ministers Meeting Chair's Statement," Washington, DC, April 12, 2012, accessed October 18, 2015, http://www.state.gov/r/pa/prs/ps/2012/04/187815.htm.

23. Millar, "Multilateral Counterterrorism."

24. Counter-Terrorism Action Group, "Building International Political Will and Capacity to Combat Terrorism: A G8 Action Plan," July 2003, accessed March 22, 2014, http://www.g8.fr/evian/english/navigation/2003_g8_summit/summit_documents/building_international_political_will_and_capacity_to_combat_terrorism_-_a_g8_action_plan.htmlQ1.

25. Oudraat, "Role of the Security Council," 163.

26. Rosand, "G8's Counter-Terrorism Group."

27. For many years the UN's counterterrorism efforts were haunted by the lack of a shared understanding, let alone a common definition, of terrorism. Between 2005 and 2008 a number of political decision makers and diplomats were able to create a "working hypothesis" of terrorism, and Resolution 1624 for the first time included education and socialization as factors. The 2006 UN Global Counter-Terrorism Strategy adopted by the General Assembly further deepened this inclusive approach (UN General Assembly, *Global Counter-Terrorism Strategy*, A/RES/60/288, September 20, 2006).

28. Lia, *Globalization and the Future of Terrorism*; Sageman, *Leaderless Jihad*.

29. For reasons that have to do with how the work of affected ministries and agencies is organized, the framing of a counterterrorism agenda within an international institution will inevitably bring out legal, conceptual, and methodological differences among governments and within expert communities.

30. Reasons not to treat security and finance as separate policy realms in the context of counterterrorism measures have been articulated and widely accepted by leading Western countries. But in order not to inadvertently damage transnational trade and commerce, a primary objective became the differentiation between "good circulation" and "bad circulation" of migrants, goods and services, and money. For all intents and purposes, this was an effort led by the United States (Duffield, *Development, Security and Unending War*, 30). Given the strong record of the G8 in this field in the past, as well as the need to engage major financial centers, it was widely considered the most appropriate vehicle for reinforcing the global counterterrorism regime.

31. Lind and Howell, "Counter-Terrorism."

32. FATF, "Money Laundering through Money Remittance and Currency Exchange Providers," June 2010, accessed May 22, 2015, http://www.fatf-gafi.org/media/fatf /ML%20through%20Remittance%20and%20Currency%20Exchange%20Providers.pdf.

33. "G8 Declaration on Counter-Terrorism," l'Aquila, July 10, 2009, accessed January 17, 2014, http://www.mofa.go.jp/policy/economy/summit/2009/declaration_t.pdf.

34. "Final Declaration," Rome, May 30, 2009, accessed July 17, 2014, http://www.icao .int/Security/mrtd/PKD%20Documents/PKDPublicityDocuments/G8Declaration -Rome-30May2009.pdf.

35. "G8 Declaration on Counter Terrorism."

36. Partly related to counterterrorism, the G8 issued the L'Aquila Statement on Non-Proliferation in support of previous summit statements on the proliferation of weapons of mass destruction and their means of delivery as a major threat to international security. It reiterated that the Treaty on the Non-Proliferation of Nuclear Weapons (NPT) remains the cornerstone of the global nuclear nonproliferation regime and praised US movement toward ratification of the Comprehensive Nuclear-Test-Ban Treaty (CTBT). The l'Aquila statement also urged states to implement UN Security Council Resolution 1540 on preventing non-state actors from obtaining WMD.

37. Scherrer, *G8 against Transnational*, 5.

38. This point should not be exaggerated. The G20 was closely involved in disseminating the anti-terrorist-financing measures in the second half of 2001, but at the time the cooperation on such issues mainly involved finance, home, and justice ministries, not heads of state and government. Interview with Paul Martin, Canada's Minister of Finance and Chair of the G20, G8 Research Group, University of Toronto, November 18, 2001, accessed August 8, 2014, http://www.g8.utoronto.ca/g20 /interviews/Martin011118.pdf.

39. Interview with Paul Martin in Scherrer, *G8 against Transnational*, 4.

40. Guebert, "Plans for the London G20."

41. US Embassy, Rome, "Italian G8 Outreach Approach Clarified; Sous Sherpa Requests Call with Climate Envoy," Wikileaks Cable Reference ID: #09ROME141, February 5, 2009, accessed July 17, 2014, https://cablegatesearch.wikileaks.org/cable.php?id=09ROME141&q=09rome141.

42. The original BRIC constellation lacked South Africa, even though it had been part of the Outreach Five. See later section on how BRIC became BRICS.

43. "Joint Statement of the BRIC Countries Leaders," Yekaterinburg, Russia, June 16, 2009, accessed July 18, 2014, http://www.brics5.co.za/about-brics/summit-declaration/first-summit/.

44. UN Security Council, S/RES/1904 (2009), December 17, 2009.

45. OSCE, "Speaking Notes of the Chairman of the UN Counter-Terrorism Committee," PC.DEL/1376/03/Rev1, November 18, 2003.

46. CTC, "Report of the Counter-Terrorism Committee to the Security Council for Its Consideration as Part of Its Interim Review of the Work of the Counter-Terrorism Committee Executive Directorate," S/2009/289, June 4, 2009.

47. Ibid.

48. CTC, "Our Mandate," accessed July 17, 2014, http://www.un.org/en/sc/ctc.

49. UN Security Council, Presidential Statement, S/PRST/2010/19, September 27, 2010, accessed July 17, 2014, 4, http://www.un.org/en/ga/search/view_doc.asp?symbol=S/PRST/2010/19.

50. UN Security Council, S/RES/1963 (2010), December 20, 2010, para. 9.

51. "CTED 2010 Communications Strategy and Action Plan," accessed February 17, 2014, http://www.un.org/en/sc/ctc/docs/policypapers/communications_strategyplan2010.pdf.

52. "Letter dated 2012/01/06 from the Chair of the Security Council Committee Established Pursuant to Resolution 1373 (2001) concerning Counter-Terrorism Addressed to the President of the Security Council," S/2012/16, accessed October 11, 2015, 25–30, http://hdl.handle.net/11176/16605.

53. "Canadian Chair's Statement," Gatineau, March 30, 2010, accessed January 15, 2014, http://www.g8.utoronto.ca/foreign/formin100330.html.

54. "G8 Conference of Senior Officials on Capacity Building: Chair's Report to G8 Sherpas," Gatineau, May 3–4, 2010, accessed July 17, 2014, http://www.g8.utoronto.ca/summit/2010muskoka/capacity.html.

55. "G8 Leaders Statement on Countering Terrorism," Muskoka, May 16, 2010, accessed January 15, 2014, http://www.g8.utoronto.ca/summit/2010muskoka/counterterrorism.html.

56. Ibid.

57. Peterson, "Using the General Assembly," 177.

58. Secretary General Annan in the newspaper *The Hindu*, cited in Beyer, *Counterterrorism*, 166.

59. UN Security Council, meeting protocol, S/PV.6390, September 27, 2010.

60. UN Security Council, meeting protocol, S/PV.6390.

61. "Letter Dated 2010/11/02 from the Chairman of the Security Council Committee Established Pursuant to Resolution 1373 (2001) concerning Counter-Terrorism Addressed to the President of the Security Council," S/2010/569, accessed October 11, 2015, http://hdl.handle.net/11176/14566.

62. Ibid., 5–6.

63. Ministry of Foreign Affairs, Japan, "Japan's International Counter-Terrorism Cooperation," August 2010, accessed January 15, 2014, http://www.mofa.go.jp/policy/terrorism/intl_coop.html.

64. "Letter Dated 2010/11/02."

65. Royal Embassy of Saudi Arabia, "Saudi Arabia Donates $100 Million to UN Counter-Terrorism Centre," August 7, 2013, accessed August 17, 2014, http://www.saudiembassy.net/press-releases/press08071301.aspx.

66. "Letter Dated 2012/06/20 from the Chair of the Security Council Committee Established Pursuant to Resolution 1373 (2001) concerning Counter-Terrorism Addressed to the President of the Security Council," S/2012/465, June 21, 2012, accessed October 11, 2015, http://hdl.handle.net/11176/17154.

67. "Deauville Declaration: Internet," May 26, 2011, accessed October 11, 2015, http://www.g8.utoronto.ca/summit/2011deauville/2011-internet-en.html.

68. Scherrer, *G8 against Transnational*, 80.

69. "Group of Governmental Experts on Developments in the Field of Information and Telecommunications in the Context of International Security: Note by the Secretary-General," A/68/98, June 24, 2013, accessed October 11, 2015, http://hdl.handle.net/11176/274239.

70. Bracht, "Plans for the 2011 G8."

71. "G8 Meeting of Foreign Ministers: Chair's Summary," Paris, March 15, 2011, accessed January 17, 2014, http://www.g8.utoronto.ca/foreign/formin110315-en.html.

72. Ibid.

73. Council on Foreign Relations, "The Global Regime for Terrorism," June 19, 2013, accessed August 18, 2014, http://www.cfr.org/terrorism/global-regime-terrorism/p25729.

74. "G8 Declaration: Renewed Commitment for Freedom and Democracy," Deauville, May 26–27, 2011, accessed July 17, 2014, http://www.g8.utoronto.ca/summit/2011deauville/2011-declaration-en.html.

75. Bracht, "Plans for the 2011 G8," 4.

76. GCTF, "Global Counterterrorism Forum Official Launch," September 22, 2011,

accessed July 17, 2014, https://www.theGCTF.org/documents/10162/13878/Political
+Declaration.pdf.

77. "Annex to the G8 Foreign Ministers Meeting Chairman's Statement," Camp
David, April 12, 2012, accessed July 18, 2014, http://www.mofa.go.jp/policy/economy
/summit/2012/g8_fm_cs_2.html.

78. "Letter Dated 2012/06/20," 4.

79. UN Security Council, S/RES/1984 (2011), June 21, 2012.

80. Eleni Tsingou argues that the Basel Committee on Banking Supervision should
be seen as part of the financial counterterrorism regime. The difference is, in my view,
that the FATF was created with the explicit purpose of combatting money laundering
and organized crime and that its activities only later were extended to anti–terrorist
financing. See Tsingou, "Global Financial Governance."

81. FATF, "IX Special Recommendations," April 20, 2012, accessed July 18,
2014, http://www.fatf-gafi.org/topics/fatfrecommendations/documents/ixspecial
recommendations.html.

82. "G20 Leaders Declaration," Los Cabos, June 19, 2012, accessed July 18, 2014,
https://www.whitehouse.gov/the-press-office/2012/06/19/g20-leaders-declaration.

83. FATF, "High-Risk and Non-cooperative Jurisdictions," February 22, 2013, accessed July 18, 2014, http://www.fatf-gafi.org/topics/high-riskandnon-cooperative
jurisdictions/documents/fatfpublicstatement22february2013.html.

84. Vladimir Nechaev, "Enhancing the Synergy between the FATF and the Egmont
Group," 21st Plenary of the Egmont Group of FIUs, Sun City, South Africa, July 3, 2013,
accessed July 18, 2014, http://www.fatf-gafi.org/documents/news/vnegmontplenary
speech.html.

85. "Rich Smell; Dirty Money," *The Economist*, December 21, 2013.

86. I believe that the assertion by Vabulas and Snidal, that the BRICS largely utilized
an informal institution to gain entry into a formal institution, the UN Security Council,
is an oversimplification. Vabulas and Snidal, "Organization without Delegation," 204.

87. "Joint Statement of the BRIC Countries Leaders."

88. "Full Text of Sanya Declaration of the BRICS Leaders Meeting," Xinhua,
April 14, 2011, accessed July 18, 2014, para. 11, http://news.xinhuanet.com/english2010
/china/2011-04/14/c_13829453.htm.

89. "G8 Foreign Ministers' Meeting Statement," London, April 11, 2013, accessed
July 18, 2014, https://www.gov.uk/government/news/g8-foreign-ministers-meeting
-statement.

90. "G7 Foreign Ministers' Statement, Joint Action to Fight the Terrorist Organisation ISIL/DAESH," September 25, 2014, accessed May 22, 2015, http://www.germany
.info/Vertretung/usa/en/__pr/P__Wash/2014/09/25-G7-ISIS.html.

91. Bracht and Kulik, "Sticking to the Core."

92. Ibid.

93. UN Security Council, Presidential Statement, S/PRST/2014/1, January 10, 2014.

94. Council on Foreign Relations, "Global Regime."

95. "Letter Dated 2010/11/02," 11.

96. UN Security Council, "Letter Dated 18 January 2012 from the Secretary-General," S/2012/45: 3, January 19, 2012.

97. "Letter Dated 2012/06/20," 4, 7–8.

Climate Change Mitigation

The UNSC has exhibited a near-complete lack of interest in the issue of climate change, with the exception of two thematic debates held in recent years. This is an issue that belongs almost exclusively to the informal dimension of institutional arrangements. Consequently, we expect that the delineation between the formal and informal institutional arrangements is sustained by the council's strong prerogatives. Climate change is widely regarded as a quintessentially nontraditional security issue; thus, the UNSC has not contested the informal institutions' control of this policy area.

Background

Climate change mitigation includes the prevention of greenhouse gas (GHG) emissions that constitute—according to the overwhelming consensus of scientists in the field—the main cause of rising global temperatures and measures by which the adverse consequences of this phenomenon could be eased. Transforming our societies so that they do not further contribute to climate change is already a complex task best tackled by a wide range of actors and institutions. So-called adaptation efforts, which are now under way in some countries and will ready societies to absorb climate change, are an even broader undertaking that requires a planning horizon spanning generations and centuries.[1] Leaving adaptation efforts aside, the following analysis considers climate change mitigation as a looming and rather elusive objective of national and international policy.[2] More specifically, I will be examining "mitigation policy as diplomacy" in the sense discussed by Joshua Busby.[3]

The issue of climate change and the need for a worldwide regulatory framework was at the outset not raised by informal great-power groups like the G7/G8 or by the UNSC. Climate change was largely an expert-driven concern put forward within the context of the United Nations and its environmental

conferences, in particular the 1979 Geneva World Climate Conference organized by the World Meteorological Organization. Only thirteen years later, at
the 1992 Rio de Janeiro Earth Summit, climate change was given large-scale
attention by top-level decision makers. One of the key documents adopted
at the summit was the United Nations Framework Convention on Climate
Change (UNFCCC), which aimed to limit GHG emissions and help governments prepare to cope with the effects of climate change.

Carbon dioxide (CO_2) emissions have received by far the most attention
in international negotiations on climate change mitigation. This is because
carbon dioxide is widely prevalent and has a residence time in the Earth's
atmosphere of between five years and two centuries depending on the circumstances. Other substances that trap solar energy in the atmosphere are
methane (CH_4), ozone (O_3), sulfur hexafluoride (SF_6), hydrofluorocarbon-23
(HFC_{23}), chlorofluourocarbon-11 (CFC_{11}), and perfluoromethane (CF_4).
Whereas most GHGs have a residence time of decades or centuries, perfluoromethane is exceptional in that it can stay in the atmosphere for some 45,000
years. Also, water vapor and clouds are technically GHGs—even though their
residence time is only nine days—because they aggravate global warming by
trapping other emissions.

The dangers and risks associated with significant climate change are not
easily summarized, as scientists disagree about the precise implications and
time span.[4] Rising sea levels, more frequent occurrences of extreme weather
conditions, and changing flora and fauna in the most affected parts of the
world are some straightforward and widely anticipated effects. Other somewhat more indirect repercussions are more contentious and difficult to predict
in the short-to-mid term. But the considerable health concerns for humans
associated with climate change are no longer controversial. In 2008 the WHO
released a report stating that a warmer and more variable climate "threatens
to lead to higher levels of some air pollutants, increase transmission of com-
municable diseases through unclean water and through contaminated food, to
compromise agricultural production in some of the least developed countries,
and increase the hazards of extreme weather."[5]

Because many realized that the UNFCCC was too weak given new scientific reports suggesting that CO_2 and other GHGs needed to be reduced
sharply, the Kyoto Protocol adopted in 1997 introduced a stricter set of rules
and targets. A total of 192 states signed the Kyoto Protocol, with the notable
exception of the United States (along with South Sudan and Andorra). Falling
short of its reduction target, Canada became the first country to repudiate
the protocol in December 2011. Meanwhile, the Intergovernmental Panel on
Climate Change (IPCC), established in 1988, began releasing scientific reports

on the state of emissions and the climate, along with projected estimates of what various levels of continued emissions would produce in terms of climate effects. The IPCC's 2007 report went so far as to state that "warming of the climate system is unequivocal."[6] The expectation that the parties to the UNFCCC would produce a universally adopted, binding agreement grew in the middle of the first decade of the twenty-first century. As the first commitment period of the Kyoto Protocol was set to expire in 2012, many hopes were pinned on the 2009 Copenhagen summit.

The debate about the Kyoto Protocol approach, aiming for a universal and mandatory regime of laws and norms that would reduce the carbon emissions at the local as well as the global level, was no doubt in part a genuine disagreement on the merits of painstaking consensus making in the spirit of multilateralism and in part a stalling device on the part of vested interests. Apart from reining in the emission levels of the vast majority of UN member states, the protocol included a Clean Development Mechanism (CDM) that helped fund hundreds of clean energy projects in the developing world.[7] But the exemption of developing countries and the refusal of the US Senate to ratify the Kyoto Protocol undermined its effectiveness and rendered the notion of a multilateral institutional arrangement deeply problematic.

Some commentators have more recently advocated decentralized regional, national, and municipal programs that would encourage creative alternatives and new technological and administrative solutions.[8] Since energy systems can only be transformed over time, a decentralized approach has the advantage of allowing for climate governance initiatives at a pace that suits communities, industries, and other stakeholders and that is sustainable over the long haul. Instead of vague, long-term commitments to targets and dates, decision makers can choose to give priority to short-term, verifiable commitments on the part of individual branches of business.[9] Also facilitated by a decentralized approach, programs such as carbon dioxide capture and storage can be explored if technologies and costs render this approach feasible and there are sufficient opportunities to experiment with the overall framework.[10]

International institutions that operate on the basis of informality would seem to have an advantage from this perspective. Ambitious regulatory frameworks are a nonstarter in the first place since informal governance is antithetical to binding rules. Yet in the case of the GX summitry, climate change only recently emerged as a self-standing agenda item. The reasons the G8 did not embrace climate change as a priority concern (or the reasons the rest of the international community assigned the G8 that role) are complex and multifaceted. But basically the G8, as a collective of industrialized great powers, has had limited credibility as the source of a fair and balanced solution.[11] The first time climate change featured as a separate issue on the G8 agenda was at the 2005 Gleneagles summit. At this point the G8 member states agreed to sixty-three nonbinding commitments and decided to make the World Bank set up a financial mechanism called the Clean Energy Investment Framework.[12] Three years later, at the Osaka summit, the group endorsed the establishment of Climate Investment Funds, the realization of which prompted independent analysts to praise the group's accomplishment in the field of energy efficiency.[13]

The leading governments' signal that a low-carbon future is a widely shared goal was now picked up by many business leaders, some of whom readily pointed out the formidable challenge of "climate financing." In November 2008 some 150 investors representing approximately US$9 trillion in assets met at the Third Investor Summit on Climate Risk in New York to show their readiness to engage in innovation and long-term investment. The United Nations Environment Programme (UNEP) Finance Initiative, which works with large-scale private investment corporations, was at the core of this dimension of UN activities on climate change.

As incontrovertible evidence of rising global temperatures accumulated, the temptation was to engage formal high-table diplomacy even though climate change traditionally is not regarded as a conventional security challenge. In mid-April 2007 the UNSC held its first-ever debate on climate change in the presence of some fifty UN delegation representatives. The meeting, called by the United Kingdom, was chaired by UK foreign secretary Margaret Beckett, who openly acknowledged that some countries were uncomfortable with the notion of the council deliberating on environmental issues. But she added that the United Kingdom was of the opinion that the unprecedented debate was justified since the threat of climate change "exacerbated" many security issues within the council's remit. The British debate, much stimulated by a famous report written by then–Oxford University professor Nicholas Stern, clearly preceded that in many other countries.[14]

The first-ever debate on climate change and its associated security challenges at the UNSC certainly received more attention than scores of international conferences and workshops devoted to the same topic. While diplomats from several countries complained about the danger of the council's undermining the work of specialized UN bodies, such as the IPCC, UNEP, and International Energy Agency (IEA), others endorsed the notion that climate change indeed represents an existing worldwide threat. Apart from raising awareness in general by having the debate at a high-table platform, another reasonable justification for convening the UNSC was to sensitize top-level decision makers in major countries to things to come. If the council now insisted on the urgency of the matter, it could later adopt binding regulatory measures for addressing major crises and emergencies that could follow from climate change and perhaps even take on a pivotal crisis-management role.[15]

In the past few years—since it became a summit-based institution—the G20 also felt considerable pressure to address climate change and thereby to contribute to raising awareness. Although the composition of the G20 suggests that it can potentially produce a world-encompassing strategic view of the challenge of climate change, format and thematic restrictions appear to limit its effectiveness. The differences in opinion and interests of industrialized and developing states with regard to historical and contemporary responsibilities for achieving a low-carbon society are well-known, as are the related concerns over conflicting energy policies, and these differences combine to render a joint approach to the vast challenge difficult to achieve. At the first G20 summits of heads of state and government, held in Washington and London in 2008–9, the issue of climate change featured only briefly in the final declarations.

In the following case study of climate change mitigation in 2009–14, the gradually expanding activities of the GX summitry and the UNSC will be analyzed in order to describe the evolving policy and decision making in both institutional arrangements. As mentioned previously, the strong prerogatives of the UNSC over its own agenda and the prevailing view that climate issues unambiguously belong to the nontraditional security agenda mean that only the GX summitry is in a position to move the issue forward. An attempt is made to assess the few examples of policy and decision making and follow-up measures that this diplomatic process so far has yielded.

Establishing a Top Priority

By early 2009 climate change had been incorporated as a self-standing agenda item at both the UNSC and the G8, though in neither case was it accompanied by mandatory programs or guidelines on mitigation. The immediate background was that the 2005 Gleneagles summit of the G8 had for the first time elevated climate change to a top priority, and follow-up meetings held at the same location for the next two years as the so-called Gleneagles Dialogue Meetings involved the twenty major GHG-emitting countries. The April 2007 UNSC debate has already been mentioned in this context, and the IPCC Working Group II assessment reports similarly helped to raise the awareness of decision makers and the general public in many parts of the world of the phenomenon and its increasingly pressing character. In 2007 IPCC chairman Rajendra Pachauri famously remarked, "If there's no action before 2012, that's too late. What we do in the next two to three years will determine our future. This is the defining moment."[16]

The decision to convene the United Nations Climate Conference in Copenhagen in 2009 heightened the sense that a universal, mandatory regime for the first time might be within political reach. As many environmental NGOs and lobbyists had always regretted the nonparticipation of the United States and Canada in the Kyoto Protocol, and viewed this as the single most important element undermining the protocol's worldwide implementation, the 2009 Copenhagen summit offered new hope. By the time of the summit, the administration of George W. Bush, demonstrably reluctant to accept binding commitments associated with climate change, had been replaced by that of Democratic successor Barack Obama, whose preelection pledges included a proactive stance on climate change.[17] Moreover, with all UN member states attending, bringing major developing countries like China and India into the fold was seen as a critically important task on the part of the pro-Kyoto coalition of governments.

Several political and diplomatic initiatives helped keep the climate issue at the top of the international agenda in 2009. A content analysis of all documents (excluding charts) coming out of the G8 during the course of two years found that 60 percent contained portions devoted to climate change in 2008, and 53.8 percent in 2009.[18] The G8 energy ministers meeting on May 24–25, 2009, was broadened to a much wider group of participating countries, among which the majority were G20 member states. On the first day of the meeting, a new initiative was unveiled, the International Partnership of Energy Efficiency Cooperation (IPEEC), which gathered all G8 member states plus Brazil, China, India, the Republic of Korea, and Mexico. The IPEEC was assigned to promote energy efficiency through exchange of best practices and improve building codes to encourage sustainable buildings, as well as elaborate detailed work plans, and invite more countries to join the initiative.

An ambitious joint statement produced at the May 24–25 G8 energy ministers meeting was approved by the governments of Algeria, Australia, Brazil, China, Egypt, India, Indonesia, Korea, Libya, Mexico, Nigeria, Rwanda, Saudi Arabia, South Africa, and Turkey. After repeating the overall commitment to the transition to a low-carbon society and to the tangible outcome at the Copenhagen summit at the end of 2009, the joint statement specified the challenges of addressing energy security, energy use, and energy availability in that context. In a fourteen-point list of measures that could help cut carbon emissions, the G8 statement urged all countries to above all improve access to energy, diversify the energy mix, substitute fossil fuels with nuclear energy and other alternatives, and redouble efforts to accomplish higher energy efficiency and saving. The document further encouraged governments to make the transition by using a sectoral approach that enhances innovation and the diffusion of low-carbon technologies and creates fiscal incentives and transparent regulatory frameworks that promote the transition process over time.

Notably, the last three points in the joint statement of G8 energy ministers narrowly concentrated on the importance of a technology-driven approach, aiming to establish a "low carbon energy technology global platform" that would enable all countries to forge their own energy policies—based on national strengths and weaknesses—in relation to the objective of reducing GHG emissions. The G8 statement ended by asking the IEA to develop a proposal for designing and implementing this low-carbon energy technology platform for its pending October 2009 meeting.[19] In 2011 the Toronto-based G8 Research Group found that member states "have largely delivered on [climate change] decisions, receiving an overall B grade."[20] As can be seen in the preamble, five non-G20 countries were engaged in the deliberations on the 2011 document, and only Argentina was missing from among the major economies. In that sense, the outcome can be said to have gained validity beyond the Western countries that form the G8 and the core of the OECD constellation.[21]

Building on the G8 energy ministers meeting and the documents it generated, the l'Aquila summit produced a declaration that linked the issues of energy and climate change closely together. That declaration, moreover, was signed by the leaders of another eight G20 countries attending the G8 summit and the so-called Major Economies Forum that Italy, the G8 chair, had carefully organized.[22] To set up the right mind-set for reaching a common, universal, and mandatory framework at Copenhagen, the phrasing conveyed a clear sense of urgency and obligation on the part of world leaders to come together:

> Climate change is one of the greatest challenges of our time. As leaders of the world's major economies, both developed and developing, we intend to respond vigorously to this challenge, being convinced that climate change poses a clear danger requiring an extraordinary global response. . . . We reaffirm the objective, provisions and principles of the UN Framework Convention on Climate Change. Recalling the Major Economies Declaration adopted in Toyako, Japan, in July 2008, and taking full account of decisions taken in Bali, Indonesia, in December 2007, we resolve to spare no effort to reach agreement in Copenhagen, with each other and with other Parties, to further implementation of the Convention.[23]

In the subsequent five points listed in the declaration, the signatory states accepted responsibilities and principles geared toward mitigation and adaptation in view of the approaching climate change. Most substantive was point number one, recognizing the need to take measures that would prevent the increase in global average temperature by two degrees Celsius above preindustrial levels and accepting that mitigation actions and measurement (plus reporting and verification) are required to meet this end. While the second point addressed the importance of not simply relying on mitigation but also preparing for adaptation efforts (as the process of climate change cannot be reversed at this point), the third point reiterated the importance of sharing technologies that further transformation to a low-carbon society. Finally, points four and five mentioned the need to urgently scale up resource mobilization and financing solutions to accelerate the process, in particular with regard to encouraging a technological shift in developing states.

More controversial was the relatively conservative fifty-by-fifty target for substantive reduction of GHG emissions, forged by consensus within the G8 community.[24] The first "fifty" referred to the target of cutting emissions in half, and the second "fifty" signaled the target date, that is, 2050. Given IPCC reports and statements by leading scientists and commentators on environmental issues, this appeared to be a least-common-denominator objective on the part of the G8. The declaration was also ambiguous as to whether all types of GHG substances were included or only CO_2 emissions. Greenhouse gas was mentioned as an encompassing term only once in the text, and not in the "operative passages" that state international obligations.

Whereas the G8 had been preparing the ground for the Copenhagen environmental summit for several years in advance, the G20—although something of a latecomer to this issue—did not seem to fall much behind. A whole host of specific references appeared in the G20 Pittsburgh summit document, adopted on September 25, 2009, with all member state governments expressing strong support for the upcoming Copenhagen conference devoted to the UNFCCC. In fact, as many as 17 of the total 128 commitments made by the group were in the field of climate change. Among the more significant pledges were those to reduce the use of fossil fuels, bolster green energy investments, and transfer clean energy technologies to developing countries.

Scandinavian Setback

The widely anticipated Copenhagen summit conference was held December 7–18, 2009, in the capital of Denmark. It was the fifteenth session of the Conference of the Parties to the UNFCCC and the fifth session of the Meeting of the Parties to the Kyoto Protocol, with its key working groups slated to hold separate sessions. The Subsidiary Body for Implementation (SBI) and the Subsidiary Body for Scientific and Technological Advice (SBSTA) reviewed progress on related issues, as did the Ad Hoc Working Group on Further Commitments for Annex I Parties under the Kyoto Protocol (AWG-KP) and the Ad Hoc Working Group on Long-Term Cooperative Action under the Convention (AWG-LCA). More than 37,000 people, including 10,500 government delegates and 119 heads of state and government, attended the conference.[25]

The preparations in terms of environmental diplomatic activities had been pursued for roughly two years in advance. Expert deliberations took place on several occasions within the subsidiary bodies and working groups of the UNFCCC process. Meanwhile, political decision makers held talks in a variety of diplomatic forums at the highest level, including the Major Economies Forum on Energy and Climate Change and the G8 and the G20 meetings on related matters.[26] The deadlines set through the Bali Road Map for the two most important working groups, the AWG-KP and AWG-LCA, contributed to raising the expectations far beyond those of previous sessions of the UNFCCC.[27] In adopting the Bali Action Plan in December 2007, the parties to the UNFCCC had committed to a "shared vision for long-term cooperative action" as well as to "enhanced action" on national mitigation, adaptation, technology development, and climate financing.

Among European countries, by most accounts, the readiness to move quickly and decisively was relatively high. In 2007 the EU had pledged to unilateral cuts of 20 percent by 2020 compared to 1990 and up to 30 percent in case other major economies would reciprocate. This approach was voted into EU law in late 2008. Japan and the so-called Umbrella Group, which was led by the United States, also made far-reaching commitments in the months leading up to the Copenhagen summit. In particular, the Obama administration promised to cut GHG emissions by 17 percent by 2020 and by 83 percent by 2050. The United States had in the past nevertheless been slow in taking credible legislative and concrete steps toward achieving such goals.

But it was the fact that Brazil, China, India, and South Africa acted in unison, or so it seemed, that effectively undermined Western and especially EU efforts to forge a binding agreement with targets and dates attached to it.[28] Little by little during the intense deliberations, the hopes and desires of the Danish and European hosts were unceremoniously dashed. In retrospect, the Scandinavian setback was described as an illustration of EU weakness as well as of starkly divergent interests between industrialized nations, on the one hand, and emerging great powers and the G77 community, on the other. There was simply no viable coalition that would pursue a serious plan for GHG emissions reduction. Brazil, China, India, and South Africa merely agreed to a deal lacking rules that might constrain economic growth. China, for its part, objected to external review of "nationally appropriate mitigation actions."[29]

The outcome of the Copenhagen summit was a failure on several counts, although for political reasons it was not universally recognized as one. As just explained, minilateral deliberations displaced the multilateral approach.[30] The United States, which drafted the Copenhagen Accord in a fast-paced dialogue with Brazil, China, India, and South Africa, was able to produce the only agreed-on text of the summit and thus was keen on describing it as a partial success. Some twenty-eight governments are said to have influenced the actual phrasing of the text.[31] Furthermore, as many as 114 countries subsequently "took note" of the accord and were listed in its chapeau text. Undeniably, the accord, which included twelve short points, provided no binding targets or dates for implementation and was never formally endorsed at the Copenhagen summit.

The core of the Copenhagen Accord was the commitment to "nationally appropriate mitigation actions," a term offering considerable leeway to all parties to the conference yet at the same time vaguely implying a political-moral pledge to accelerate GHG emissions reduction in accordance with national capacities. In particular, the different opportunities and constraints available to developing and developed countries, respectively, were acknowledged, with the former expected to assist the latter in enhancing implementation of national efforts. The accord established two funds: one devoted to the adaptation needs of small island states and the second called the Copenhagen Green Climate Fund. Once the financing mechanism is settled, the Copenhagen Green Climate Fund will support "projects, programmes, policies and other activities in developing countries related to mitigation . . . adaptation, capacity-building, technology and transfer."[32]

Post-Copenhagen Blues and the Elusiveness of Global Governance

Blame for the failure to reach a universal, binding agreement at Copenhagen was apportioned to several actors, not merely Beijing and New Delhi, whose governments received the bulk of overt criticism at and beyond the negotiating tables. It was widely perceived that China and India, along with Brazil and South Africa, by announcing unilateral mitigation targets in the weeks leading up to the Copenhagen conference had undermined an alternative, multilateral agreement.[33] Some were adamant that a number of small and midsize developing countries had failed to take their responsibility in that they had not resisted attempts to block ambitious proposals by representatives of larger and more active countries. Yet others argued that the lack of success was primarily a result of European and Western insensitivities and continual neglect of the viewpoints of large and small developing states.[34] And finally, some criticized the Danish organizers for allowing too many civil society representatives to attend, thereby diluting the influence of individual NGOs over the proceedings.[35]

Beyond the responsibilities of national delegations, a procedural lesson was that large negotiating blocs like the EU and the G77 were at a disadvantage when improvised bargaining ensued.[36] A number of commentators and attendees were prepared to declare the summit an outright failure. Following the partial and inconclusive agreements coming out of the Copenhagen summit, many analysts observed that in 2010 the attention paid to climate change at major diplomatic venues was roughly half of that in 2007–9.[37] In all documents coming out of the G8, the attention devoted to climate change was down almost as much, according to independent analysts.[38] A lesson widely drawn was that intergovernmental consensus making may not after all be the way forward on climate change, given the increasing urgency of robust action. As the economist William Nordhaus put it, succinctly and with a tinge of sarcasm, "Progress on reaching a more binding agreement has been glacial at best."[39]

Other observers said the one positive outcome of the Copenhagen Accord consisted of large developing countries coming together for the first time and agreeing to undertake mitigation actions and subject those actions to a moderate level of transparency and oversight by the international community.[40] Optimists further emphasized that the two-degree ceiling for CO_2 and other GHG emissions was in fact reaffirmed by the Copenhagen Accord and that significant funding was offered to deal with mitigation. Appendixes I and II of the accord specify the different obligations of developed and developing countries, along with the incentives created for the latter to take part in an international regime aimed to enhance implementation. Although only developed countries are subject to measurement, reporting, and verification (MRV), developing countries that accept funding also fall under the regime. Countries obliged to conduct nationally appropriate mitigation actions without MRV are supposed to submit biannual national communications that detail their CO_2 reduction pledges and mitigation actions either to MRV or to "international consultations and analysis."[41] The Copenhagen Accord thereby has, optimists insisted, the potential of speeding up the financing of mitigation actions and the enactment of domestic climate change legislation.[42]

Such optimism was not reflected in official G8 statements post-Copenhagen.

In fact, there was a virtual consensus that the mitigation measures coming out of the Copenhagen Accord fell well short of what the IPCC and other expert groups believed would be adequate for the world to remain below the two-degree ceiling. And given that large-scale mitigation measures were postponed, major actors realized that it would be significantly more expensive than hitherto acknowledged to reach that target.[43] By 2009 not even all G8 countries had implemented the financial arrangements that were intended to underwrite the climate regime after the first commitment period expired in 2012. Especially Italy and Russia, according to a report by the G8 Research Group at the University of Toronto, consistently performed well below commitments.[44]

In fact, in late 2010 it appeared that the G20 was picking up some of the slack of advancing the climate agenda following the Copenhagen debacle and the lower profile adopted by G8 countries in its aftermath. The G20 Toronto summit, held June 26–27, 2010, produced a summit declaration that reaffirmed the readiness of member states to the UNFCCC and the reduction of greenhouse gas emissions:

> We reiterate our commitment to a green recovery and to sustainable global growth. Those of us who have associated with the Copenhagen Accord reaffirm our support for it and its implementation and call on others to associate with it. We are committed to engage in negotiations under the UNFCCC on the basis of its objective provisions and principles including common but differentiated responsibilities and respective capabilities and are determined to ensure a successful outcome through an inclusive process at the Cancun Conferences.[45]

Although the commitments were less extensive and precise than those pledged by the G8, the G20 Research Group at the University of Toronto found that six out of sixty-one commitments made at the Toronto summit directly or indirectly concerned climate change. Soon after the Toronto summit was wrapped up in late 2010, moreover, Seoul signaled it would work to reinvigorate climate change at the 2011 summit.[46]

By late 2010 it was increasingly clear that there was no politically viable alternative to the UN process in terms of advancing the climate change mitigation agenda. The two main working groups, the AWG-KP and the AWG-LCA, continued their respective activities. In November–December 2010 the parties to the UNFCCC held another large-scale climate conference in Cancun, Mexico. This conference made progress on establishing a green climate fund and adopted a declaration in which all participating countries agreed to adopt a universal and binding agreement by 2015, with effective implementation starting at 2020.

Taking Climate Change to First Avenue, Again

As mentioned in the beginning of this chapter, the UNSC broke new ground in 2007 by holding a debate devoted to the problem of climate change. On that occasion a large number of countries took part in the deliberations, but the majority of them were expressly skeptical or ambivalent about whether the council was the appropriate forum for these discussions. Four years later, the tenor of the analogous debate was markedly different, with a small majority of countries now in favor of linking the council to the climate change issue.[47]

Part of the reason for the change in tone and emphasis may have been the way in which the two debates were framed. In 2007 the United Kingdom initiated the debate, while it was chair of the UNSC. Margaret Beckett, the British foreign secretary, had set off the debate by introducing "drivers of conflict" as an intervening variable to justify tying climate change to the mandate of the council. Citing the widely circulated Stern report, Secretary Beckett explained, "An unstable climate will exacerbate some of the core drivers of conflict, such as migratory pressures and competition for resources. The recent Stern Review Report on the Economics of Climate Change speaks of potential economic disruption on the scale of the two world wars and of the great depression. That alone will have an impact on the security of all of us—developed and developing countries alike."[48]

In a study of all fifty-five interventions made during the 2007 debate, Detraz and Betsill found that as many as twenty-seven speakers perceived a clear link between climate change and drivers of conflict in the sense described by Beckett.[49] The foreign secretary had then gone on to make a generic argument for the UNSC to consider, or at least not to ignore, the direct threat to human life of a variety of repercussions that according to the majority of climate scientists may not be avoided unless governments act in unison. Recognizing the importance of not undermining national and international authorities already dealing with the problem at various levels, she had similarly emphasized the value of raising awareness of people and decision makers so that they more clearly understood the potential repercussions of climate change on international conflict and thereby were better prepared to respond adequately: "So today is about the world recognizing that there is a security imperative, as well as economic, developmental and environmental ones, for tackling climate change and for our beginning to build a shared understanding of the relationship between energy, climate and security."[50]

Four years later, in 2011, Gerhard Wittig, the permanent representative of Germany, chaired the climate debate at the UNSC. This time the drivers of conflict were placed only in the background of the narrative, not as a means to justify raising the issue at the council. Wittig chose to take a different approach, inviting Secretary General Ban Ki-Moon and the executive director of UNEP, Achim Steiner, to make the first interventions. Ban Ki-Moon's remarks on the "double-barrelled challenge of climate change and international security" lasted for only a few minutes, whereas Steiner was given extensive time to address the audience. Steiner gave a lengthy yet unambiguous statement interlaced with expert assessment, including repeated references to research conducted under UN auspices during three decades.

He opened his statement with reaffirmed empirical observations concerning the global warming of 0.13 degrees Celsius per decade in the past fifty years. This, he emphasized, is double the increase of the previous century, as noted in the IPCC's fourth assessment report. The head of the UNEP also referenced fresh evidence regarding the frequency of extreme weather situations over the past five decades. He concluded that international research results speak very clearly "to the fact that climate change is happening. Not only is it happening; it is also accelerating. Not only is it accelerating, but indeed the latest science being published by scientific institutions across the planet is in many respects overtaking the rather conservative scenarios, predictions and models that the IPCC brought to our attention four years ago."[51]

Although briefly cautioning that science cannot exhaustively account for climate change's future implications for economies, societies, and life-support systems, Steiner agreed with observers who use the term "threat multiplier" when trying to account for the likely impact. He insisted that the interconnectedness and complexity of climate change and its security implications make it particularly hard to precisely predict and plan for contingencies ahead, other than saying that the global economy, the global community of states, and humanity at large "are confronted with scenarios of natural resource scarcities, droughts and floods, and corresponding instabilities in global markets for food and other commodities that are putting in question some of the gains that we have achieved in sustainable development in recent decades."[52]

Steiner's rather forceful message to the members of the UNSC could not be easily misunderstood. While acknowledging the ongoing debate about the appropriateness of the council's becoming engaged in the climate change issue, the head of UNEP asked the council members not to shy away from the geopolitical and security perspective of the matter at hand and to address cooperatively a phenomenon that is "unprecedented in its implications for civilization."[53]

First to speak after Steiner were the permanent representatives of the United States and Brazil, Ambassadors Susan Rice and Monica Viotti. Rice and Viotti endorsed Steiner's overall message and furthermore seemed to fully agree with one another about the need to be flexible and practical when it came to using UN institutional resources and arenas to meet the challenges caused by climate change. According to Rice, the council "needs to be prepared for the full range of crises that may be deepened or widened by the effects of climate change."[54] Viotti emphasized that food security was a particular concern for her government and then echoed her American colleague's point about not neglecting any of the instruments at the disposal of the relevant decision makers: "Effectively fighting climate change and dealing with its myriad implications must be a priority for the international community. To do so, we must take advantage of all the tools that the United Nations system has to offer, especially in the area of sustainable development, and redouble our efforts to achieve ambitious results in the international negotiations on climate change."[55]

The permanent representative of China, however, then broke the pattern by disagreeing with the underlying premise that climate change is linked to international security and called the appropriate procedures for addressing climate challenges problematic. Ambassador Wang Min stated that climate change "may affect security, but it is fundamentally a sustainable development issue. The Security Council lacks expertise in climate change and the necessary means and resources. Moreover, the Council is not a forum for decision-making with universal representation."[56] In the remainder of his statement, Wang expressed China's support for the views of the G77—represented by Argentina in this debate—and pledged to work with heavily affected small island states in finding solutions to their pressing problems with rising sea levels.

The additional sixty representatives of UN member states who took part in the ensuing debate, including most council members, defended a position somewhere in between these extremes. Because the initial framework was more generously defined than it had been in 2007, the focus was more on the pending impact on biological and human life than on drivers of conflict arguably unleashed by climate change. The debate was also seemingly affected by a greater recognition that further scientific results had accumulated in the meantime and that scholars were growing increasingly confident that contemporary empirical evidence was bearing out extrapolations made in the past. Unlike in 2007, in 2011 several ambassadors commented explicitly on the accumulating evidence and sided with the interpretation that sea-level rise and extreme weather already appeared to be having an impact on local and global weather conditions.

There was also a noticeable shift regarding whether the UNSC might be instrumental in dealing with the problem, in one capacity or another. Drawing on the discursive approach used in 2009 by Detraz and Betsill, who assessed the support or nonsupport of the fifty-five UN member states taking part in the 2007 debate, Cousins found that the 2011 deliberations (with sixty-three diplomats making statements on behalf of their governments) reflected a significant shift in state positions compared with four years earlier. Despite the absence of a consensus on an exact boundary that the council must not transgress, a 44 percent minority in favor of "a role for the Security Council in addressing climate change" had grown to a 57 percent majority. At the same time the 24 percent share expressly rejecting such a role had shrunk to 17 percent, whereas the 33 percent stating "no position" had decreased to 27 percent.[57]

Although the 2007 and 2011 debates were far from seeking to assign the UNSC a concrete and specific role in addressing climate change, the deliberations appeared to clarify the options that may be available at a later point in time. Senior diplomats and political leaders who want to revisit the issue may in the future build on what the debates explicitly aimed for, namely, to raise awareness and help elevate the climate change issue on the agendas of national decision makers by "securitizing" it. The same goes for the UN Secretariat. Were the secretary general to demand regular reports and briefings on the progress of addressing the climate threat in connection to regional or thematic agenda items, it would most likely be given more thought and consideration in the UN's various institutional units and policy-making processes, with likely domino effects in the national contexts of many countries.

Rio+20: A Road to Nowhere?

By the fall of 2011, governments were acutely aware that the first commitment period of the Kyoto Protocol was about to expire and that no new universal, mandatory regulatory framework had been created in its place. Copenhagen had not delivered on its promise of a universal and binding agreement with the potential of substantially mitigating and, in the long run bringing to a complete halt, the growth of CO_2 and other GHGs in the atmosphere. Moreover, the minilateral deal struck between merely five of the major emitter-states could not make up for the absence of a formal and negotiated agreement among all, or at least most, UN member states.[58]

At the first five-country summit of BRICS, held June 14, 2011, on the island of Hainan in China, the non-Western great powers appeared to want to capitalize on the failure at Copenhagen and at the same time respond to the criticisms blaming several of its key members for the collapse of negotiations on a universal and binding agreement. At the Hainan summit, in the city of Sanya, the most precise commitments eventually agreed to were made in the area of climate change.[59] These commitments, moreover, primarily pertained to the kind of agreement—though in the abstract—that the 2009 Copenhagen summit had failed to produce, to many observers precisely because of the opposition of emerging great powers. In Sanya BRICS expressly declared, "We commit ourselves to work towards a comprehensive, balanced and binding outcome to strengthen the implementation of the United Nations Framework Convention on Climate Change and its Kyoto Protocol."[60]

Meanwhile, however, diplomatic activities during 2011 and much of 2012 saw a partial regrouping of coalitions pursuing various goals with regard to climate change and associated policies. Although China, South Africa, and India had been able to demonstrate their newfound diplomatic clout and avert an ambitious international agreement that might have limited their potential for economic growth, that success began to ring hollow in many quarters. In fact, there seemed to be a growing realization that the South was not in such a strong bargaining position after all, precisely because it was likely to suffer more than the industrialized North from the effects of climate change, especially in the short-to-mid term.[61]

Self-criticism among some BRICS countries, along with pushback from disappointed, smaller, and more vulnerable developing countries, thus ushered in a new dynamic in the complicated diplomatic politics of climate change. A first sign of that dynamic was visible in the breaking up of previous coalitions of developing countries within the G77 in the months preceding the Durban climate conference in December 2011.[62] The realignments were formalized at the conference itself. A second sign of a new dynamic was that during the negotiations at the Durban conference, India was eventually left to fend for itself and its position, as Brazil, South Africa, and China chose to enter a compromise on the question of whether the widely anticipated 2015 international agreement (coming out of the Paris climate conference summit scheduled for December) would be legally binding. India fought hard to water down the language to concern a "legal outcome," grudgingly accepting the principle of a strong commitment four years down the road, though insisting that it would take effect no earlier than in 2020.[63]

From June 13 to 22, 2012, the United Nations Conference on Sustainable Development, "Rio+20" for short, was held in Rio de Janeiro. The conference nickname referred to the twenty years that had passed since the 1992 Earth Summit, held in the same city, which had produced the Climate Change Convention and thereby prompted the establishment of the Commission on Sustainable Development. More directly, the Earth Summit had given rise to initiatives that eventually produced the Kyoto Protocol, Agenda 21, and the Convention on Biological Diversity, all signature agreements associated with the global environmental movement.

Although the focus of the 2012 conference was renewing political commitments and improving implementation of sustainable development, expectations that a breakthrough on climate change mitigation might be forthcoming and compensate for the Copenhagen debacle preceded the deliberations. The first preparatory committee convened as early as two years in advance, and two more committees, supplemented by numerous informal consultations at the UN Headquarters in New York, were put together in the months ahead. Some of the preconditions for an important decision were certainly in place. In the end Rio+20 became the biggest conference ever organized by the UN, with some 45,000 attendees, including 57 heads of state and 31 heads of government, taking part in the end portion of the conference.

Although parts of the sustainability agenda, for instance, the greening of cities, advanced significantly through the Rio+20 conference, there was no movement on climate change mitigation. In fact, realizing the considerable gap between outsiders' expectations and the political and diplomatic realities of the major governments may have led the latter to cancel their participation. In the end US president Obama, UK prime minister David Cameron, and German chancellor Angela Merkel opted not to travel to Rio. Whether these political leaders would not sufficiently prioritize the sustainability agenda or whether they were trying to avoid aggravating already serious differences on how to deal with climate change and associated (development and financing) issues is difficult to conclusively establish.[64]

In the end roughly half of all G8 and G20 leaders attended the Rio+20 conference. No doubt as a result of the high-profile cancellations, out of the 130 heads of state and government originally slated to participate in the final stage of the conference 42 political leaders never showed up. To those who value the multilateral character of diplomacy and international relations, and believe that the UN system continues to provide unique legitimacy to international accords adopted under its auspices, this augured a second blow—after Copenhagen in 2009—to the entire notion of a global environmental regime devoted to climate change. Even though the forty-nine-page conference document called "The Future We Want" managed to successfully paper over many of the deeper divisions among countries, the nonparticipation of several of the world's most influential political leaders directly undermined its significance.

The snub to UN multilateralism was all the more striking given that none of the G20 leaders neglected attending the Los Cabos summit of June 18–19, 2012, under Mexican stewardship. At the Los Cabos summit, which as usual paid most attention to economic growth and financial regulation, a total of eight paragraphs concerned the environment, including sustainable development and climate change. On the latter issue, it was paragraph 71 that formulated the relatively elaborate, common stance of the G20, strongly endorsing the UN-led negotiation process and recalling what auxiliary measures the group had agreed to undertake in its support:

> Climate change will continue to have a significant impact on the world economy, and costs will be higher to the extent we delay additional action. We reiterate our commitment to fight climate change and welcome the outcome of the 17th Conference of the Parties to the UN climate change conferences. We are committed to the full implementation of the outcomes of Cancun and Durban and will work with Qatar as the incoming Presidency towards achieving a successful and balanced outcome at COP-18. We emphasize the need to structurally transform economies towards a climate-friendly path over the medium term. We welcome the creation of the G20 study group on climate finance, in order to consider ways to effectively mobilize resources taking into account the objectives, provisions and principles of the UNFCCC in line with the Cancun Agreement and ask to provide a progress report to Finance Ministers in November. We support the operationalization of the Green Climate Fund.[65]

With the UN approach of convening large conferences and adopting far-reaching international accords coming to a screeching halt in 2009–11, others besides G20 member states needed to assume the initiative. Thus, the reaffirmations of the cause of climate change mitigation from the G20 and BRICS were helpful for sustaining a limited momentum through modest progress made at the Cancun and Durban conferences. At this point the US presidency and the State Department saw an opportunity to make headway.

The Nudge: Obama Presides at Camp David

The main political obstacle that the US government has faced at home for many years is entrenched resistance to mandatory climate change legislation in the US Congress, especially the Senate, which needs to ratify international agreements before they come into effect. A related problem in advancing the issue diplomatically is the credibility gap that has widened over the years, in part because of the skeptical approach taken by the George W. Bush administration and in part because the financial backing behind anti-climate activism and ideology tends to be US-based. At the same time, though, many of the technological and political innovations that might solve the global problem of greenhouse gas emissions are likely to originate in America.

Even under the Bush administration, some states—such as California—adopted environmental and energy policies that recognized the problem of climate change. More recently, the discovery of new methods to extract large quantities of shale gas at a reasonable cost caused American coal and oil consumption to stagnate, meaning US GHG emissions have actually decreased.[66] But the US government under Obama did not stop at mitigation as a long-term strategy. It also created the Interagency Climate Change Adaptation Task Force (ICCAT) on the premise that climate change is inevitable. The ICCAT is tasked with advancing policies and programs that will help the United States adapt to climate change.

As far as external policies go, the US State Department paid significant attention to the issue of climate change from the beginning of the Obama administration. Secretary of State Hillary Clinton appointed a special envoy on climate change, Todd Stern, in January 2009. Stern made several speeches and held press conferences at which he spoke bluntly about the serious challenge posed in the coming decades by climate transformation. Former senator and chairman of the Senate Foreign Relations Committee John Kerry, who took over the foreign affairs portfolio from Secretary Clinton in early 2013, demonstrated a personal commitment that went even further than that of his predecessor. In 1992 Kerry had attended the Rio Earth Summit, the first summit to highlight environmental sustainability. In 2013–14 the US Agency for International Development (USAID) diplomatically engaged some of the most vulnerable countries and regions, such as small island states in the Western Hemisphere, and provided financial support in small quantities through two different funds, the Least Developed Countries Fund and the Special Climate Change Fund.

The G8 Camp David summit on May 18–19, 2012, presented a particularly timely opportunity to address new American initiatives on climate change. The Fukushima nuclear plant disaster, along with the weakened multilateral process under UN auspices, had renewed pressure on the group to set targets for CO2 and GHG emission reductions. Already at the G8 foreign ministers meeting six weeks earlier in Washington, DC, the participants were ready to "recognize climate change as a contributing factor to increased security risks globally; and intend to continue to work domestically and multilaterally to address climate change."[67] At Camp David the extensive six paragraphs dealing with environmental challenges were all prominently placed, and climate change made up the bulk of concerns and pledges outlined in three of them.[68]

Paragraph 13 was the most specific and far-reaching of the latter three, reiterating the two-degree ceiling and the 2015 deadline for adopting a "protocol, another legal instrument or an agreed outcome with legal force" that would apply to "developed and developing countries alike." The exact wording was unusually unambiguous and can be interpreted as a clear signal to China, South Africa, and, above all, India, given the reservations that the latter had uttered on previous occasions:

> We agree to continue our efforts to address climate change and recognize the need for increased mitigation ambition in the period to 2020, with a view to doing our part to limit effectively the increase in global temperature below 2°C above pre-industrial levels, consistent with science. We strongly support the outcome of the 17th Conference of the Parties to the U.N. Framework Convention on Climate Change (UNFCCC) in Durban to implement the Cancun agreements and the launch of the Durban Platform, which we welcome as a significant breakthrough toward the adoption by 2015 of a protocol, another legal instrument or an agreed outcome with legal force applicable to all Parties, developed and developing countries alike. We agree to continue to work together in the UNFCCC and other fora, including through the Major Economies Forum, toward a positive outcome at Doha.[69]

This last sentence acknowledges that other forums, such as the Major Economies Forum, are needed to compensate for the previous failure to arrive at a universal, binding agreement. The following paragraph, number 14, further recognized the relevance of new research results anticipating that a warming climate will inevitably produce additional effects, a particularly significant one being the release of short-term air pollutants. These pollutants, the G8 agreed, should be the subject of parallel targeted mitigation efforts:

> Recognizing the impact of short-lived climate pollutants on near-term climate change, agricultural productivity, and human health, we support, as a means of promoting increased ambition and complementary to other CO2 and GHG emission reduction efforts, comprehensive actions to reduce these pollutants, which, according to UNEP and others, account for over thirty percent of near-term global warming as well as 2 million premature deaths a year. Therefore, we agree to join the Climate and Clean Air Coalition to Reduce Short-lived Climate Pollutants.[70]

The final paragraph devoted to climate change, number 15, consisted of merely one sentence, one that represented a near truism. Still, cutting fossil fuel subsidies across the board is supposedly one of the most important mitigation efforts for states to engage in, as not doing so undercuts other policies: "In addition, we strongly support efforts to rationalize and phase-out over the medium term inefficient fossil fuel subsidies that encourage wasteful consumption, and to continue voluntary reporting on progress."[71]

In line with US thinking about climate change as a "threat multiplier," but without mentioning a specific link to climate change, the next four paragraphs in the Camp David summit declaration dealt with "food security and nutrition." The declaration began by noting the decade-long G8 engagement with Africa, highlighting the pledges made at the 2009 l'Aquila summit and the expansion of collaboration in agricultural research. It went on to launch the New Alliance in Food Security and Nutrition, aimed at lifting fifty million Africans out of poverty over the coming decade, and a collective commitment on the part of G8 countries to invest in "credible, comprehensive and country-owned plans," along with other efforts to mobilize private capital, spur innovation, and leverage the capacity of private-sector partners. The declaration also reaffirmed the G8's commitment to improving the conditions of the world's poorest and most vulnerable people, implicitly recognizing that many of them reside in Africa.

From a climate change mitigation perspective, furthermore, the Camp David summit declaration recognized "the importance of meeting our energy needs from a wide variety of sources ranging from traditional fuels to renewables to other clean technologies." G8 countries were committed to establishing and sharing best practices on energy exploration and energy production as well as industrial and building efficiency through energy management procedures. According to the declaration, "increasing energy efficiency and reliance on renewables and other clean energy technologies can contribute significantly to energy security and savings, while also addressing climate change and promoting sustainable economic growth and innovation."[72]

The emphasis on technology development, business-friendly innovation, and economic growth as a means to secure long-term energy needs bore the distinctive hallmarks of the Obama administration, striving to provide the climate change issue with a new impetus that would not be associated with the Kyoto process. Another characteristic trait of Obama's first term was to focus on building government and expert networks that move non-legislative policies and standards, some of which can be elaborated at state and municipal levels. Among federal initiatives the presidential administration also worked to enhance fuel energy efficiency, modernize the electricity grid, curb carbon and methane emissions, and render building codes more conducive to a low-carbon energy policy.[73]

Still, the fall 2012 presidential election could not help but slow down US-driven international environmental initiatives. Journalists found that climate change was virtually absent from the platforms of the main contenders for the presidency.[74] And even if polls suggested that a significant number of undecided voters could be swayed, at least in part, by a strong position in support of measures to combat climate change, the presidential candidates appear to have decided they had little to win from displaying activism.[75] In the aftermath of Hurricane Sandy, which devastated the East Coast the week before Election Day, presidential candidate Mitt Romney and incumbent Obama did their best to make up for this omission. Some polls indicated that the Obama administration's more forward-leaning handling of Sandy may actually have affected the election results in its favor.[76]

A Partial Breakthrough on Financing

The original climate financing mechanism coming out of the UNFCCC in 1992 was modeled on the system of international development bank lending, with donors that exert considerable influence throughout the funding process. At the center of the UNFCCC approach to climate financing was the Global Environment Facility. Yet before the system had begun to operate on a large scale, developing countries moved to insist that the arrangement be restructured by forming a secretariat and an assembly made up of so-called constituencies. Thirty-two such constituencies were established. Half of them were drawn from developing countries and the rest from developed countries, including two votes offered to Central and Eastern Europe and the former Soviet Union. This setup allowed for a significant recalibration of leverage from the industrialized countries in the West and North to developing countries in the East and South.[77]

Given that relevant financial institutions and banks for the most part continue to be located in Western capitals, the rebalancing of voting power in the Global Environment Facility has not put an end to the tug-of-war between governments representing developing and developed countries. Since the mid-1990s donor countries have increasingly demanded MRV in most development and aid projects, purportedly to ensure the minimum level of wasteful funding, graft, and corruption by recipient and donor organizations and institutions. As anticipated, an analogous requirement was also included in the 2009 Copenhagen Accord.[78] In reality, though, many developing countries today are sufficiently competent to assess their own needs and capacities to administer projects and are closer to the circumstances in which funds are put to use. Moreover, when a substantial portion of funds earmarked for climate financing is used on said MRV measures, it may limit the overall effectiveness of development aid and assistance.[79]

A first set of significant breakthroughs in climate financing came to pass in 2009. Notably, the so-called Adaptation Fund (AF), officially launched in 2007, started functioning that year. Originally the AF, which is set to prepare developing countries for changes to the world climate, was supposed to have been funded through certified emission reduction sales. But as the carbon-credit market subsequently weakened, the Adaptation Fund Board, based in Washington, DC, under the supervision of the World Bank acting as trustee, embarked on a fund-raising program primarily targeting industrialized countries. At the end of 2013, the AF was able to surpass its fund-raising objectives and stabilize its balance sheet. Since AF funds can be accessed directly by national and regional implementing agencies, project financing and implementation through AF is faster and less cumbersome than most other forms of climate financing.

The AF initiative and climate financing in general were further helped by the substantive deal made in Copenhagen, through which a broad agreement on responsibilities for costs, instead of a universal binding outcome, materialized. As was alluded to previously, the emerging great powers in the South were able to convince representatives of industrialized states to accept building up a vast fund for climate mitigation and adaptation, which by 2020 is supposed to generate $100 billion annually. The fund, labeled the Green Climate Fund, was made operational in mid-2014, but its principals have yet to specify to what extent private funding will be required to meet the full commitment. In the meantime, the Transitional Committee for the Green Climate Fund was appointed at the UNFCCC's 2010 climate conference in Cancun, with the World Bank selected as a temporary trustee. The Climate and Development Knowledge Network has promised to provide analyses of how to best allocate resources, in an ambitious project funded by China, India, the United States, and Switzerland.[80] The fund was opened for capitalization in September 2014, prompting concrete funding pledges from Germany, France, Japan, the United States, and others.[81]

A second set of significant breakthroughs in climate financing materialized in 2012–14, with a large number of big international corporations and key public entities more pointedly leveraging governments, foundations, and international organizations to enhance their activities and speed up the pace at which effective action is taken. At the fifth Investor Summit on Climate Risk and Energy Opportunities held at the UN Headquarters in New York in January 2012, the US-based Investor Network on Climate Risk (INCR) adopted an action plan. With the backing of the European Institutional Investors Group on Climate Change (IIGCC) and the Investors Group on Climate Change (IGCC) in Australia and New Zealand, the INCR listed a number of new corporate practices that help incorporate and manage climate risk in investment portfolios. At the same time the action plan encouraged proactive measures in finance and industry with a view of shifting to a low-carbon economy and engaging regulators in creating business-friendly rules and norms conducive to that goal. A third plank of the INCR action plan highlighted the expansion of important business opportunities in the growing fields of energy conservation and low-carbon technology development. By September 2014 the INCR represented private business interests worth some $24 trillion in aggregate assets, together urging political leaders to take measures to address climate change and above all to provide stable and meaningful pricing on carbon.[82]

At the December 2012 UN Climate Change Conference in Doha, Qatar, another initiative was launched showcasing public-private partnerships in climate financing but similarly highlighting investment opportunities for the private sector in particular. This initiative built on a previous project demonstrated at the 2011 Durban climate conference. A year later, the hugely influential World Economic Forum, based in Switzerland, had joined the sponsors. The initiative was important in part because it dovetailed with the World Economic Forum's Green Growth Action Alliance, which organizes fifty of the world's largest energy companies, development finance banks, and international financial institutions. The Green Growth Action Alliance was unveiled at the 2012 Los Cabos summit, and a year later, it sponsored an extensive report assessing the prospective investment opportunities in sustainable energy, water, transport, and agriculture to tens of billions of US dollars per year. The vast majority of these opportunities, the report says, will arise in the developing world.[83]

The chief message of the Green Growth Action Alliance was that public spending generates private investment, which in turn makes public spending worthwhile and drives costs down for everybody involved in green growth and climate financing projects, including consumers. The investment figures projected by the alliance in fact come close to the projections of leading economists who have assessed the funding needed to deal with climate change on a global scale. As stated in the first annual progress report released by the alliance in 2013, if "annual public sector investment can be increased from the current US$96 billion to US$130 billion and be more effectively targeted, it could mobilize private capital in the range of US$570 billion. This would come close to achieving the US$700 billion of investment required to address climate change."[84]

The B20 Green Growth Task Force was an initiative similarly geared toward

emphasizing environmental opportunities and productive public-private relations, primarily by engaging businesses and corporations in G20 countries in
green growth projects. Germany spearheaded this movement, with 95 percent
of all climate financing coming from private sources.[85] At the 2012 Los Cabos
summit, this agenda received considerable attention, with a specific B20 Task
Force on Green Growth listing five key priorities for engagement with government leaders and regulators:

1. promoting free trade in green goods and services;
2. achieving robust pricing on carbon;
3. ending inefficient fossil-fuel subsidies;
4. accelerating low-carbon innovation;
5. dramatically increasing efforts to target public funding to leverage
    private investment.[86]

In the capacity of conference host, the Mexican G20 presidency managed
to get B20 attendees to agree to a joint statement awarding priority to green
growth, endorsing these five priorities.[87] Unfortunately, however, momentum
was lost as the B20 virtually abandoned climate financing and green growth
issues during the 2013 and 2014 presidencies. Russia, which in the 1990s actively helped bring the Kyoto Protocol to fruition, now refrained from listing
environmental issues as a priority for the B20 deliberations. As part of Russia's
G20 priorities, energy sustainability was the sole issue under which environmental concerns featured, and the St. Petersburg summit consequently failed
to rekindle political momentum. Nor did Australia, led by a prime minister—Tony Abbott—well-known for his climate skepticism. At the nineteenth
and twentieth UN climate conferences, held in Warsaw (November 2013) and
Lima (December 2014), divisions between industrialized and developing nations were reaffirmed, once more blocking a positive outcome.[88]

In the meantime 2013 saw a growing interest among defense planners in
climate change, in terms of both strategic opportunities, such as summertime
transport in the Arctic region, and new threats and vulnerabilities. Indeed,
military organizations have begun to systematically examine the issue of climate change in an effort to assess its short- and long-term implications. The
United States included such an analysis in the 2011 Quadrennial Defense Review, at the request of US secretary of defense Robert Gates.[89] The US Navy
was clearly at the forefront of this development.[90]

In the course of 2013, experienced military commanders openly addressed
the pending challenges and placed them on the agenda of the US military in
particular. For instance, in early March 2013 the US Navy Pacific commander,

Adm. Samuel J. Locklear III, in a newspaper interview included the problem of climate change at the very top of his list of overall structural national security challenges, in that it "is probably the most likely thing that is going to happen . . . that will cripple the security environment, probably more likely than the other scenarios we all often talk about."[91] Such statements are potentially at least as important as the political message that they imply in that public resources could be directed at mitigation as well as adaptation measures. Given that the US Navy annually spends some $500 billion, Locklear's remarks could have real consequences if they were acted upon—and the US Congress endorsed such action—prompting major research endeavors and technological investments. Considerable attention was paid to sea-level rise on the American Atlantic coast, which hosts the major US Navy ports, primarily in Virginia and Maryland, following the consequences of severe storms and flooding in recent years, especially 2011–13.[92]

National and international research projects aimed at nurturing innovative technologies for energy conservation and renewable and alternative energy could conceivably address the problem of climate change more effectively and rapidly than experts so far have been able to forecast. That being said, it remains important to more accurately determine how much GHG emissions are entering the atmosphere and how the climate is changing in order for decision makers and the public to know how the problem is likely to evolve in the coming years. It is encouraging that corporate leaders involved in the Global Compact, UNEP's Global Reporting Initiative, the Carbon Disclosure Project, and the International Integrated Reporting Council have called for a global policy commitment to reduce the problem of free riders and ensure more rapid implementation of sustainability norms. The Corporate Sustainability Reporting Coalition, representing US$3 trillion in assets, in 2012 requested voluntary disclosures to be replaced with regular requirements.[93]

While recent commitments are a significant development that came about in a short space of time, they will not be sufficient to meet projected financial needs. The IEA estimated in 2012 that at least $531 billion of annual global investments in green and low-carbon technology is warranted to meet the challenge of climate change.[94] The funding of a robust and extensive infrastructure for systematic collection of high-quality climate data in developing states, where much of the severe consequences are expected in the coming years and decades, was also clearly identified as a priority. In October 2012 an extraordinary congress of the World Meteorological Organization—the same organization that spearheaded the first international conference on climate change in 1979—pledged to undertake speedy measures to consolidate the Global Framework for Climate Services. Reinforcing a truly global network of observation, organizations will require the creation of a secretariat and a mechanism for garnering nonvoluntary financial means.

A Bilateral Deal to Pave the Way for Others

The accumulated achievements in climate financing had by 2013–14 amounted to substantial sums of investment capital earmarked for a variety of purposes. None of these funding sources was by itself in a position to make a significant dent in countering the massively harmful industrial processes and consumption patterns that prevail in most parts of the world, but together they could be put to work to expand the opportunities for reducing GHG-generating practices and, over a longer period, for replacing them with alternatives that release much less carbon into the atmosphere.

A strong push for the development of new technologies is under way in the United States, Europe, and increasingly, Asia, where most of the world's rapid economic development is taking place. Japan's virtual abandonment of nuclear power energy within the space of a few months after the Fukushima nuclear disaster is an interesting example for other countries, as it shows how aggressive energy conservation methods can accomplish a rapid reduction of energy consumption. In India biomass and other renewable fuel sources make up more than a fifth of the energy consumption, which, among other things, reduces the environmental and economic costs of long-distance transportation. Experiments on several new technologies—in particular, carbon capture, utilization, and storage—are ongoing in China. The United States has, under the Obama administration, set up Joint Clean Energy Research Centers with China and India that serve to expand networks of scholars with cutting-edge competence to address a host of related issues.

In terms of climate negotiations, however, cooperation has been more difficult to achieve, especially beyond bilateral agreements. Given the debacle of the Copenhagen conference of 2009, the policymaking community had by 2014 certainly become more mindful of the delicate sequencing of climate change negotiations. The EU, which needs to strike a compromise among its own twenty-nine member states before it can seriously engage others around the table, is a predictably inflexible party in climate negotiations. Its role is at best one of stepping out ahead of the others. This is what the EU often has done in the past by making commitments that go further than those expected of others and thereby showing the way.[95] In October 2014 the EU repeated this tactic, pledging to reduce GHG emissions by 40 percent below 1990 levels by the year 2030.

More important, however, on November 11, 2014, the presidents of the

United States and China put in place "a floor" of commitments to which other parties will have to relate their own policies on climate change. During a state visit to Beijing by President Obama, the two countries made an unprecedented Joint Announcement on Climate Change, upsetting the previously existing coalitions in climate change politics. For its part Washington pledged to reduce its emissions by 26–28 percent below its 2005 level by 2025, primarily striving for the higher target. China said it would work toward peaking in GHG emissions in 2030 and by then have a 20 percent share of nonfossil fuels in its primary energy consumption.[96]

Albeit substantively of lesser significance, the US-China agreement rendered a comprehensive realignment of partners on the issue of climate change more feasible. The first strike against the Gordian knot of climate change gridlock was delivered at the Copenhagen summit, it can be argued, in that the United States peeled off China and India from the G77 coalition of developing countries and the latter two managed to break up the EU-US constellation. Through the US-China deal of November 2014, the United States succeeded in peeling off China from India, whose government appears to have been caught by surprise.[97] India, which continues to rely primarily on endemic energy resources but to a great extent uses coal-driven power plants, has been among the most reluctant emerging powers to issue pledges that might hamper its path toward economic growth.

In terms of sequencing negotiations for a comprehensive climate regime, India has long found itself at a pivotal position. It has associated closely with the positions of China and the G77 in the past and could probably bring along other G20 countries. Substantively, the US-China announcement did little to alter the fundamental dynamic of climate politics. Part of the US-China announcement in mid-November 2014 was a vague promise to perform a "peer review" on inefficient fossil fuel subsidies within the G20 framework. This is far from the ban on fossil fuel subsidies that NGOs have urged the G20 to develop. That was also the major objection raised by the NGO community against the outcome of the 2014 announcement. The C20 network provided its own commentary on the results of the Brisbane summit, especially deploring the lack of a "strong time-limited commitment to ending subsidies for fossil fuels."[98]

Another disappointment was the group's preparedness to relegate responsibility for measures that limit carbon emissions to "nationally determined contributions," efforts that render it near impossible to hold anybody accountable for future failures to rein in accelerating rates of greenhouse gases.[99] This goes to the core of the preparedness of G20 countries, as a collective, to assume ownership of the climate issue. As in past communiqués, however, the least common denominator was a renewed pledge to continue working in the UN-led diplomatic process. Although climate change was devoted only a single paragraph in the Brisbane communiqué, that paragraph confirmed the objective of forging a universal, formal agreement in the framework of the UNFCCC process: "We will work together to adopt successfully a protocol, another legal instrument or an agreed outcome with legal force under the UNFCCC that is applicable to all parties at the 21st Conference of the Parties (COP21) in Paris in 2015. We encourage parties that are ready to communicate their intended nationally determined contributions well in advance of COP21." By the end of 2014, the distance between the bilaterally agreed-to floor that the two biggest emitters introduced in November and the elusive goal of a universal and binding agreement among the parties to the UNFCCC process remained vast. Somewhere in the middle, roughly equidistant from a "G2 bargain" and a multilateral accord signed by 190-plus governments, is the arena of high-table diplomacy.[100]

Given the nature of the issue, that arena would most naturally be represented by the major emitters or the Major Economies Forum, in other words, the countries with the most to contribute to solving the problem at hand.[101] Comprising the seventeen largest economies including the EU, the Major Economies Forum encompasses the most asset-rich countries of the world and would therefore be a logical choice of arena. But the problem is that this forum was never active at a high level or included all the major energy-producing and energy-consuming countries. The G20, which adds Argentina, Turkey, and Saudi Arabia to the mix, would therefore be a better "fit."[102] Saudi Arabia, with its huge fossil fuel deposits and its significance in the Islamic world, is of course the most important addition. Like the Major Economies Forum, the G20 is hierarchically speaking also located "beneath" the US and China, the two largest economies, yet "above" the rank-and-file membership of the UN.

The Empirical Findings: Too Little, Too Late?

As in chapters 3 and 4, I will now turn attention to the question, How do contemporary great and middle powers employ existing formal and informal institutional arrangements to address challenges in climate change mitigation, spanning traditional and nontraditional security concepts? The US UN delegation, in summarizing the general debate at the opening session in September 2009, noted, "Almost all of the 192 member states [which] addressed the General Assembly highlighted the deleterious impact of climate change and the global financial, food, and energy crises on their economies."[103] But over the next five years, the issue of climate change did not find consistent support among first-tier great powers, as the greatest attention to climate in the annual debate of the UN General Assembly was paid by the Republic of Korea, Mexico, South Africa, Australia, and India (the latter three being tied). All except India, here viewed as a second-tier great power, belong to the middle power category. Interestingly, Korea and Mexico, which ranked the highest, held the G20 presidency in 2010 and 2013, respectively. India and South Africa are both BRICS members and among countries that scholars say may suffer the most from a rapidly changing climate. Australia, meanwhile, had been a leader in the field before the government changed hands in 2013 and the new prime minster, Tony Abbott, drastically redirected Canberra's stance toward climate change skepticism.

At the bottom of the list of countries devoting attention to climate change in their UN General Assembly speeches was Russia, which did not mention the issue in any of the six years, followed by China, Canada, and the EU. Russia's blatant disinterest in climate change is presumably partly a reflection of its dependence on the oil and gas industry for government revenues and the strategic interest that the administrations of Presidents Medvedev and Putin attribute to this sector. The same can be said for Canada, but the appearance of China and the EU in this category is more surprising. China certainly does not want to be tied down by binding commitments, and the low profile of the EU representative may be because he is the chair of the European Council, not the European Commission, which has a more elaborate policy on environmental matters.

In 2009 the problem of how to mitigate, as well as adapt to the consequences of, pending climate change featured prominently on the agendas of the diplomatic high tables. Instrumental in raising awareness were the UN, the European Commission, and the UNFCCC, along with a coalition of like-minded experts and decision makers throughout the world. The diplomatic efforts aimed at extending, renewing, or expanding the Kyoto Protocol and at adopting mandatory, universally binding rules and targets to be met by each UN member state culminated at the 2009 Copenhagen conference. Because an agreement was not reached in a multilateral setting, however, many believe that the prospects for bringing down the level of GHG emissions in the atmosphere before the global temperature rises two degrees Celsius were severely set back.

The great-power deal among the United States and the four largest emerging economies at Copenhagen in 2009 is a striking illustration of nested informality created to reduce expectations of a binding set of rules and to avert a breakdown of climate negotiations. By espousing the two-degree ceiling for growth of CO_2 emissions and agreeing to introduce nationally appropriate mitigation measures, the four most important developing countries were brought, via the flexibility of informal diplomatic practices, into the fold of Kyoto norms, albeit without the requisite enforcement demands.

Following a post-Copenhagen lull in the climate change debate during 2010, the diplomatic high tables eventually picked up the issue anew in 2011 and 2012. Noteworthy is the second installment of a seminar-like discussion on climate change at the UNSC in 2011, another example of nested informality given the choice of deliberation format and the slight shift in viewing the council as a legitimate arena in which to raise this problem. The UK and Pakistan also cochaired an Arria formula meeting at the council, in mid-February 2013, on "the security dimensions of climate change." In the meantime the BRICS countries worked to fend off the impression that they had effectively scuttled a broader agreement at Copenhagen, adopting joint statements at their own summits that reaffirmed a general commitment to a universal and binding legal outcome of future negotiations under the auspices of the UNFCCC.

More promising in that they pointed to concrete steps ahead were the G8 and G20 summits in 2012. The Camp David summit led by US president Obama gave an unprecedented amount of attention and time to environmental concerns, with climate change at the top of that list. The summit also produced an unusually fine-tuned joint statement that reiterated the G8 member states' ambition to speed up mitigation efforts until 2010 and arrive at a "protocol" by 2015. Most commentators perceived this as a renewed pledge to forge a mandatory legal arrangement akin to the Kyoto Protocol. And although the leaders of the most prominent and asset-rich G20 countries chose not to show up at the Rio+20 conference devoted to environmental sustainability, the same leaders at the June Los Cabos summit restated their joint obligation to arrive at a balanced and successful outcome of climate change negotiations and promised to move the issue of climate financing forward.

Climate financing is also the area in which moderate progress was, indeed, achieved in 2012–13. In the absence of a major push forward on genuine and effective climate change mitigation measures at the global level in the previous five years, individual states, cities, corporations, and civil society organizations picked up some of the slack. Equally important, international organizations, governments, and major corporations and investor groups demonstrated a growing interest in climate financing. If public and private funding arrangements more often than hitherto could work hand in glove, experts in environmental financing suggested, the economies-of-scale problem would be significantly reduced.

Still, the problem of identifying a suitable institutional venue for climate change mitigation efforts remains and was clearly accentuated by the Copenhagen conference debacle. As illustrated by the UNSC debate in 2011, the resistance to having the council take charge of the climate change issue continues to be widespread. The G7/G8, on the other hand, has the economic resources but lacks the political legitimacy to satisfactorily handle the problem. This leaves the G20 as the most promising venue, even though the group has long been reluctant to take on this matter in a comprehensive manner.

A minilateralist partnership, placing the United States, China, and India at the center of the arrangement, could potentially bring other countries along.[104] Japan and Germany have already invested considerable political prestige and financial resources in climate change mitigation, although both are simultaneously trying to reduce their dependence on nuclear power. Major producers of oil and gas, such as Saudi Arabia and Russia, cannot be expected to be in the forefront of an energy shift away from fossil fuels. An informal body that gathers the major producers and consumers of energy, and therefore the main emitters of GHGs, might be a crucial forum for forging a deal that balances utilities and vulnerabilities and thereby circumvents the so-called Giddens's paradox that renders timely action so difficult to realize.[105]

A more ambitious approach would be to engage the UNSC in outright dispute resolution in the area of preventive conflict management. Cousins has suggested that the council could insist on negotiations among the countries most severely affected by sea-level rise, namely, the small island states and those governments resisting the target global temperature increase of no more than 1.5–2.0 degrees Celsius, on the other. In a manner consistent with the threat multiplier understanding of climate change, the council's acceptance of a role as a proactive facilitator of dispute resolution between stakeholders on opposite sides of the conflict would seem appropriate in principle. Yet without an acute sense of crisis, this thought experiment would from a political standpoint no doubt be exceedingly difficult to realize, let alone use as a vehicle to reconcile opposing views on climate change.[106]

Finally, there is a third possibility, so far not given much credence but embedded in the prerogatives of the UNSC as a body that can adopt binding resolutions in the field of peace of security.[107] If the worst-case scenarios of climate scientists were to materialize over the coming years and decades—and no binding rules were agreed to through some other arrangement even though the crisis became aggravated and started producing immediate and irrefutable consequences for peace and security—it is feasible that people around the world would consider it incumbent on the council to act, in the interest of humanity at large. This reasoning would seem consistent with the views of Ambassadors Rice and Viotti and others who partook in the 2011 debate.

The council's unique legitimacy and authority under international law, so the argument goes, makes it an obvious candidate to create a subsidiary organ that could execute a crisis-response role under its supervision.

The overall findings on climate change mitigation are that contemporary great and middle powers increasingly resort to informal institutional arrangements to address challenges in this policy area, with debates in formal settings such as the UNSC and the UN General Assembly's annual opening session at most helping to remind governments of the issue. Attempts to forge an agreement on measures that would transcend the traditional-nontraditional security nexus are highly contested by a number of major actors, though, such as China, India, and Russia.

NOTES

1. Solomon, *Climate Change 2007*; Giddens, *Politics of Climate Change*, 3–4, 91–128; Moser and Boykoff, *Successful Adaptation to Climate Change*; Dalby, "Rethinking Geopolitics."

2. Stern, *Economics of Climate Change.*

3. Busby, "Climate Change and National Security."

4. Cox, *Climate Crash.*

5. World Health Organization, *Protecting Health from Climate Change—World Health Day* 2008 (Geneva: World Health Organization, 2008).

6. Solomon, *Climate Change 2007*, 5.

7. Giddens, *Politics of Climate Change*, 9, 190–91.

8. Hoffmann, *Climate Governance at the Crossroads.*

9. Victor, *Global Warming Gridlock.*

10. Metz, *IPCC Special Report.*

11. Giddens, *Politics of Climate Change*, 221.

12. Kirton and Kokotsis, "Gleneagles Performance."

13. Van De Graaf and Westphal, "G8 and G20 as Global."

14. Stern, *Economics of Climate Change.*

15. Cousins, "UN Security Council."

16. Elisabeth Rosenthal, "U.N. Report Describes Risks of Inaction on Climate Change," *New York Times*, November 17, 2007, accessed January 15, 2014, http://www .nytimes.com/2007/11/17/science/earth/17cnd-climate.html?pagewanted=print& _r=0.

17. Barack Obama, "Obama's Speech on Climate," *New York Times*, September 22, 2009, accessed February 16, 2014, http://www.nytimes.com/2009/09/23/us /politics/23obama.text.html?pagewanted=all&_r=0.

18. Guebert, Shaw, and Vassallo, "G8 Conclusions on Climate Change."

19. "Joint Statement by the G8 Energy Ministers and the European Energy Com-

missioner," Rome, May 24, 2009, accessed October 15, 2015, http://www.g8italia2009
.it/static/G8_Allegato/Energia%203%2c0.pdf.

20. Kirton, Guebert, and Bracht, "Climate Change Accountability."

21. In the wider community of environmental NGOs, the invitation of increasingly influential developing countries was viewed as an opportunity to prepare the ground for the Copenhagen summit in December 2009, not just for the G8 l'Aquila summit in July that same year.

22. The Major Economies Forum gathers sixteen countries that together account for some 80 percent of total CO2 emissions (Kirton, Guebert, and Bracht, "Climate Change Accountability," 11).

23. Major Economies Forum, "Declaration of the Leaders of the Major Economies on Energy and Climate," l'Aquila, July 9, 2009, accessed March 9, 2014, http://www .majoreconomiesforum.org/past-meetings/the-first-leaders-meeting.html.

24. Bodansky, "Copenhagen Climate Conference," 235.

25. Dimitrov, "Inside UN Climate Change Negotiations," 796.

26. Ibid., 797.

27. Bodansky, "Copenhagen Climate Conference," 233–34.

28. Gowan, "Asymmetrical Multilateralism," 167.

29. Bodansky, "Copenhagen Climate Conference," 236.

30. McGee, "Exclusive Minilateralism."

31. Bodansky, "Copenhagen Climate Conference," 230.

32. UNFCCC, "Copenhagen Accord," September 18, 2009, accessed July 19, 2014, http://unfccc.int/meetings/copenhagen_dec_2009/items/5262.php.

33. Hurrell and Sengupta, "Emerging Powers," 471.

34. Bodansky, "Copenhagen Climate Conference," 234.

35. Fisher, "COP-15 in Copenhagen."

36. Gowan, "Asymmetrical Multilateralism," 175–77.

37. Nowhere was this more obvious than in the annual General Assembly opening debates, as seen in table 2.2.

38. Guebert, Shaw, and Vassallo, "G8 Conclusions on Climate Change."

39. Nordhaus, "Economic Aspects of Global Warming," 11721.

40. Doelle, "Legacy of the Climate Talks," 91.

41. Bodansky, "Copenhagen Climate Conference," 240.

42. Doelle, "Legacy of the Climate Talks," 91.

43. Van Vliet et al., "Copenhagen Accord Pledges."

44. Kirton and Guebert, "Climate Change Accountability," 4.

45. "The G20 Toronto Summit Declaration," June 26–27, 2010, accessed October 15, 2015, https://g20.org/wp-content/uploads/2014/12/Toronto_Declaration_eng.pdf.

46. Bracht, "Plans for the 2011."

47. Cousins, "UN Security Council."

48. UN Security Council, S/PV.5663, April 17, 2007.

49. Detraz and Betsill, "Climate Change and Environmental Security," 311; Gaouette, "U.S. 'Not Encouraged.'"

50. UN Security Council, S/PV.5663, 2.

51. UN Security Council, S/PV.6587, July 20, 2011, 3.

52. Ibid., 5.

53. Ibid., 6.

54. Ibid., 7.

55. Ibid., 8–9.

56. Ibid., 9.

57. Cousins, "UN Security Council," 203.

58. Ibid., 207–9.

59. Kirton and Bracht, "Prospects for the 2013 BRICS."

60. "Full Text of Sanya Declaration."

61. Hurrell and Sengupta, "Emerging Powers," 473–74.

62. Ibid.

63. Eugene Robinson, "Reason to Smile about the Durban Climate Conference," *Washington Post*, December 12, 2011, accessed February 15, 2014, https://www.washingtonpost.com/opinions/reason-to-smile-about-the-durban-climate-conference/2011/12/12/gIQA80nZqO_story.html.

64. Suzanne Goldenberg, "Barack Obama Skips Rio+20 Earth Summit," *Guardian*, June 12, 2012, accessed February 20, 2014, http://www.theguardian.com/environment/2012/jun/13/barack-obama-skips-rio.

65. "G20 Leaders Declaration," Los Cabos, June 19, 2012, accessed October 19, 2015, https://www.whitehouse.gov/the-press-office/2012/06/19/g20-leaders-declaration.

66. Julie M. Carey, "Surprise Side Effect of Shale Gas Boom: A Plunge in U.S. Greenhouse Gas Emissions," *Forbes*, December 7, 2013, accessed February 18, 2014, http://www.forbes.com/sites/energysource/2012/12/07/surprise-side-effect-of-shale-gas-boom-a-plunge-in-u-s-greenhouse-gas-emissions/.

67. "G8 Foreign Ministers Meeting Chair's Statement," Washington, DC, April 12, 2012, accessed July 18, 2014, http://www.state.gov/r/pa/prs/ps/2012/04/187815.htm.

68. "Camp David Declaration," May 18–19, 2012, accessed July 18, 2014, https://www.whitehouse.gov/the-press-office/2012/05/19/camp-david-declaration.

69. Ibid.

70. Ibid.

71. Ibid.

72. Ibid.

73. Executive Office of the President, "The President's Climate Action Plan," June 2013, accessed May 22, 2015, 6–11, https://www.whitehouse.gov/sites/default/files/image/president27sclimateactionplan.pdf.

74. Tom Zeller Jr. and Joanna Zelman, "Climate Change Not Mentioned in Presidential Debates for the First Time in a Generation," *Huffington Post*, October 23, 2012, accessed February 20, 2014, http://www.huffingtonpost.com/2012/10/23/climate-change-presidential-debate_n_2004067.html.

75. Yale Project on Climate Change Communication and George Mason University Center on Climate Change Communication, "Climate Change in the American Mind: The Potential Impact of Global Warming on the 2012 Presidential Election," September 2012, accessed February 20, 2014, http://environment.yale.edu/climate-communication/files/Global-Warming-2012-Election.pdf.

76. Dan Cash, "CBS News Early Exit Poll Information Says 60 Percent of Voters Consider Economy Most Important Issue," WKZO, November 6, 2012, accessed February 20, 2014, http://wkzo.com/news/articles/2012/nov/06/cbs-news-early-exit-poll-information-has-economy-at-60-percent-as-voters-most-important-issue/.

77. Graham and Thompson, "Financing Climate Adaptation," 5–10.

78. Winkler, "Measurable, Reportable and Verifiable."

79. International Partnership on Mitigation and MRV, "Elements and Options for National MRV Systems," German Federal Ministry for the Environment, Nature Conservation and Nuclear Safety, August 2013, accessed April 4, 2014, http://mitigationpartnership.net/sites/default/files/mrv_knowledge_product_130830.pdf.

80. Climate and Development Knowledge Network (CDKN), "Climate Finance," accessed July 19, 2014, http://cdkn.org/themes/theme-climate-finance/?loclang=en_gb.

81. Lattanzio, "International Climate Change Financing."

82. UN Environmental Program News Center, "World's Leading Institutional Investors Managing $24 Trillion Call for Carbon Pricing, Ambitious Global Climate Deal," September 18, 2014, accessed February 24, 2014, http://www.unep.org/NEWSCENTRE/Default.aspx?DocumentID=2796&ArticleID=10984#sthash.wavuByaN.dpuf.

83. Green Growth Action Alliance, "Progress Report from the First Year of Catalysing Private Investment, World Economic Forum," June 2013, accessed April 4, 2014, http://www.weforum.org/reports/green-growth-action-alliance-progress-report-first-year-catalysing-private-investment.

84. Ibid., 6.

85. Juergens, *Landscape of Climate Financing.*

86. B20 Task Force on Green Growth, "Concrete Actions for Los Cabos," *Mexico Today*, June 22, 2012, accessed July 19, 2014, http://mexicotoday.org/article/b20-summit-los-cabos-wrap.

87. Marca Pais, "B20 Global Business Leaders Announce Their Prioritised Recommendations for Economic Recovery and Growth," *PR Newswire Europe*, June 5, 2012, accessed May 22, 2015, http://www.prnewswire.co.uk/news-releases/b20-global-business-leaders-announce-their-prioritised-recommendations-for-economic-recovery-and-growth-157341195.html.

88. "UN Framework Convention on Climate Change," November 11–22, 2013, accessed July 19, 2014, http://unfccc.int/meetings/warsaw_nov_2013/session/7767.php; "UN Framework Convention on Climate Change," December 1–12, 2014, http://unfccc.int/meetings/lima_dec_2014/meeting/8141/php/view/dailyprogramme.php.

89. Department of Defense, *Quadrennial Defense Review* (Washington, DC, 2011); National Research Council, *National Security Implications of Climate Change for U.S. Naval Forces* (Washington, DC: National Academies Press, 2011).

90. National Research Council, *National Security Implications*, 6.

91. Bryan Bender, "Chief of US Pacific Forces Calls Climate Biggest Worry," *Boston Globe*, March 9, 2013, accessed April 4, 2014, http://www.bostonglobe.com/news/nation/2013/03/09/admiral-samuel-locklear-commander-pacific-forces-warns-that-climate-change-top-threat/BHdPVCLrWEMxRe9IXJZcHL/story.html.

92. Ryan McNeill and Deborah J. Nelson, "Coastal Flooding Has Surged along Eastern Seaboard, Investigation Finds," Reuters, July 10, 2014, accessed August 9, 2014, http://www.huffingtonpost.com/2014/07/10/coastal-flooding_n_5574703.html; Center for Coastal Resources Management, *Recurrent Flooding Study for Tidewater* (Gloucester Point, VA: Virginia Institute of Marine Science, 2013).

93. Achim Steiner and David Pitt-Watson, "Global Sustainability Reporting: The Corporate Path to a Green Economy," *G20 Newsdesk*, June 2012, accessed May 22, 2015, http://www.g8.utoronto.ca/newsdesk/loscabos/g20loscabos2012-08.pdf, 128–29.

94. International Energy Agency, *Energy Technology Perspectives* (Paris: International Energy Agency, 2012).

95. Vogler, "European Contribution."

96. Office of the Press Secretary, "US-China Joint Announcement on Climate Change," November 11, 2014, accessed May 22, 2015, https://www.whitehouse.gov/the-press-office/2014/11/11/us-china-joint-announcement-climate-change.

97. Janaki Lenin, "US-China Climate Deal's Ambition Fails to Impress India," *Guardian*, November 18, 2014.

98. "C20 Response to the G20 Leaders. Communiqué," November 16, 2014, accessed May 22, 2015, http://www.c20.org.au/2014/11/c20-statement-on-the-g20-leaders-communique/Q2.

99. Kirton, "Summit of Significant, Selective Success."

100. Garnaut, "G-20 and International Cooperation," 223.

101. Keohane and Victor, "Regime Complex for Climate Change," 10–11.

102. Ibid.

103. US UN Delegation, "64th UN General Assembly: East Asian and Pacific Islands' Performance," Wikileaks cable reference ID: #09USUNNEWYORK1129, December 18, 2009, accessed July 25, 2014, https://cablegatesearch.wikileaks.org/cable.php?id=09USUNNEWYORK1129&q=elected%20member%20unsc.

104. Engelbrekt, "Minilateralism Matters More?"

105. Giddens's paradox appears to obtain especially in countries where expert views are subordinated to those held by the public and by interest groups, which normally is the case in democratic societies. It states that the dangers of global warming are not sufficiently tangible, immediate, or visible to generate massive political mobilization on the issue of climate change, which in turn means that only highly disruptive effects will precipitate such action. By that time, however, it will most likely be too late to avert catastrophic scenarios for much of humankind; Giddens, *Politics of Climate Change*, 1–4.

106. Cousins, "UN Security Council," 209.

107. This point has so far received virtually no attention from scholars. For instance, in a recent volume exclusively devoted to the global governance of climate change, the UN Security Council was not mentioned at all. Held, Fane-Hervey, and Theros, *Governance of Climate Change.*

Conclusions

The analysis in the three preceding chapters described the ways international security institutions responded to the challenges of conflict management, counterterrorism cooperation, and climate change mitigation in 2009–14 and the extent to which high-table diplomacy formed part of that response by using formal and informal settings and facilitating diplomatic practices across the traditional/nontraditional security nexus. At the center of this last chapter are the concept of high-table diplomacy and the nexus of formality-informality and traditional-nontraditional security in the realm of international security. I begin by summarizing why high-table diplomacy is appealing and why informal institutional arrangements are likely to occupy a greater role in future international relations than they did in the twentieth century, especially its latter half. I then proceed to describe the theoretical insights on rival propositions regarding the two nexuses and their relationship to the three policy areas examined. The feasibility of a one-stop shop for international security is discussed, and then an attempt is made to condense the empirical findings into two governance mechanisms. Finally, I revisit the analytical themes—polarity, prestige, and process—introduced at the outset and assess the importance of high-table diplomacy in international security, including the promise it may hold for global governance at large, from a normative angle.

High-Table Diplomacy: A Work in Progress

The appeal of high-table diplomacy appears to lie, at least in part, in the experience of multilateralism not working in the way it did during much of the twentieth century. The high level of transnational interdependence already achieved may indeed be a factor weakening multilateral decision making, as this interdependence raises the bar for additional pooling of national sovereignty. A handful of countries always have high stakes in existing regulatory frameworks and rules, and major actors presumably have less leverage over smaller ones in a globalized world characterized by the absence of interstate conflict. The governments of major countries, in other words, cannot discipline countries with fewer resources to the degree that they were able to during the Cold War era.

For great and middle powers, meanwhile, the absence of existing conflict in the system makes cooperative arrangements among peers feasible. The prospects for achieving convergence among a smaller number of countries are less daunting than in multilateral negotiations based on equality and expectation of reaching universal consensus. There are certainly ways in which full-fledged multilateralism can be bracketed at some stage of establishing a new international framework or institution, as pointed out by Martin and described in chapter 1, but minilateralism presently appears all too tempting to be abandoned. Among other advantages it offers opportunities to manage power relations directly within a wide group of peers that want the global power configuration to remain relatively stable and power shifts to take place as smoothly as possible.

In *conflict management* between 2009 and 2014, the peace-building agenda developed by the UNSC involved a pattern of recurrent shifts between formal and informal institutional arrangements. "Peace building" is a term used by governments and international organizations to describe traditional security activities, such as military training, modernization of defense equipment, and enhancement of combat and policing skills. These tasks are supposed to enable future, collaborative peacekeeping missions on the African continent, while at the same time minimizing the risk that the increased capabilities could be turned against neighboring countries. A comprehensive peace-building agenda beyond traditional security, as explained in chapter 3, would include a wide range of additional objectives, including conflict resolution, political reconciliation, security sector reform, restorative justice, institution building, gender equality, and development.

It is evident that peace building as carried out in 2009–14 relies on decades of previous conflict management experience within the UN and its Security Council and therefore may be slow to take on nontraditional security challenges. But a more immediate precursor to recent peace-building efforts was the informal setting of the G8, which used the capacities of its member states to launch the so-called G8 Africa Clearing House and to provide it, eventually, with adequate resources to take on major tasks in this field of activity. The initiative originated with the US presidency of the G8, in 2004, and clearly envisaged a broader mandate. More specifically, at the sixth meeting of the Africa Clearing House, held July 2009 in conjunction with the G8 summit at l'Aquila, Italy, an agreement on moving from policy proposal to large-scale implementation was reached. At l'Aquila G8 countries agreed to set up a network of training centers for not only military but also civilian peace-building measures and to widely disseminate information about projects launched and initiatives taken within the broader framework.[1]

Already as this initiative was unfolding, African security received renewed attention from within the UN system, opening up opportunities to marry traditional with nontraditional security tasks. Only one year after the original establishment of the Africa Clearing House, in 2005, the PBC was forged under the joint auspices of the UN General Assembly and the UNSC. Operating in the formal setting of the UN and two of its most important bodies, the PBC was promptly set up as a subsidiary organ in its own right through UNSC Resolution 1645 and UN General Assembly Resolution 60/180. Although the PBC was given primarily an advisory function, the coordination of field missions that encompass a variety of traditional and nontraditional security objectives effectively ensures a key role in all UN missions undertaken on the African continent. Having held its first session in 2007, the PBC for the first time began to affect situations on the ground with its direct involvement in the Burundi and Sierra Leone peace process in 2008.

The Africa Clearing House had gathered governments with resources to spend on peace-building efforts in the same way informal groups previously had acted with the consent of the UN secretary general and the P5 member states. Following the 2009 l'Aquila summit, it was decided that the PBC could rely on a more regulated process, and work began to identify countries with the greatest need for this holistic form of peace building. By late 2014 thirty-one member states formed part of the PBC's Organizational Committee: the P5 and two E10 UNSC member states (Argentina, Chad), the five top financial contributors (Canada, Japan, Germany, Spain, and Sweden), the five major troop-contributing nations (Bangladesh, India, Egypt, Nigeria, and Pakistan), seven countries appointed by the General Assembly (Brazil, Bosnia and Herzegovina, Guatemala, Kenya, Malaysia, Peru, and South Africa), and another seven by the ECOSOC (Croatia, Denmark, Dominican Republic, Ethiopia, Indonesia, Nepal, and Tunisia).

To the thirty-one countries should be added the World Bank, the IMF, the EU, and the Organization of Islamic Cooperation, together representing the biggest donors. These bodies, and the extraordinarily rich and varied experience they represent, further ensure that nontraditional security activities are included. It is nevertheless incumbent on the Organizational Committee to select a chair and decide on the so-called country-specific configurations that take charge of specific issues and dossiers, which so far are made up of

African countries in great need of post-conflict reconstruction and institution building (namely, Burundi, Sierra Leone, Guinea, Liberia, Guinea-Bissau, and the Central African Republic).

As a result, between 2009 and 2014 PBC institutional arrangements unfolded in ways that may ensure their consolidation in the medium to long term. Six different country-specific configurations were set up, and the record of achievements so far appears to be one of progress, especially in conflict management and post-conflict reconstruction. At the same time, the rate of setting up new country-specific configurations tapered off after an initial outburst of interest. The question is whether weakening interest was due to the waning generosity of rich countries and international organizations in the wake of the financial and economic crisis or whether other factors were affecting its performance. By rendering peace building less flexible and contingent on the desire of a coalition of countries, and by reducing the visibility of governments that may want to take credit for making substantive contributions, the convoluted combination of formal and informal diplomatic practices might be undercutting the potential strengths of informal governance. Notably, middle and second-tier great powers have rarely chaired the Organizational Committee or the country-specific configurations, which may indicate efforts made to include the wider UN membership and somewhat limit the influence of the former over the PBC.[2]

In *counterterrorism cooperation* a more intense pattern of shifts, even reversals, between formal and informal settings and diplomatic practices could be observed in 2009–14. This is a field that conventionally has belonged to nontraditional security but which following, and in response to, the 9/11 attacks against the United States increasingly came to rely on military and other coercive resources. As described in chapter 4, transnational efforts in this area originally emerged in the informal setting of the G8, with a dramatic expansion of activities taking place after 9/11.

UNSC Resolutions 1267, 1373, 1540, and 1624 established formal legitimation and enforcement measures for counterterrorism cooperation within the regularized setting of the council, complete with oversight procedures. As should be expected in the UN context, the creation of the CTC as a full-fledged subsidiary body of the council introduced higher transaction costs, bureaucratic complexity, and inflexibility, yet also reinforced opportunities for repeated action and uniform implementation of all relevant resolutions. Besides the two annual council meetings devoted to counterterrorism, each P5 member state exerted direct leverage over the appointment of chairs to the CTC, the sanction committees, and other subsidiary bodies.

A second twist in the evolution of counterterrorism cooperation can be described as going in the opposite direction, as the CTED was created to offset some of the constraints inherent in the relatively inflexible CTC framework. Essentially, the UNSC fashioned an office and a top management position over which the council diplomats would not exert day-to-day control. The management position came into existence after the adoption of Resolution 1535 (2004), which established the duty to oversee the implementation of Resolution 1373 in the shape of a mandate subsequently expanded through Resolution 1624 (2005). It was decided that unlike the CTC, which has a chair appointed for each UN session who thus only serves one year at a time, the CTED would have a director who held his or her position for several consecutive years. With a staff of some forty international civil servants, half of whom are legal experts, the CTED was given powers to supervise the enactment of counterterrorism laws and regulations and to conduct visits to countries that face significant challenges in meeting the requirements of Resolutions 1373 and 1624.

Insofar as the CTED needed to develop a range of diplomatic activities to fulfil its expanded tasks, it could paradoxically no longer operate solely as an informal, technically oriented body in the realm of counterterrorism. If it were to discharge its extensive outreach and traveling activities, in other words, the CTED had to acquire more nuanced diplomatic routines and skills and to communicate effectively with governments of countries that face difficulties implementing aspects of the counterterrorism framework. This development made the work of the CTED cumbersome, as senior (national) diplomats started looking over its shoulders. In a third reversal of the formality-informality dynamic, the P3 countries, China, and several E10 member states in early 2010 asked that the CTED be able to treat a wider range of procedures and documents as "internal" and not circulate them within the council for prior approval.[3]

This could have been the end of a story with several wrinkles concerning the formality-informality nexus. But bringing the CTED into the formal sphere of UNSC activities simultaneously also meant reducing the space for nested informality and its associated informal governance. The directorate became principally engaged in capacity-building measures, some of which have an outreach dimension that requires carefully gauged diplomatic practices. A corollary to this development was therefore a renewed momentum toward technical cooperation under the auspices of the CTC, now less burdened by enforcement tasks. As a result, an initiative promoted by the US permanent representation in New York gathered national prosecutors of counterterrorism cases in a series of seminars and workshops to compare notes and best practices.[4] The CTC later hosted other technically oriented seminars on problems of counterterrorism referred to as "special meetings."

Although the boundary between traditional and nontraditional security concepts has tended to be blurred in this area, it is probably the case that international security institutions until recently considered counterterrorism as distinct from conflict management and thereby also from military and state coercion. Military intelligence resources were previously used almost exclusively for purposes of nationally organized defense and security policy, with limited exchange between governments and organizational units that had developed mutual trust. Only in 2014, with the rise of ISIL in Iraq and Syria, did conflict management and counterterrorism become fused in ways that started to require a restructuring of international efforts. By mid-2015 coordinated use of international resources in overlapping areas of responsibility remained limited.

In *climate change mitigation* a basic problem is that neither formal nor informal settings so far have provided a proper venue for addressing the issue, let alone defining the scope of a mandate. Considered far removed from traditional security normally handled by the UNSC, the problem of climate change was in the past never raised in that context. Still, the scientific community of climate scholars and the majority of governments appear to agree that high-table diplomacy can and should play a key role in addressing the issue. The multilateral, formal setting of recurrent UN conferences was for several decades used to try to identify a mitigation formula that worked for all UN member states. Repeated attempts to forge an ambitious agreement had by mid-2015 so far failed to produce results that would slow down the acceleration of GHG emissions. Also, the widely anticipated 2009 Copenhagen climate summit, as described in chapter 5, was unsuccessful on most counts.

Given that climate change mitigation has not been achieved in multilateral negotiations since the late 1970s, it could make sense to explore a minilateral framework instead.[5] Given what we know about the strengths and weaknesses of formal versus informal governance, furthermore, the latter may very well be more conducive to a diplomatic breakthrough. Above all minilateral frameworks allow great powers to think that they can maintain control over (at least some of the) information and a measure of political flexibility in negotiations with peer governments. This control and flexibility might persuade them to let down their guard and strike a compromise deal. The Copenhagen Accord, a result of informal communication before and during the 2009 climate summit in the Danish capital, bears witness to the potential of minilateral negotiations.

As already established the G7/G8 has too few members to make an agreement on climate change mitigation that is sufficiently legitimate and effective. Representing the industrialized world of post-1945 economic great powers and excluding non-democracies like China (and, since the spring of 2014, semi-democracies like Russia), the G7 lacks the credibility necessary for authoritative deliberations on climate change. Before the upgrade of the G20 to a summit of heads of state and government, in other words, GX summitry was not an institutional arrangement within which the looming problem of climate change could have been successfully and sustainably handled.

For a variety of reasons, though, the G20 engaged only partially in the issue of climate change in 2009–14. Up until the Copenhagen summit of December 2009, multilateral negotiations were sustained almost exclusively in order to achieve a universal and binding agreement on the part of the entire world community. For most of 2010, following the 2009 Scandinavian debacle, the main protagonists had little appetite for creating new initiatives on climate change, and only in 2011–12 did the great powers recommit to working on the issue. In the meantime US president Obama was able to bring up narrower environmental proposals loosely associated with climate change at the 2012 G8 Camp David summit. The emphasis of American climate diplomacy was on creating business-friendly, technology-driven collaboration among corporations and nations that, with or without a universal agreement, would help advance the broader agenda.

Even by 2013–14 making progress through formal diplomatic practices had not been ruled out. Some governments considered the 2015 Paris climate summit, and other future summits, as additional opportunities for binding commitments. Others began debating the prospects for short-circuiting efforts at climate change mitigation, and adaptation, that had long made up the bulk of UN activities. Apart from the rather unrealistic idea of creating an entirely new body to address the challenge of climate change—an equivalent to the UNSC in the area of environmental threats—a number of permanent representations and commentators took to outlining some preliminary ideas about using the existing council for that purpose.[6]

Interestingly, the 2007 and the 2011 UNSC debates on climate change helped break the taboo of seriously engaging the council in deliberations on matters other than traditional security concerns. While it remains unrealistic to imagine that the council will take further steps in the same direction without a powerful political impetus, a successive widening of the mandate proceeded throughout the post–Cold War period and could hypothetically extend to ecological matters as well. Crucially, the council's prerogatives as the sole international security institution with a legal mandate to adopt international law binding on all UN member states would have to be applied to a new policy area. If its mandate were expanded, the council's sweeping powers to create and interpret international law could be exploited to make the world absorb tough regulations that individual nations remain reluctant to make. The most likely scenario in which the council's mandate might thus be reinterpreted, tragically enough, is if atmospheric transformations associated with climate change precipitate large-scale environmental damage and humanitarian emergencies and a direct causal connection between the two is widely recognized.

The Propositions Revisited

It is now time to revisit the two sets of propositions outlined in chapter 1. First, a hybridity proposition was juxtaposed with a differentiation proposition in relation to the formality-informality nexus. It is at once clear that the findings for the three policy areas are not unequivocal and therefore should not be reported as falling exclusively on one side of the dichotomy. Instead, figure C.1 shows that the findings fall on a sliding scale between hybridity and differentiation.

The aggregate outcome of the analysis in chapters 3–5 demonstrates with considerable clarity that conflict management is the policy area where differentiation between formal and informal institutional arrangements is most distinct. As the analysis shows, UNSC member states and the P5 in particular vigilantly upheld the distinction and would not allow GX summitry to engage in what is seen as the council's legitimate domain. Even second-tier great powers, themselves seeking permanent membership in the UNSC, appear to strongly prefer differentiation to hybridity in this field.

On the opposite side of the sliding scale, counterterrorism cooperation is characterized by a significant degree of hybridity. This is above all reflected in the interrelationship between informal expert networks and institutional bodies established by the G7/G8 summits, on the one hand, and the formal legitimacy and subsidiary bodies of the UNSC underpinning transnational counterterrorism cooperation, on the other. In terms of origins as well as current modes of operation, the international counterterrorism regime relies on the combination of both formal and informal institutional arrangements.

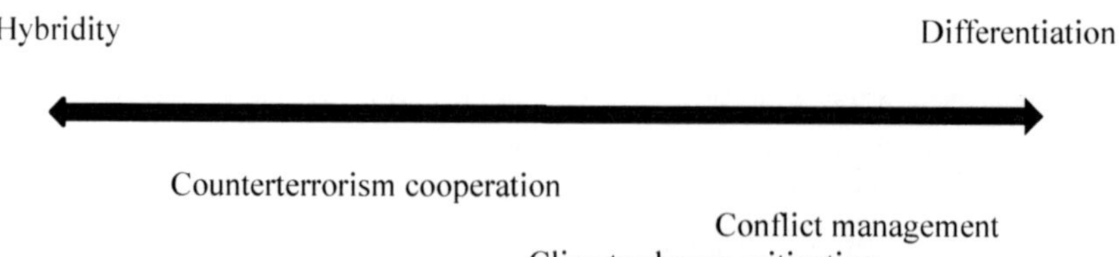

Figure C.1. Formality versus Informality Proposition Outcomes

While the UNSC has a relatively robust set of procedures governing a variety of institutional arrangements in place today, the supplementary role that the GX summitry contributes to transnational counterterrorism cooperation remains one of its major assets.

The analysis suggests climate change mitigation falls in between the two previous policy areas, leaning slightly toward differentiation. Whereas the UNSC as a collective remains committed to differentiation, the UN more broadly appears increasingly flexible on the issue of how the international community may arrive at a satisfactory solution to the problem of rising GHG emissions and their rapidly growing repercussions for the planet's ecosystems and for humanity. This seems to be even more the case following the diplomatic debacle of the 2009 Copenhagen summit, during which the five major powers forged a minilateral deal instead of contributing to a multilateral, universal agreement. Ambivalence about whether a formal or an informal solution should be pursued was in mid-2015 still noticeable among the G20 countries. In summit communiqués from the six years examined here, G20 leaders time and time again expressed deep concern about the slow progress of UN-based negotiations as the main vehicle of climate negotiations leading toward mitigation (and adaptation).

Second, a complementarity proposition was juxtaposed with a contestation proposition in relation to the traditional-nontraditional nexus. The aggregate outcome of the analysis in chapters 3–5 along the complementarity-contestation sliding scale shows a pattern that in part resembles that just described for differentiation and hybridity and in part deviates from it (fig. C.2). Counterterrorism cooperation is a policy area characterized not only by hybridity among formal and informal institutional arrangements but also by complementarity between traditional and nontraditional concepts of security. This characterization appears most immediately related to the increased use of military and state coercion, as well as the entire spectrum of intelligence and security agencies, to map, identify, predict, and respond to terrorist threats in national and international contexts. But it is also the result of resorting to

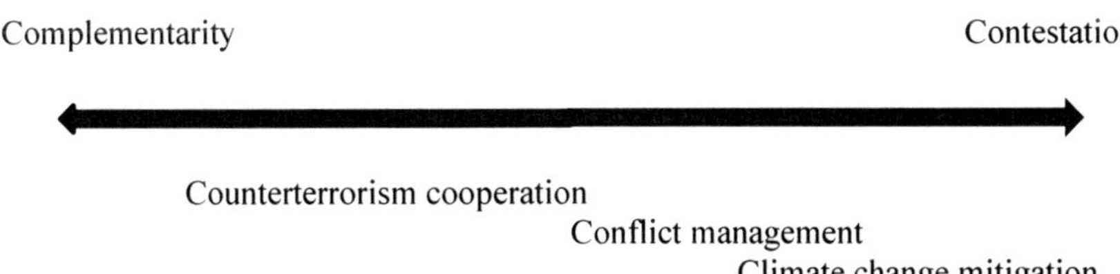

Figure C.2. Traditional versus Nontraditional Security Proposition Outcomes

all available legal and institutional resources as counterterrorism cooperation expanded dramatically in the beginning of the twenty-first century. Some of those resources were existing UN conventions; others institutional monitoring bodies, such as the FATF; and a third category professional networks of intelligence and police officers with experience in combatting terrorism, as well as organized crime and drug and arms trade.

In conflict management the UNSC continues to insist on the primacy of the formal binding character of carefully worded resolutions. But as pointed out earlier in this chapter, the PBC represents an attempt to introduce complementarity to formal frameworks with informal leverage by virtue of commitments made by the biggest donors and contributors of personnel to peacekeeping missions or prominence in the economic and social field of the UN via ECOSOC. If this innovation is deemed successful and adds value to the UN, it may generate other attempts to forge similar solutions.

In climate change mitigation, however, the most obvious pattern is one of contestation. Within the UN many countries certainly prefer the climate issue to be handled entirely outside the UNSC. In the debate China and Russia face the United Kingdom and small island nations that believe climate change is now so pressing that it should be viewed as a threat to international peace and security. At the same time, in the GX summitry the mere introduction of the issue on the agenda of serial summits has been controversial. The climate change issue was repeatedly raised at G20 summits immediately before the 2009 Copenhagen summit, but afterword it receded in the larger scheme of serial summit priorities.

The Feasibility of a One-Stop Shop in International Security

Given the perceived mismatch between existing international security institutions, with formal bodies including the UNSC and a range of other international organizations, on the one hand, and informal groups composed of emerging great and middle powers, on the other, pragmatic attempts to bridge the gap between high-table platforms and the underlying power configuration are to be expected.[7] The 2009–14 transformation of the G20 to a summit of heads of state and government helped make representatives of emerging great powers aware that they could exercise more influence over global affairs, and the macroeconomic parameters of growth and investments in particular. This influence, real and potential, could also be translated into leverage over international security institutions. Within the UNSC, some expected that more subtle sources of diplomatic leverage, such as procedures and working methods, would become unsettled.

At this critical juncture of the changing global power configuration, the informal power resources wielded by emerging second-tier and middle powers were redirected into halting the economic and social fallout of the 2008–9 financial crisis by way of G20 summits convening twice a year. Presumably, one of the main reasons why the P5 countries helped several BRICS countries to join the UNSC in a non-permanent capacity at the same time was so that their growing leverage could be channeled through a formal power structure. As described in chapters 1 and 3, the 2010 and 2011 councils contained an especially unprecedented number of second-tier great powers and regionally influential middle powers, with Japan, Turkey, Mexico, Germany, Brazil, and India serving simultaneously or consecutively. Although the unleashed resources of these countries were temporarily reined in once they had representatives in the council, regional groups of UN and E10 member states started holding more regular consultations—in 2012–13 once a month—demanding greater transparency and more consequential assignments.[8]

Regarding the growing practice of forum shopping and forum shifting in international relations at large, it seems reasonable to interpret the rise of high-table diplomacy as a systematic development capable of constraining the temptation of great and middle powers to "shop" or "shift" issues and responsibilities in the realm of international security. Although the first-tier, incumbent great powers have predictably sought to delay the restructuring of international institutions to their disadvantage, their second-tier and middle-power counterparts have been invited into informal platforms and institutional arrangements and thereby elevated above the roughly 170 smaller countries that also make up the UN membership. Because formal rules are upheld and informal agreements that restrict opportunities for addressing various issues at the UNSC or in one of the GX formats have been reached, in some cases there is often only one place to take a specific dispute or problem related to international security.

With regard to forum shifting, Daniel Drezner has reasonably pointed out that "the weakening of legal obligations disproportionately enhances great powers" at the expense of smaller countries.[9] But what will also be important in a world in which no single government is preeminent is that a one-stop shop in international security on core issues, such as the legitimate use of military violence outside one's own borders, will create a more predictable environment for all major powers, including potential contenders for preeminence, for the foreseeable future. Even though countries like China and Russia have made normative commitments to a world of "multipolarity" (without clarifying the normative content of this concept), one can imagine that a stable set of institutional arrangements spanning formal and informal settings and diplomatic practices would also be in their interest.

Mutual Nestedness, Mutual Reinforcement

Whereas most of this study has borrowed the conceptual universe of diplomacy, international relations, and security studies, I will now try to summarize the findings of chapters 3–5 that relate to political science and public policy more broadly. Two separate governance mechanisms manifested in this study appear to make forum shopping and forum shifting obsolete in international security. One is mutual nestedness, which operates across the formality-informality nexus we have observed throughout this study. The second is mutual reinforcement, which similarly operates across the traditional-nontraditional security nexus. I will now deal with each in turn, using what I regard to be the clearest illustrations of both mechanisms in the 2009–14 period.

First, we will turn to the obvious example cited already in chapter 1, namely, the striking overlap in 2010–12 of E10 and G20 member states not part of the P5 or G8. In terms of the management of UNSC membership, all P5 countries clearly supported—and in part actively promoted through informal consultations—the idea of G20 member states' serving in the E10 category. It is difficult to imagine that this proactive stance was not preceded by deliberations among first-tier great powers. There are some indications that China and Russia, which helped put together BRICS, for once were at the forefront of a council initiative. By mid-2009 the BRICS countries met regularly to coordinate their stance on conflict management issues involving the council. While serving on the 2011–12 UNSC, though, the second-tier great powers spent a lot of time "eyeing each other," according to one participant in council deliberations at that time.[10]

Also at the highest political level, mutual nestedness helped ease tension over the handling of contentious issues in the Middle East, such as the crises in Libya and Syria, in the UNSC. In the 2011 Libya crisis, the P3 for the most part remained far ahead of Beijing and Moscow. As core members of the G8, France, the UK, and the United States used that informal setting to sway other G8 and UNSC members into actively or passively supporting Western intervention at the council. In the G8 context China was absent and then–Russian president Medvedev was sympathetic to the notion of protecting civilians and thereby would tolerate some form of UN action; thus, the P3 was able to press ahead in the fast-paced developments of March 2011. After having secured a thin majority behind the "necessary means" formula implying authorization of military force, the P3 mobilized their allies in NATO to design and execute the defeat of the Libyan armed forces within six months.

In Syria, however, al-Assad did not have Muammar Gaddafi's record of recklessness, and there was no equivalent to the "Benghazi moment," when Western leaders apparently faced an opportunity to avert a large-scale massacre of civilian Libyans. Therefore, in 2012–14 the tables were turned as Chinese and Russian diplomats provided each other moral cover by using, or threatening to use, their combined veto power over the issue. This informal constellation, apparently cemented in the second half of the period investigated here, not only could stand up to the P3 and the wider West but had the capacity to begin altering the political dynamics of the UNSC. In the wider UN membership, both countries actively sought to justify their positions against growing concerns about spillover effects and humanitarian consequences of allowing the Syrian conflict to evolve into a full-scale civil war.

But nested informality was also present at the more technical levels of conflict management under UNSC auspices. It is well-known that the asymmetry between P5 and E10 rights in the council strongly influences the appointment of chairs of subsidiary organs and of "penholders" on issues and dossiers before the council, which in turn reinforces the bias toward P5 preferences. By using their privileged positions to constrain constructive action by E10 member states, P5 countries are able to shape the game beyond the rules laid down in the 1940s. That asymmetry—and the particularly strong position of the United States, the P2, and the P3 within the council—requires a concerted response if multilateral principles also embodied by the council are to be successfully defended by the E10 on the part of the wider UN membership.

The three case studies nevertheless generated evidence of subtle changes lessening the grip of the P5 countries over the rest of the UN membership. Indeed, in recent years a marked trend toward closer coordination within regional groups and among E10 country ambassadors, along with meetings at the level of political coordinators in charge of scheduling, appears to have gently softened the unbridled influence of the P5.[11] In 2013 and 2014, notably, all regional groups except one (the WEOG) held clean-slate elections for E10 membership, based on an agreed-to rotating system for each group member, and thereby undercut the beauty contest dimension of the poll.[12] Non-P5 member states were also consulted more concerning either specific conflict situations or generic issues, such as appointment procedures or working methods, and informal Arria formula meetings and wrap-up sessions were more frequent, providing additional opportunities for non-UNSC member states to gain insight into the council's work.[13]

As described in chapter 4, G8 cooperation on justice and home affairs formed the nucleus of transnational counterterrorism activities that rapidly expanded after 2001, in particular when it came to anti–money laundering and intermittent exchange of intelligence information. The FATF regime was critical to the success of anti-terrorist-financing measures, as they largely relied on the same institutional infrastructure set up in the 1990s. Faced with insurgencies in Afghanistan in 2009, the United States further reinforced the anti-terrorist-financing regime through domestic and bilateral measures; above all, an interagency Illicit Financial Task Force was set up with the Treasury Department.[14] Meanwhile, G7/G8 working groups, such as the Roma-Lyon Group and its various subgroups, redirected much of their work from other issues to dealing with counterterrorism. Other examples of nested informality arising in a predominantly formal setting were P5 contacts with the head of the CTED and a seminar series launched by the CTC.

Albeit in a less complicated and tangled way, mutual nestedness also featured in climate change mitigation in 2009–14. In fact, nested informality drove climate change mitigation through nearly the entire six years systematically covered in this study. The result coming out of the Copenhagen conference was a short text agreed to by the United States, China, India, South Africa, and Brazil, acting outside the framework of multilateral negotiations. Another clear example was the UNEP Financial Initiative, which successfully mobilized private investors, though it remains lodged within the formal setting of the UN, as described in chapter 5. The more flexible setting of GX summits did not achieve much more. Only the G8 summit at Camp David, from which the Russian president was conspicuously absent, produced tangible progress by broadening the climate change agenda to food security and related health issues.

At the same time, the GX summitry offered several examples of nested formality within a predominantly informal setting, ensuring actors participating in the deliberations political flexibility, control of information, and limited transaction costs. The years 2008–9 in particular, as described in the introduction, were a time of recurrent affirmation of the joint commitments to a climate change mitigation agreement that would be binding and universal. The 2011 formal UNSC meeting devoted to climate change also clearly contributed to catapulting the issue back to the top of the international agenda, roughly eighteen months after the failed Copenhagen summit.

The second governance mechanism manifested in the three policy areas in 2009–14 pertains to the traditional-nontraditional security nexus. In international security institutions there are two particularly conspicuous illustrations of mutual reinforcement of policies across this boundary, one concerning the PBC and the other concerning the horizontal complementarity upheld in counterterrorism cooperation in particular. In the first case policy frameworks and professional networks formed part of institutional arrangements in the traditional dimension of security, addressing peacekeeping, and then branched out to nontraditional peace building by drawing on many of the same resources. In the second case rudimentary transnational cooperation among the GX summitry on nontraditional questions such as organized crime and drug trafficking later, when terrorism became viewed as an existential threat on a much larger scale, expanded to traditional security in terms of resource allocation and force generation.

When it comes to measures directly geared toward conflict management, the work done to organize peace-building efforts under the newly established PBC and its Organizational Committee stands out. The PBC was an attempt to institutionalize and subject to formal rule making the well-established yet unofficial practice of allowing asset-rich UN member states, when not serving on the UNSC, to take the lead and bring their considerable diplomatic skills and material wherewithal to bear on conflict situations. When P5 governments either lacked interest or could not agree on a joint approach, this practice was especially useful to UN objectives. But the legitimacy of allowing voluntary coalitions, typically led by a midsize OECD country, to assume the leadership of UN missions was always uncertain. The PBC formula, consolidated in 2009–14, in that respect offered an attractive solution to the problem.

If the PBC example was horizontal policy management at the political level, counterterrorism has evolved into a more technical, specialized set of rules handled by professionals from national governments and international civil servants. With regard to counterterrorism the development and further entrenchment of UNSC subsidiary bodies was not the result of organizational improvisation in the first decade of the twenty-first century, even though transnational collaboration had always been patchy. The CTC was in a position to use the existing transnational collaborative structures and networks—above all G8 working groups and their protocols—as building blocks when establishing and consolidating institutional arrangements within the UN. It could do so in part because several of these working groups had acquired quasi-permanency over the years, with regular meetings, shared agendas and protocols, and a habit of coordination on legislative and policy proposals. Some of those practices of nested formality were carried over into the governance mechanisms created within the UN, breaking down barriers between conflict management and counterterrorism cooperation (and therefore also between traditional and nontraditional security concepts).

Thematic Lessons

Although this study was not designed to validate general claims that international relations are entering into a transformative phase in which relations between contemporary great and middle powers are changing in profound ways, nothing in the previous analysis contradicts such predictions. It is quite feasible that observations regarding patterns of polarity since the early 1990s reflect a global power configuration that edged from hegemonic unipolarity to non-hegemonic unipolarity and that the world is headed toward a multipolar pattern in the second half of the twenty-first century. It would nevertheless seem warranted to insist on a more nuanced understanding of the current state of affairs than sometimes offered in contemporary international relations literature, in which some predict an abrupt end to American-led unipolarity. Even if important indicators suggest that American and European power is waning, continued US military primacy and success in sustaining extensive alliances around the world may very well ensure that unipolarity comes in for a soft landing.

Had the study focused on areas other than international security, it would then have had to pay more attention to the repercussions of Asian countries, and China in particular, gaining weight in relative economic terms. This leveling of the playing field is no longer taking place at the breakneck speed we witnessed over the past twenty-five years, when the emerging Asian societies transformed from low- to high-productivity economies. As the latter are becoming more mature, complex, and similar to their already industrialized counterparts, and as the demands of consumers and citizens precipitate investments in sophisticated governance and public policy on health care, education, transportation, and the environment, annual GDP growth in the double digits is unlikely to obtain. That being said, there is nothing to indicate that GDP growth in China, Indonesia, Vietnam, and other Asian countries will be lower than that in today's OECD in the foreseeable future.

Success in maintaining free trade and robust international security institutions will enable power relations to change gradually rather than abruptly, as second-tier great powers and middle powers, figuratively and literally, expand their influence in the world at the expense of incumbents. The fact that China already is a permanent member state of the UNSC, and thus almost a full-fledged incumbent, would seem to facilitate that development. A gradual rather than rapid and potentially disruptive shift ought to be in the long-term interest of all three categories of great and middle powers, as well as of virtually all of the world's small powers. An open world economy and an international system in which the some 170 small powers do not experience a need to defer to great and middle powers on issues of particular salience to the latter are particularly valuable to the former. Only a multipolar power configuration that does not compel individual units to align geographically or ideologically with great powers offering patronage in exchange for security, but rather encourages economic and political relations to thrive across power asymmetries, is one that allows for widespread peace, prosperity, and societal and environmental resilience.

Minilateral high-table diplomacy constitutes a potential threat to, but ultimately also a safeguard in defense of, that vision of mitigated polarity and constrained power competition. Judging by the overview of the twentieth century in the introduction and chapter 1, plus descriptions of the six-year period analyzed in chapters 3–5, minilateralism has asserted itself rather swiftly, historically speaking, and so far without generating much overt opposition or sharp twists and turns in policymaking. Instead of viewing high-table diplomacy and the reshaping of international security institutions as divorced from, or merely constituting the reflective image of, a long-term trend toward a more multipolar world, the results of this study suggest that global power configurations and the evolution of institutional arrangements are intimately intertwined. Our analysis suggests that both the expectation and reality of a more level playing field among great powers that affect power relations, and the perceived opportunity to nudge developments further in that direction, induce the aspirations of leaders of increasingly asset-rich countries.

The clearest illustration of awakened aspirations is in the desire of representatives of second-tier great powers and middle powers to be acknowledged as top-level actors and accepted as permanent, or at least frequent, guests at platforms of high-table diplomacy, as a matter of prestige. This pits each of the three categories against the other two. The complex diplomatic struggles that accompany the attempts to reform and enlarge the UNSC, in order to make it more representative and aligned with the twenty-first-century global power configuration, offer an especially vivid example of how the interests of the second-tier great powers and middle powers are at odds, with the latter trying to prevent the former from taking up permanent seats in the council (or at least to postpone that development). So far the first-tier great powers—the P5 incumbents—have been more successful at disguising their own discomfort at the prospect of extending great-power privileges to their rising peers. But the resistance is compact, and the actions of the former typically speak much louder than their words.

The preoccupation with prestige and social status, also expressed in other contexts of international security, in fact seemed to grow even in the relatively short time span of six years covered in this study. Interlocutors who partook in UNSC debates on which countries to lead subsidiary bodies or country-specific configurations in charge of peace building in Africa were witnesses to backroom games in which governments would use their relative leverage to impose themselves in positions of diplomatic prestige. Another illustration, highlighted in chapter 5, is the 2009 Copenhagen climate conference, at which Brazil, India, and above all China appeared more concerned with sending a message of strength than with consenting to an international agreement over which they had only marginal influence. Although the way in which the negotiations were structured may have been flawed in more than one respect, the prestige factor made it even more difficult to reconcile global environmental concerns with institutional arrangements operating in accordance with multilateralist principles.

The connections between minilateralism and great-power prestige concerns at high-table platforms have not yet been systematically examined by international relations scholars but appear analytically promising given recent developments in East Asia, Central Europe, and the Middle East. The Senkaku/Diyaou islands dispute between China and Japan, the tug-of-war between Russia and the EU over influence in Ukraine, and Brazil's and India's desire to enhance their diplomatic presence in all corners of Africa—even where historic and business ties are lacking—underscore the great powers' preoccupation with how they present themselves to the world and how they are perceived by others, above all their "peers." Since participation in international security institutions and commitments to alliances represent cornerstones of any country's foreign and defense policy, the relationship between interests and prestige presumably becomes more pronounced in a multipolar power configuration than in situations where one or two first-tier great powers act as the ultimate guarantor(s) of peace and stability (as was the case during much of the Cold War).

In turn, the aspirations of second-tier great powers and middle powers now increasingly come up against the entrenched procedures and institutional arrangements in the existing panoply of international organizations, regimes, and network structures. The findings of this study indicate that the diplomatic process conducted in a variety of institutional arrangements has been significantly influenced by cross-cutting dynamics in recent years. The most obvious outcomes of this heightened tension are the adjustments that have been made in the GX summitry since 2009, including the rise of the G20 to prominence and the relegation of the G8 to noneconomic affairs. The exact nature and scope of GX summitry agendas continue to be the subject of considerable disagreement. By contrast, changes to the well-entrenched diplomatic practices of the UNSC are less conspicuous. These changes mainly concern the composition of the elected member states, working methods and established diplomatic practices, and the way in which subsidiary committees interact with countries that contribute funding, troops, and other resources that underwrite specific missions.

As the diplomatic process serves to channel shifts in power relations and changes in aspirations of individual governments and leaders, it cannot avoid influencing how interests and demands are articulated. The articulation of interests and demands can be tangible or intangible, depending on the openness of the process and the availability of a paper (or electronic) trail that nonparticipants can access and interpret. In and of itself, the bifurcation of high-table diplomacy into a predominantly formal and a predominantly informal institutional arrangement is a phenomenon that seems greatly underappreciated in the study of international relations, forming an implicit premise of the discourse insofar as we cannot easily imagine a world without either the UNSC or the GX summitry. Informal great-power condominiums do have a previous history in international relations, with the nineteenth-century Concert of Europe representing its clearest expression. But a great-power condominium with first-tier great powers accorded formal veto rights is, in fact, a unique institutional arrangement engineered in the mid-1940s.

International Security Institutions and the Future of Global Governance

At last the time has come to draw on the whole spectrum of empirical findings—the lessons from the analytical themes just discussed, in conjunction with our theoretical and conceptual ambitions—in order to elicit a couple of general conclusions and try to respond to the normative question: Does high-table diplomacy provide a solution to complex governance issues in the realm of international security so promising that the experience can be emulated in other policy areas? Is the theory of a stakeholdership of the few, implicit in high-table diplomacy, plausible?

As mentioned in chapter 2, Stone's theoretical prediction, loosely based on his own study, was that "international governance improves when the distribution of power becomes more egalitarian." That notion is squarely based on a liberal premise, and scholars sympathetic to realism or hegemonic stability theory would certainly object. The three cases examined here do not, quite frankly, offer corroboration for such an optimistic scenario. The most dysfunctional policy area of the three is climate change mitigation, the only issue on which the United States does not (or will not) assert its full authority and mobilize its leverage over formal and informal settings. In conflict management and counterterrorism, policy areas in which Washington holds more resources by far than any other country, American leverage appears to contribute to the higher performance of relevant institutional arrangements.

Whereas Washington continues to be of two minds about climate change mitigation and the use of its considerable leverage over other great powers in this policy area, China and Russia appear not to pay much attention to the issue. The combination of vacillation in large Western countries and a reluctance to address climate change in many emerging countries, at least until recently, goes some way toward explaining the failure of formal and informal institutional arrangements to mobilize domestic and international constituencies in this field. Beijing and, above all, Moscow do not actively pursue a mitigation strategy as part of their great-power diplomacy, apparently regarding mitigation as something that could potentially undercut future economic opportunities presented by a warmer climate in the High North.

Meanwhile, it is not clear that the United States, although seemingly acting with growing restraint today compared with twenty-five (or even five) years ago, is becoming more inclined to engage in formal governance even though decision makers realize it may very well solidify international security institutions. Stone, though himself a liberal theorist, acknowledged that temptations to rely on informal influence remain powerful for the preeminent power. It is possible that Washington continues to optimize outcomes for its current policy agenda and therefore avoids taking a principled stance for multilateralism or minilateralism and for formal or informal governance. The lack of overt support for one or the other may, in turn, indicate that the US government is postponing making a decision about such matters or that its leadership has not yet sufficiently thought through the ramifications of acting in one way or another. The slow rise of a sense of stakeholdership among middle and second-tier great powers, illustrated in this volume, is seen by some to vindicate the cautious approach adopted by US policymakers and the Obama administration.

The shift toward minilateralism would not be taking place without American acceptance of it as a means to distribute risk and to sustain US preeminence. High-table diplomacy was established a half century ago and has since then largely exerted a stabilizing influence in the world. Acknowledging its significance in the realm of international security, including nontraditional security, could even be a way to harness that role while trying to reinvigorate multilateralism in other spheres. The G8 helped enhance and implement conflict management, through the Africa Clearing House and the PBC. The G8 created the precursor framework to the UNSC's counterterrorism activities and the institutional arrangements that ensure the continuity of those efforts, with the FATF as a particularly valuable achievement. But the G8, and even less the G7, is not representative enough to play the role of reinvigorating global governance at large, as perhaps suggested by the lack of major progress on climate change mitigation. The G20 could possibly assume that role over time.

Scholars who complain about the lack of a basic definition of terrorism in international security institutions at the same time readily acknowledge that transnational counterterrorism has scored substantive successes through enhanced financial transparency at the global level. International security institutions undoubtedly need reshaping, and the establishment of a G20 summit of heads of state and government represents a promising first step. Some form of UNSC reform will also be required. But less critical than the exact shape of the future council is how it ties into and amplifies the activities of other less formal settings, and vice versa. The alignment of polarity, prestige, and process with existing international security institutions might be a sufficiently robust test of the resilience and robustness of the relevant arrangements that deliberately utilize (and are not impeded by) the bifurcated nature of high-table diplomacy.

In the past the UNSC has consistently been slow to adapt, and as a rule it has been directly prodded to do so by momentous events or great-power governments. This inertia, requiring a crisis or a massive political impetus, is likely to remain a key feature of most UN-based institutional arrangements. The scourge of international conflicts was acknowledged in the 1940s and led to the creation of the UN and its Security Council. But it was only in the 1960s that UN-based conflict management produced an effective method to reduce instability and human suffering, namely, peacekeeping. Similarly, the council and the General Assembly recognized the challenge of terrorism in the mid-1970s, yet it was not until the late 1990s and early 2000s that institutional arrangements were set up, within and outside the UN, to respond to the challenge via transnational measures. Climate change was expressly accepted as a potential challenge to international security no earlier than in 2011. As we have seen, there is still no institutional arrangement in place to forge a coordinated response.

The mutual nestedness and mutual reinforcement of policies involving the principal two high tables, as demonstrated in this study, have long been overlooked and require closer attention if we are to understand their implications and to ensure that the strengths of existing institutional arrangements are exploited to the fullest. A cursory examination of the mainstream criticism of high-table diplomacy is telling: the most common critique of the UNSC concerns its lack of effectiveness and political realism, whereas the GX summitry is rebuked for its legitimacy deficit and inflexibility. The major flaws ascribed to both bodies are, in other words, the key assets of the other, leaving us with an ostensible paradox that obscures and suppresses the bifurcated nature of contemporary high-table diplomacy.

Mutual nestedness, as well as the seesaw pattern of tactically shifting between formal and informal arrangements described previously, in reality provides useful contributions to our study of international security institutions. Mutual nestedness is essentially a cross-cutting dynamic relationship that is, some would say, inherent to diplomatic practice itself. Mutual nestedness allows predominantly formal settings to compensate for several of their most serious weaknesses—such as bureaucratic complexity, inflexibility, and high transaction costs—by introducing nested informality that alleviates the latter. Conversely, lodging formality in predominantly informal settings, for instance, by institutionalizing the role of Sherpas and agenda setting in GX summitry, helps develop institutional arrangements' capacity to improve collective oversight, joint control of information, and weak enforcement.

Mutual reinforcement, the horizontal management of national and international resources across policy areas and thematic boundaries—in our case in the realm of international security—is in important ways a more prosaic phenomenon than mutual nestedness. Mutual reinforcement lacks a basis in international law and the compartmentalization of policy areas into jurisdictions and functional logics of international relations. Yet that does not make the traditional-nontraditional security nexus inconsequential. The use of military force has political, legal, and symbolic repercussions that must not be underestimated, which is why preparedness and capacity to operate across organizational and territorial boundaries matter. That capacity, if carefully harnessed, may significantly improve the prospects for future international security institutions to successfully fulfill the tasks assigned by their principals.

In other words, there is little doubt that high-table diplomacy already contributes to global governance by addressing international security challenges. In fact, it might be argued that for normative reasons precisely these challenges should be at the very top of the list of issues handled by high-table platforms. The seesaw shifts and reversals described previously suggest that the formality-informality nexus in high-table diplomacy at times functions as a self-correcting device that, albeit fraught with tension, essentially constitutes a productive relationship. The underlying logic of that productive relationship seems to bolster one of two values—effectiveness or legitimacy—without entirely eschewing the other. When the device operates at its full potential, nested informality in a formal setting strengthens effectiveness, whereas nested formality in an informal setting reinforces legitimacy.

The relationship between traditional and nontraditional security is more straightforward. As described previously, this nexus has a functional logic, striving to identify solutions to problems that increasingly blur the dividing line between coercive and noncoercive means and modes of operation. This logic has been relaxed over a period of several decades, yet it appears the boundary is upheld to different degrees, depending on the relevant policy area. In this study it has been demonstrated that counterterrorism cooperation is the area most directly and comprehensively affected by this relaxation.

Let us end by recalling table 2.3 (see page 65) showing the three policy areas of international security, the ideal objectives and mandates of the UNSC and GX summits, and the (formal or informal) mode of operation. The three policy areas were juxtaposed with primary objectives and thereby provide the first-order justifications of high-table diplomacy's seeking to avert large-scale wars, terrorist acts, and human-induced natural disasters with major consequences for nations and peoples across the planet. The secondary objectives cater to less existential threats yet offer significant opportunities to mitigate conflict, terrorism, and environmental and societal repercussions resulting from climate change. Given the severity and scale of these challenges and the weak performance of multilateralism in recent years, it would appear that high-table diplomacy is here to stay. Normatively speaking, this should be the case especially when it comes to the primary objectives corresponding to the policy areas examined in this study.

As stated in chapter 1, high-table diplomacy is conducted within platforms and institutional arrangements where great powers enjoy special status or to which they have privileged access. Some will on normative grounds, in the spirit of multilateralism and the equality of states, reject what they regard as a growing asymmetry among great, middle, and small powers in international relations at large, to the detriment of the latter. This study has nonetheless suggested that such lopsidedness can be softened through a more direct involvement of the E10 in all or most aspects of the UNSC's work, as well as through extensive consultations by the GX summitry with all members of the international community. If the UNSC is expanded in some shape or form and the mandate of serial summits is broadened in the coming years and decades, traditional notions of diplomacy are not necessarily undermined or made redundant. Even in the era of minilateralism, that is, diplomacy as the employment of leverage can be reconciled with diplomacy as negotiation and representation.

NOTES

1. "G8 Leaders Declaration: Responsible Leadership for a Sustainable Future," l'Aquila, July 10, 2009, accessed July 28, 2014, http://www.g8italia2009.it/G8/Home/Summit/G8-G8_Layout_locale-1199882116809_Atti.htm.

2. Brazil is in charge of the Guinea-Bissau configuration, and Canada chairs the Liberia configuration.

3. US Permanent Representation, "Meeting with New Turkish Counter Terrorism Committee Chairman" (signed Rice), WikiLeaks Cable ID: #10USUNNEWYORK22, January 10, 2010, accessed July 28, 2014, https://cablegatesearch.wikileaks.org/cable.php?id=10USUNNEWYORK22&q=elected%20member%20unsc.

4. Ibid.

5. Naim, "Minilateralism"; Oye, "Explaining Cooperation under Anarchy," 21. In mid-2014 the Obama administration seemed to be reasoning along the same lines; see Coral Davenport, "Obama Pursuing Climate Accord in Lieu of Treaty," *New York Times*, August 26, 2014.

6. On a separate UN Climate Council, see Eckersley, "Moving Forward."

7. Weitz, *War and Governance*.

8. Author's interviews. See also Engelbrekt, "Responsibility Shirking."

9. Drezner, "Power and Perils," 66.

10. Author's interviews.

11. Ibid.

12. Ibid.

13. Engelbrekt, "Responsibility Shirking."

14. US Department of State, "Terrorist Finance: Action Request for Senior Level Engagement on Terrorism Finance" (signed Clinton), WikiLeaks Cable ID: #09STATE131801, July 30, 2014, accessed May 22, 2015, https://wikileaks.org/cable/2009/12/09STATE131801.html.

List of Interviewees

Anonymous, Department of Political Affairs, UN Secretariat
Anonymous, Office of the President of the General Assembly, UN Secretariat
Anonymous, UN Mission of China
Anonymous, UN Mission of France
Anonymous, UN Mission of Greece
Anonymous, UN Mission of India
Anonymous, UN Mission of Latvia
Anonymous, UN Mission of Morocco
Anonymous, UN Mission of Pakistan
Anonymous, UN Mission of Sweden

Angel Angelov, Third Secretary, UN Mission of Bulgaria
Ertuğrul Apakan, Permanent Representative, UN Mission of Turkey
Emmanuel Bonne, Political Counselor, UN Mission of France
Germán Calderón, Second Secretary, UN Mission of Colombia
Ruggiero Corrias, First Counselor, UN Mission of Italy
Bruce Cronin, Associate Professor of Political Science, City College of New York
Michael C. Doyle, Harold Brown Professor of US Foreign and Security Policy, Columbia University
Dmitry Filatkin, Second Secretary, UN Mission of Russia
Tomoaki Ishigaki, Counselor, UN Mission of Japan
B. Z. Lolo, Minister, UN Mission of Nigeria
Edward C. Luck, Special Adviser to the Secretary General and Professor in the Professional Practice of International Affairs, Columbia University
Miguel Madureira, Counselor, UN Mission of Portugal
Anne-Marie Maskay, First Secretary, UN Mission of France
Kosei Nomura, Counselor, UN Mission of Japan
Philip Parham, Deputy Permanent Representative, UN Mission of the United Kingdom
Park Chul-min, Minister Counselor, UN Mission of Korea
James A. Paul, Global Policy Forum

Rodrigo Pintado, Second Secretary, UN Mission of Mexico
Gert Rosenthal, Permanent Representative, UN Mission of Guatemala
Stefan Tafrov, Permanent Representative, UN Mission of Bulgaria
Zahir Tanin, Permanent Representative, UN Mission of Afghanistan
Calin Trenkov-Wermut, Assistant Professor, New York University
Daniel Tumpal S. Smianjuntak, First Secretary, UN Mission of Indonesia
Eugenio Vargas Garcia, Counselor, UN Mission of Brazil
Christian Wenaweser, Permanent Representative, UN Mission of Liechtenstein

BIBLIOGRAPHY

Adibe, Clement E. "The Liberian Conflict and the ECOWAS-UN Partnership." *Third World Quarterly* 18, no. 3 (1997): 471–88. http://dx.doi.org/10.1080/0143659 9714821.

Agha, Hussein, Shai Feldman, Ahmad Khalidi, and Zeev Shiff. *Track-II Diplomacy: Lessons from the Middle East.* Cambridge, MA: Belfer Center / Kennedy School / Harvard University, 2003.

Alexandroff, Alan S., and Andrew F. Cooper. *Rising States, Rising Institutions: Challenges for Global Governance.* Washington, DC: Brookings Institution and CIGI, 2010.

Alter, Karen, and Sophie Meunier. "Nested and Overlapping Regimes in the Transatlantic Banana Trade Dispute." *Journal of European Public Policy* 13, no. 3 (2006): 362–82. http://dx.doi.org/10.1080/13501760600560409.

Amicelle, Anthony. "Trace My Money If You Can: European Security Management of Financial Flows." In *Security, Accountability and Risk Management: Transforming the Public Security Domain*, edited by Karin Svedberg Helgesson and Ulrika Mörth, 110–31. London: Routledge, 2012.

Anderson, Matthew S. *The Rise of Modern Diplomacy, 1450–1919.* New York: Longman, 1993.

Apl, Sigrid. *Die sicherheitspolitischen Dimensionen der G20: Zu Global Governance und internationaler politischer Ökonomie.* Berlin: Akademie-Verlag, 2013.

Badie, Bertrand. *La diplomatie de connivence: Les derives oligarchiques du système international.* Paris: Éditions la Découverte, 2011.

Bailey, Sydney D., and Sam Daws. *The Procedure of the UN Security Council.* 3rd ed. Oxford: Clarendon Press, 1998. http://dx.doi.org/10.1093/0198280734.001.0001.

Barclay Roger, Charles. "Varieties of Networks: Agents and Agency in Transnational Cooperation." Presented at the annual convention of the International Studies Association, New Orleans, February 18–21, 2015.

Barnett, Michael, and Liv Coleman. "Designing Police: Interpol and the Study of Change in International Organizations." *International Studies Quarterly* 49, no. 4 (December 2005): 593–620. http://dx.doi.org/10.1111/j.1468-2478.2005.00380.x.

Bates, Robert H., Avner Greif, Margaret Levi, Jean-Laurent Rosenthal, and Barry R. Weingast. *Analytic Narratives.* Princeton, NJ: Princeton University Press, 1998.

Baturo, Alexander, Niheer Dasandi, and Slava Mikhaylov. "Analysis of State Preferences from the General Debates in the General Assembly." Paper presented at the annual general conference of the European Political Science Association, Edinburgh, June 19–21, 2014.

Bayne, Nicholas. *Staying Together: The G8 Summit Confronts the 21st Century*. Aldershot, UK: Ashgate, 2005.

Bernstein, Steven, and Erin Hannah. "Coherence and Global Sustainable Development Governance." Paper presented at the annual convention of the International Studies Association, Toronto, March 26–29, 2014.

Berridge, Geoff R. *Diplomacy: Theory and Practice*. 4th ed. Basingstoke, UK: Palgrave Macmillan, 2010.

———. "'Old Diplomacy' in New York." In *Diplomacy at the UN*, edited by Geoff R. Berridge and Anthony Jennings, 175–90. London: Macmillan, 1985.

Berridge, Geoff R., Maurice Keens-Soper, and Thomas G. Otte. *Diplomatic Theory from Machiavelli to Kissinger*. New York: Palgrave, 2001. http://dx.doi .org/10.1057/9780230508309.

Beyer, Anna Cornelia. *Counterterrorism and International Power Relations: The EU, ASEAN and Hegemonic Global Governance*. London: Tauris, 2010.

Biscop, Sven, and Daniel Fiott, eds. *The State of Defence in Europe: State of Emergency?* Egmont Paper 62. Brussels: Egmont Royal Institute for International Relations, November 2013.

Bodansky, Daniel. "The Copenhagen Climate Change Conference: A Postmortem." *American Journal of International Law* 104, no. 2 (2010): 230–40. http://dx.doi .org/10.5305/amerjintelaw.104.2.0230.

Bosco, David L. *Five to Rule Them All: The UN Security Council and the Making of the Modern World*. New York: Oxford University Press, 2009.

Bracht, Caroline. "Plans for the 2011 G8 Deauville Summit: May 26–27 2011." G8 Research Group, University of Toronto, January 17, 2011, accessed January 22, 2014. http://www.g8.utoronto.ca/evaluations/g8plans/g8plans-110117.pdf.

Bracht, Caroline, and Julia Kulik. "Sticking to the Core, Ignoring the Current: The 2014 Brisbane G20 Summit." G20 Research Group, University of Toronto, November 16, 2014, accessed January 22, 2014. http://www.g20.utoronto.ca /analysis/141116-kulik-bracht.html.

Bradford, Colin I., and Wonhyuk Lim, eds. *Global Leadership in Transition: Making the G20 More Effective and Responsive*. Washington, DC: Brookings Institution, 2011.

Bradford, Colin I., and Wohnyuk Lim. "Introduction: Toward the Consolidation of the G20: From Crisis Committee to Global Steering Committee." In Bradford and Lim, *Global Leadership in Transition*, 9–13.

Brenton, Anthony. "Great Powers in Climate Politics." *Climate Policy* 13, no. 5 (2013): 541–46. http://dx.doi.org/10.1080/14693062.2013.774632.

Brooks, Stephen G., G. John Ikenberry, and William C. Wohlforth. "Don't Come Home, America: The Case against Retrenchment." *International Security* 37, no. 3 (Winter 2012–13): 7–51. http://dx.doi.org/10.1162/ISEC_a_00107.

Brummer, Chris. *Minilateralism: How Trade Alliances, Soft Law, and Financial Engineering Are Redefining Economic Statecraft.* Cambridge: Cambridge University Press, 2014. http://dx.doi.org/10.1017/CBO9781107281998.

Bull, Hedley. *The Anarchical Society: A Study of Order in World Politics.* London: Macmillan, 1992.

Busby, Joshua W. "Climate Change and National Security: An Agenda for Action." CSR no. 32. New York: Council on Foreign Relations, November 2007.

Buzan, Barry. *The United States and the Great Powers: World Politics in the Twenty-First Century.* Cambridge: Polity Press, 2004.

Buzan, Barry, and Lene Hansen. *The Evolution of International Security Studies.* Cambridge: Cambridge University Press, 2009. http://dx.doi.org/10.1017/CBO9780511817762.

Cameron, Fraser. *An Introduction to European Foreign Policy.* Oxon, UK: Routledge, 2007.

Chivvis, Christopher S. *Toppling Qaddafi: Libya and the Limits of Liberal Intervention.* Cambridge: Cambridge University Press, 2013. http://dx.doi.org/10.1017/CBO9781139649704.

Clark, Ian. *The Hierarchy of States: Reform and Resistance in the International Order.* Cambridge: Cambridge University Press, 1989. http://dx.doi.org/10.1017/CBO9780511521683.

Claude, Inis L. *The Changing United Nations.* New York: Random House, 1967.

———. "Multilateralism—Diplomatic and Otherwise." *International Organization* 12, no. 1 (1958): 43–52. http://dx.doi.org/10.1017/S0020818300008390.

———. *Swords into Ploughshares: The Problems and Progress of International Organization.* 3rd rev. ed. New York: Random House, 1964.

Clunan, Anne L. "The Fight against Terrorist Financing." *Political Science Quarterly* 121, no. 4 (2006): 569–96. http://dx.doi.org/10.1002/j.1538-165X.2006.tb00582.x.

Coady, C., and J. Anthony. "The Morality of Terrorism." *Philosophy* 60, no. 231 (1985): 47–70. http://dx.doi.org/10.1017/S0031819100068182.

Cooper, Andrew F. "Squeezed or Revitalized? Middle Powers, the G20, and the Evolution of Global Governance." *Third World Quarterly* 34, no. 6 (2013): 963–84. http://dx.doi.org/10.1080/01436597.2013.802508.

Cooper, Andrew F., and Asif B. Farooq. "BRICS and the Privileging of Informality in Global Governance." *Global Policy* 4, no. 4 (2013): 428–33. http://dx.doi.org/10.1111/1758-5899.12077.

Cooper, Andrew F., and Richard Higgot. *Relocating Middle Powers: Australia and Canada in a Changing World Order.* Vancouver: UBC Press, 1993.

Cooper, Andrew F., and Mo Jongryn. "The Middle 7." In Jongryn, *Middle Powers and G20 Governance,* 63–126.

Cooper, Andrew F., and Ramesh Thakur. *The Group of Twenty (G20).* London: Routledge, 2013.

Cooper, David. "Between Great and Small: Disentangling the Conceptual Jumble of

Middle, Regional and 'Niche' Powers." *Journal of Diplomacy and International Relations* 14, no. 2 (2013): 32–58.

Cousins, Stephanie. "UN Security Council: Playing a Role in the International Climate Change Regime?" *Global Change, Peace & Security* 25, no. 2 (2013): 191–210. http://dx.doi.org/10.1080/14781158.2013.787058.

Cox, John. *Climate Crash: Abrupt Climate Change and What It Means for Our Future.* Washington, DC: Joseph Henry Press, 2005.

Crawford, Timothy W. "Pivotal Deterrence and the Kosovo War: Why the Holbrooke Agreement Failed." *Political Science Quarterly* 116, no. 4 (2001–2): 499–523. http://dx.doi.org/10.2307/798219.

Crocker, Chester, Fen Osler Hampson, and Pamela Aall, eds. *Managing Global Chaos: Sources and Responses to International Conflict.* Washington, DC: US Institute of Peace, 1996.

Cronin, Bruce, and Ian Hurd, eds. *The UN Security Council and the Politics of International Authority.* London: Routledge, 2008.

Dalby, Simon. "Rethinking Geopolitics: Climate Security in the Anthropocene." *Global Policy* 5, no. 1 (February 2014): 1–9. http://dx.doi.org/10.1111/1758 -5899.12074.

Dayton, Bruce W., and Louis Kriesberg, eds. *Conflict Transformation and Peacebuilding: Moving from Violence to Sustainable Peace.* London: Routledge, 2009.

Derviş, Kemal, and Peter Drysdale. "G-20 Summit at Five: Time for Strategic Leadership." In *The G-20 Summit at Five: Time for Strategic Leadership*, edited by Kemal Derviş and Peter Drysdale, 3–20. Washington, DC: Brookings Institution, 2014.

Detraz, Nicole, and Michele M. Betsill. "Climate Change and Environmental Security: For Whom the Discourse Shifts." *International Studies Perspectives* 10, no. 3 (2009): 303–20. http://dx.doi.org/10.1111/j.1528-3585.2009.00378.x.

Deutsch, Karl W., and J. David Singer. "Multipolar Power Systems and International Stability." *World Politics* 16, no. 3 (April 1964): 390–406. http://dx.doi.org /10.2307/2009578.

Dewar Viscarra, Diego A. "Exercising Responsibility: Non-P5 Member States and the Development of the UN Collective Security System." Paper presented at the annual convention of the International Studies Association, New Orleans, February 17–20, 2010.

Dimitrov, Radoslav S. "Inside UN Climate Change Negotiations: The Copenhagen Conference." *Review of Policy Research* 27, no. 6 (2010): 795–821. http://dx.doi .org/10.1111/j.1541-1338.2010.00472.x.

Doelle, Meinhard. "The Legacy of the Climate Talks in Copenhagen: Hopenhagen or Brokenhagen?" *Carbon & Climate Law Review* 1 (March 2010): 86–100.

Doyle, Michael W., and Nicholas Sambanis. *Making War and Building Peace: United Nations Peace Operations.* Princeton, NJ: Princeton University Press, 2006.

Drezner, Daniel W. *All Politics Is Global: Explaining International Regulatory Regimes.* Princeton, NJ: Princeton University Press, 2008. http://dx.doi.org /10.1515/9781400828630.

———. "The Power and Perils of International Regime Complexity." *Perspectives on Politics* 7, no. 1 (March 2009): 65–70. http://dx.doi.org/10.1017/S1537592709090100.

———. *The System Worked: How the World Stopped Another Great Depression*. New York: Oxford University, 2014.

Duffield, Mark. *Development, Security and Unending War: Governing the World of Peoples*. Oxford: Polity, 2007.

Eckersley, Robyn. "Moving Forward in the Climate Negotiations: Multilateralism or Minilateralism?" *Global Environmental Politics* 12, no. 2 (May 2012): 24–42. http://dx.doi.org/10.1162/GLEP_a_00107.

Eckstein, Harry C. "Case Study and Theory in Political Science." In *Regarding Politics: Essays on Political Theory, Stability, and Change*, edited by Harry Eckstein, 117–76. Berkeley: University of California Press, 1992.

Eistrup-Sangiovanni, Mette. "Network Theory and Security Governance." In Sperling, *Handbook of Security Governance*, 42–62.

Ekpe, Bassey. "The Intelligence Assets of the United Nations: Sources, Methods, and Implications." *International Journal of Intelligence and CounterIntelligence* 20, no. 3 (2007): 377–400. http://dx.doi.org/10.1080/08850600701249709.

Engelbrekt, Kjell. "Minilateralism Matters More? Exploring Opportunities to End Climate Negotiations Gridlock." *Global Affairs* 1, no. 3 (2015): 1–11. Published online September 14, 2015. doi: 10.1080/23340460.2015.1077607.

———. "Mission Creep? The Non-Traditional Security Agenda of the G7/G8 and the Nascent Role of the G20." *Global Governance* 21, no. 4 (2015): 537–56.

———. "Responsibility Shirking at the United Nations Security Council: Constraints, Frustrations, Remedies." *Global Policy* 6, no. 4 (2015): 369–78.

———. "Why Libya? Security Council Resolution 1973 and the Politics of Justification." In *The NATO Intervention in Libya: Lessons Learned from the Campaign*, edited by Kjell Engelbrekt, Marcus Mohlin, and Charlotte Wagnsson, 41–62. London and New York: Routledge, 2014.

Engelbrekt, Kjell, and Jan Hallenberg, eds. *The European Union and Strategy: An Emerging Actor*. London: Routledge, 2010.

Etzioni, Amitai. "International Prestige, Competition and Peaceful Coexistence." *Archives Européennes de Sociologie* 3, no. 1 (1962): 21–41. http://dx.doi.org/10.1017/S0003975600000515.

Finkelstein, Lawrence S. "The United Nations: Then and Now." *International Organization* 19, no. 3 (1965): 367–93. http://dx.doi.org/10.1017/S0020818300012352.

Fisher, Dana R. "COP-15 in Copenhagen: How the Merging of Movements Left Civil Society out in the Cold." *Global Environmental Politics* 10, no. 2 (2010): 11–7. http://dx.doi.org/10.1162/glep.2010.10.2.11.

Follett, Mary Parker. *Dynamic Administration: The Collected Papers of Mary Parker Follett*. New York: Harper & Brothers, 1941.

Fontaine, Richard, and Kristin M. Lord, eds. *America's Path: Grand Strategy for the Next Administration*. Washington, DC: Center for a New American Security, 2012.

Foot, Rosemary, and Andrew Walter. *China, the United States, and Global Order.* Cambridge: Cambridge University Press, 2011.

Franck, Thomas M., and Georg Nolte. "The Good Offices Function of the UN Secretary-General." In *United Nations, Divided World: The UN's Roles in International Relations*, 2nd ed., edited by Adam Roberts and Benedict Kingsbury, 143–82. Oxford: Clarendon Press, 1993.

Franke, Ulrik, Johan Norberg, and Fredrik Westerlund. "The Crimea Operation: Implications for Future Russian Military Interventions." In *A Rude Awakening: Ramifications of Russian Aggression towards Ukraine*, edited by Niklas Granhom, Johannes Malminen, and Gudrun Persson, 41–49. Stockholm: Swedish Armed Forces Research Institute (FOI), 2014.

Friedberg, Aaron. "Ripe for Rivalry: Prospects for Peace in a Multipolar Asia." *International Security* 18, no. 3 (1993): 5–33. http://dx.doi.org/10.2307/2539204.

Gaddis, John Lewis. *We Now Know: Rethinking Cold War History.* Oxford: Oxford University Press, 1997.

Gadinis, Stavros. "The Financial Stability Board: The New Politics of International Financial Regulation." *Texas International Law Journal* 48, no. 2 (2013): 157–76.

Gardner, Kathy L. "Fighting Terrorism the FATF Way." *Global Governance* 13, no. 3 (2007): 325–45.

Garnaut, Ross. "The G-20 and International Cooperation on Climate Change." In *The G-20 Summit at Five: Time for Strategic Leadership*, edited by Kemal Derviş and Peter Drysdale, 223–45. Washington, DC: Brookings Institution, 2014.

Gartner, Scott Sigmund, and Jacob Bercovitch. "Overcoming Obstacles to Peace: The Contribution of Mediation to Short-Lived Conflict Settlements." *International Studies Quarterly* 50, no. 4 (December 2006): 819–40. http://dx.doi.org/10.1111/j.1468-2478.2006.00427.x.

Gathorne-Hardy, Geoffrey M. *A Short History of International Affairs 1920–1939.* Oxford: Oxford University Press, 1950.

Geithner, Timothy F. *Stress Test: Reflections on Financial Crises.* New York: Random House, 2014.

George, Alexander L., and Andrew Bennett. *Case Studies and Theory Development in the Social Sciences.* Boston: MIT Press, 2005.

Giddens, Anthony. *The Politics of Climate Change.* Cambridge: Polity, 2009.

Gilpin, Robert. *War and Change in International Politics.* Cambridge: Cambridge University Press, 1981. http://dx.doi.org/10.1017/CBO9780511664267.

Gorodetsky, Gabriel. *Russia between East and West: Russian Foreign Policy on the Threshold of the 21st Century.* London: Frank Cass, 2003.

Gowan, Richard. "Asymmetrical Multilateralism: The BRICS, the US, Europe and the Reform of Global Governance (2005–2011)." In Renard and Biscop, *European Union and Emerging Powers*, 165–83.

Graber, Doris A. *Crisis Diplomacy: A History of U.S. Intervention Policies and Practices.* Washington, DC: Public Affairs Press, 1959.

Graham, Erin R., and Alexander Thompson. "Financing Climate Adaptation: The

North-South Politics of Institutional Design." Paper prepared for the annual conference of the American Political Science Association, Chicago, August 29–September 1, 2013.

Gray, Christine. *International Law and the Use of Force*. Oxford: Oxford University Press, 2008.

Guebert, Jenilee. "Plans for the London G20 Summit 2009." G20 Research Group, University of Toronto, February 21, 2009, accessed January 17, 2014. http://www .g20.utoronto.ca/g20plans/g20leaders090221.pdf.

Guebert, Jenilee, Zaria Shaw, and Sarah Jane Vassallo. "G8 Conclusions on Climate Change, 1975–2011." G8 Research Group, University of Toronto, June 20, 2011. http://www.g8.utoronto.ca/conclusions/climatechange.pdf.

Haas, Richard N. "The Age of Nonpolarity: What Will Follow U.S. Dominance." *Foreign Affairs* 3 (May/June 2008): 44–56.

Hajnal, Peter I. *The G8 System and the G20: Evolution, Role and Documentation*. Aldershot, UK: Ashgate, 2007.

Hale, Thomas, David Held, and Kevin Young. "Gridlock: From Self-Enforcing Interdependence to Second-Order Cooperation Problems." *Global Policy* 4, no. 3 (2013): 223–35.

———. *Gridlock: Why Global Cooperation Is Failing When We Need It Most*. Cambridge: Polity Press, 2013.

Hallenberg, Jan. "Anti-Money Laundering in the United States." In *Security, Accountability and Risk Management: Transforming the Public Security Domain*, edited by Karin Svedberg Helgesson and Ulrika Mörth, 56–69. London: Routledge, 2012.

Hameiri, Shahar, and Lee Jones. "The Politics and Governance of Non-Traditional Security." *International Studies Quarterly* 57, no. 3 (2013): 462–73. http://dx.doi .org/10.1111/isqu.12014.

Hassler, Sabine. *Reforming the UN Security Council Membership: The Illusion of Representativeness*. Oxon, UK: Routledge, 2013.

Hayter, William. *The Diplomacy of the Great Powers*. London: H. Hamilton, 1960.

Heinbecker, Paul. "Kosovo." In Malone, *UN Security Council*, 537–50.

———. "The United Nations and the G20: Synergy or Dissonance?" In Bradford and Lim, *Global Leadership in Transition*, 236–48.

Held, David, Angus Fane-Hervey, and Marika Theros, eds. *The Governance of Climate Change: Science, Economics, Politics and Ethics*. Cambridge: Polity, 2011.

Helmke, Gretchen, and Steven Levitsky. "Informal Institutions and Comparative Politics: A Research Agenda." *Perspectives on Politics* 2, no. 4 (2004): 725–40. http:// dx.doi.org/10.1017/S1537592704040472.

Hilderbrand, Robert C. *Dumbarton Oaks: The Origins of the United Nations and the Search for Postwar Security*. Chapel Hill: University of North Carolina Press, 1990.

Hiscocks, Richard. *The Security Council: A Study in Adolescence*. New York: Free Press, 1973.

Hobsbawm, Eric. *The Age of Revolution: Europe, 1789–1848*. London: Abacus, 1962.

Hodges, Michael. "The G8 and the New Political Economy." In *The G8's Role in the New Millennium*, edited by Michael Hodges, John J. Kirton, and Joseph Daniels, 69–74. Aldershot, UK: Ashgate, 1999.

Hoffmann, Matthew J. *Climate Governance at the Crossroads: Experimenting with a Global Response after Kyoto*. New York: Oxford University Press, 2011. http://dx.doi.org/10.1093/acprof:oso/9780195390087.001.0001.

Hook, Glenn D., ed. *Japan's International Relations: Politics, Economics and Security*. Oxon, UK: Routledge, 2001.

Houseman, Robert F., and Durwood J. Zaelke. "Making Trade and Environmental Policies Mutually Reinforcing: Forging Competitive Sustainability." *Environmental Law* 23, no. 2 (1993): 545–74.

Hurd, Ian. *After Anarchy: Legitimacy and Power in the UN Security Council*. Princeton, NJ: Princeton University Press, 2007.

Hurrell, Andrew. *Power, Values, and the Constitution of International Society*. Oxford: Oxford University Press, 2007.

Hurrell, Andrew, and Sandeep Sengupta. "Emerging Powers, North-South Relations and Global Climate Politics." *International Affairs* 88, no. 3 (May 2012): 463–84. http://dx.doi.org/10.1111/j.1468-2346.2012.01084.x.

Iji, Tetsuro. "Contact Group Diplomacy: The Strategies of the Western Contact Group in Mediating Namibian Conflict." *Diplomacy and Statecraft* 22, no. 4 (2011): 634–50. http://dx.doi.org/10.1080/09592296.2011.625819.

Ikenberry, G. John. "The Emerging Powers and the Future of the Global Order." Transcript from a seminar held at the Brookings Institution, Washington, DC, February 6, 2014.

———. John. *Liberal Leviathan: The Origins, Crisis, and Transformation of the American World Order*. Princeton, NJ: Princeton University Press, 2012.

Ikenberry, G. John, Michael Mastanduno, and William C. Wohlforth, eds. *International Relations Theory and the Consequences of Unipolarity*. Cambridge: Cambridge University Press, 2011. http://dx.doi.org/10.1017/CBO9780511996337.

Ilgit, Asli, and Binnur Ozkececi-Taner. "Turkey at the United Nations Security Council: 'Rhythmic Diplomacy' and the Quest for Global Influence." *Mediterranean Politics* 19, no. 2 (2014): 183–202. http://dx.doi.org/10.1080/13629395.2013.829329.

Jenkins, Rob. "The UN Peacebuilding Commission and the Dissemination of Norms." Working Paper 38, Ralph Bunche Institute for International Studies, New York, 2008, accessed January 19, 2014. http://www.lse.ac.uk/internationalDevelopment/research/crisisStates/download/wp/wpSeries2/WP382.pdf.

Jones, Bruce D., and Richard Gowan. "New Members Make for a Real Security Council at Last." *World Politics Review*, October 20, 2010.

Jongryn, Mo, ed. *Middle Powers and G20 Governance*. New York: Palgrave Macmillan, 2013.

Jönsson, Christer, and Martin Hall. *Essence of Diplomacy*. Basingstoke, UK: Palgrave Macmillan, 2003.

Juergens, Ingmar. *The Landscape of Climate Financing in Germany*. San Francisco: Climate Policy Initiative, 2012.

Kang, David. "Stability and Hierarchy in East Asian International Relations, 1300–1900 CE." In Kaufman, Little, and Wohlforth, *Balance of Power*, 199–227.

Kaufman, Stuart J., Richard Little, and William C. Wohlforth, eds. *The Balance of Power in World History*. Basingstoke, UK: Palgrave Macmillan, 2007. http://dx .doi.org/10.1057/9780230591684.

Keating, Colin. "Reforming the Working Methods of the UN Security Council." Friedrich-Ebert-Stiftung, December 2011, accessed May 23, 2015. http://library .fes.de/pdf-files/iez/08728-20111216.pdf.

Keohane, Robert O. "The Contingent Legitimacy of Multilateralism." In *Multilateralism under Challenge? Power, International Order, and Structural Change*, edited by Edward Newman, Ramesh Thakur, and John Tirman, 56–76. Tokyo: United Nations University, 2006.

———. "Lilliputians' Dilemmas: Small States in International Politics." *International Organization* 23, no. 2 (1969): 291–310. http://dx.doi.org/10.1017 /S002081830003160X.

———, ed. *Neorealism and Its Critics*. New York: Columbia University Press, 1986.

Keohane, Robert O., and David G. Victor. "The Regime Complex for Climate Change." *Perspectives on Politics* 9, no. 1 (2011): 7–23. http://dx.doi.org/10.1017 /S1537592710004068.

Kerr, Pauline, and Geoffrey Wiseman, eds. *Diplomacy in a Globalizing World: Theories and Practices*. New York: Oxford University Press, 2014.

Kirton, John J. "The G8: Legacy, Limitations, and Lessons." In Bradford and Lim, *Global Leadership in Transition*, 16–35.

———. "Standing Together on Security at Camp David." G8 Research Group, University of Torontoo, May 20, 2012, accessed November 17, 2014. http://www.g8 .utoronto.ca/evaluations/2012campdavid/kirton-security.html.

———. "A Summit of Significant, Selective Success: Prospects and Possibilities for the Brisbane G20." G20 Research Group, University of Toronto, November 10, 2014, accessed January 22, 2015. http://www.g8.utoronto.ca/g20/analysis/141110 -kirton-g20prospects.html.

———. "A Summit of Small Selected Success: Deep Disappointment at the Brisbane G20 in 2014." G20 Research Group, University of Toronto, November 16, 2014, accessed February 14, 2015. http://www.g20.utoronto.ca/analysis/141116-kirton -performance.html pdf.

Kirton, John J., and Caroline Bracht. "Prospects for the 2013 BRICS Durban Summit." BRICS Research Group, University of Toronto, March 22, 2013, accessed February 18, 2014. http://www.brics.utoronto.ca/commentary/130322-kirton -bracht-prospects.html.

Kirton, John J., Jenilee Guebert, and Caroline Bracht, "Climate Change Accountability: The G8's Compliance Record from 1975 to 2011." G8 Research Group,

University of Toronto, December 2, 2011, accessed October 19, 2015. http://www
.g8.utoronto.ca/.../climate-acc-111205.pdf.

Kirton, John J., and Elena Kokotsis. "Gleneagles Performance: Number of Documents, Words and Commitments." 2005 Gleneagles Summit Analytical Studies, G8 Research Group, University of Toronto, July 8, 2005, accessed January 17, 2014. http://www.g8.utoronto.ca/evaluations/2005gleneagles/2005commitments .html.

Kissinger, Henry. *A World Restored*. New York: Grosset and Dunlap, 1964.

Kleine, Mareike. "Informal Governance in the European Union." *Journal of European Public Policy* 21, no. 2 (2014): 303–14. http://dx.doi.org/10.1080/13501763.2013 .870023.

Knutsen, Torbjorn L. *History of International Relations Theory*. 2nd ed. Manchester, UK: Manchester University Press, 1997.

Kolbert, Elizabeth. *The Sixth Extinction: An Unnatural History*. London: Bloomsbury, 2014.

Larionova, Marina, Peter I. Hajnal, and John J. Kirton. *G-X Summitry*. Moscow: International Organizations Research Institute, 2010.

Larson, Deborah Welch, and Alexei Shevchenko. "Status Seekers: Chinese and Russian Responses to U.S. Primacy." *International Security* 34, no. 4 (Spring 2010): 63–95. http://dx.doi.org/10.1162/isec.2010.34.4.63.

Lattanzio, Richard K. "International Climate Change Financing: The Green Climate Fund (GCF)." Congressional Research Service, Washington, DC, November 17, 2014, accessed May 23, 2015. http://fpc.state.gov/documents/organization /235012.pdf.

Layne, Christopher. *The Peace of Illusions: American Grand Strategy from 1940 to the Present*. Ithaca, NY: Cornell University Press, 2006.

Lee, Seryon. "The Feasibility of Reforming the UN Security Council: Too Much Talk, Too Little Action?" *Journal of East Asia and International Law*, no. 2 (2011): 405–18.

Lehmann, Volker. "Reforming the Working Methods of the UN Security Council: A New ACT." Friedrich-Ebert-Stiftung, August 2013, accessed May 23, 2015. http:// library.fes.de/pdf-files/iez/global/10180.pdf.

Lia, Brynjar. *Globalization and the Future of Terrorism: Patterns and Predictions*. London: Routledge, 2005.

Lind, Jeremy, and Jude Howell. "Counter-Terrorism and the Politics of Aid: Civil Society Responses in Kenya." *Development and Change* 41, no. 2 (2010): 335–53. http://dx.doi.org/10.1111/j.1467-7660.2010.01637.x.

Llewellyn, Jennifer J., and Daniel Philpott, eds. *Restorative Justice, Reconciliation, and Peacebuilding*. Oxford: Oxford University Press, 2014. http://dx.doi.org /10.1093/acprof:oso/9780199364862.001.0001.

Lundestad, Geir. "Empire by Invitation in the American Century." *Diplomatic History* 23, no. 2 (1999): 189–217.

Lynch, Marc, and Dean Freelon. "Social Media and Transnational Involvement in Civil War." Paper prepared for the annual convention of the International Studies Association, Toronto, March 26–29, 2014.

MacFarlane, S. Neil, and Thomas G. Weiss. "The United Nations, Regional Organisations and Human Security: Building Theory in Central America." *Third World Quarterly* 15, no. 2 (1994): 277–95. http://dx.doi.org/10.1080/01436599408420380.

Mahbubani, Kishore. "The Permanent and Elected Council Members." In Malone, *UN Security Council*, 253–66.

Malone, David, ed. *The UN Security Council: From the Cold War to the 21st Century.* Boulder, CO: Lynne Rienner, 2004.

Manning, Carrie, and Monica Malbrough. "Bilateral Donors and Aid Conditionality in Post-Conflict Peacebuilding: The Case of Mozambique." *Journal of Modern African Studies* 48, no. 1 (March 2010): 143–69. http://dx.doi.org/10.1017/S0022278X09990255.

Markey, Daniel Seth. "The Prestige Motive in International Relations." PhD diss., Princeton University, 2000.

Martin, Lisa L. "The Rational State Choice of Multilateralism." In *Multilateralism Matters: The Theory and Praxis of an Institutional Form*, edited by John G. Ruggie, 91–121. New York: Columbia University Press, 1993.

McGee, Jeffrey Scott. "Exclusive Minilateralism: An Emerging Discourse within International Climate Change Governance?" *PORTAL Journal of Multidisciplinary International Studies* 8, no. 3 (2011): 1–29. http://dx.doi.org/10.5130/portal.v8i3.1873.

McLaughlin Mitchell, Sara, and Paul R. Hensel. "International Institutions and Compliance with Agreements." *American Journal of Political Science* 51, no. 4 (2007): 721–37. http://dx.doi.org/10.1111/j.1540-5907.2007.00277.x.

Metz, Bert, ed. *IPCC Special Report on Carbon Dioxide Capture and Storage: A Special Report of Working Group III of the Intergovernmental Panel on Climate Change.* Cambridge: Cambridge University Press, 2005.

Millar, Alistair. "Multilateral Counterterrorism: Harmonizing Political Direction and Technical Expertise." Policy Analysis Brief 1210, Stanley Foundation, Muscatine, IA, December 2010, accessed January 22, 2014. http://www.stanleyfoundation.org/publications/pab/millarpab1210.pdf.

Morawiecki, Wojciech. "Problems Connected with the Organs of International Organizations." *International Organization* 19, no. 4 (1965): 913–28. http://dx.doi.org/10.1017/S0020818300012662.

Morgan, Patrick M. *International Security: Problems and Solutions.* Washington, DC: CQ Press, 2006.

———. "Multilateralism and Security: Prospects in Europe." In *Multilateralism Matters: The Theory and Praxis of an Institutional Form*, edited by John G. Ruggie, 327–64. New York: Columbia University Press, 1993.

Morse, Julia. "International Institutions and Indirect Market Enforcement: Analyzing the Regime to Combat Terrorist Financing." Paper presented at the annual convention of the International Studies Association, New Orleans, February 18–21, 2015.

Moser, Suzanne C., and Maxwell T. Boykoff, eds. *Successful Adaptation to Climate Change: Linking Science and Policy in a Rapidly Changing World*. London: Routledge, 2013.

Murray, Donette, and David Brown, eds. *Multipolarity in the 21st Century: A New World Order*. Milton Park, Abingdon, UK: Routledge, 2012.

Nahory, Céline. "The Hidden Veto." Global Policy Forum, May 2004, accessed July 11, 2014. https://www.globalpolicy.org/component/content/article/185/42656.html.

Naim, Moisés. "Minilateralism: The Magic Number to Get Real International Action." *Foreign Policy* 173 (July-August 2009): 135–36.

Nikonov, Vyacheslav. "BRICS: Analysing the Security Dimension." BRICS Research Group, University of Toronto, 2013, accessed January 17, 2014. http://www.brics.utoronto.ca/newsdesk/durban/nikonov.html.

Nordhaus, William D. "Economic Aspects of Global Warming in a Post-Copenhagen Environment." *Proceedings of the National Academy of Sciences of the United States of America* 107, no. 26 (2010): 11721–26. http://dx.doi.org/10.1073/pnas.1005985107.

Nye, Joseph A. *Bound to Lead: The Changing Nature of American Power*. New York: Basic Books, 1991.

O'Connor, Brandan, and Martin Griffiths, eds. *The Rise of Anti-Americanism*. London: Routledge, 2006.

Odinius, Daniel. "Between Forum Shopping and Forum Shifting: The Relationship of Institutionalized Summits and Formal International Intergovernmental Organizations." Paper presented at the annual convention of the International Studies Association, New Orleans, February 18–21, 2015.

Olson, Mancur. *Collective Action: Public Goods and the Theory of Groups*. Cambridge, MA: Harvard University Press, 1965.

Organski, Abramo F. K., and Jacek Kugler. *The War Ledger*. Chicago: University of Chicago Press, 1980.

Oudraat, Chantal de Jonge. "The Role of the Security Council." In *Terrorism and the UN: Before and After September 11*, edited by Jane Boulden and Thomas G. Weiss, 151–76. Bloomington: Indiana University Press, 2004.

Oye, Kenneth A., ed. *Cooperation under Anarchy*. Princeton, NJ: Princeton University Press, 1986.

———. "Explaining Cooperation under Anarchy: Hypotheses and Strategies." *World Politics* 38, no. 1 (1985): 1–24. http://dx.doi.org/10.2307/2010349.

Patrick, Stewart M. "Irresponsible Stakeholders? The Difficulty of Integrating Rising Powers." *Foreign Affairs* 89, no. 6 (2019): 44–53.

Paul, James. "Arria Formula." Global Policy Forum, October 2003, accessed March 28, 2014. https://www.globalpolicy.org/component/content/article/185/40088.html.

Paul, T. V., Deborah Welch Larson, and William C. Wohlforth, eds. *Status in World Politics*. New York: Cambridge University Press, 2014. http://dx.doi.org/10.1017/CBO9781107444409.

Pentillä, Risto E. J. *The Role of the G8 in International Peace and Security*. Oxford: Oxford University Press, 2003.

Peters, B. Guy. "Concepts and Theories of Horizontal Policy Management." In Peters and Pierre, *Handbook of Public Policy*, 115–38.

Peters, B. Guy, and Jon Pierre, eds. *Handbook of Public Policy*. London: Sage, 2006.

Peterson, M. J. *The UN General Assembly*. London: Routledge, 2006.

———. "Using the General Assembly." In *Terrorism and the UN: Before and after September 11*, edited Jane Boulden and Thomas Weiss, 173–97. Bloomington: Indiana University Press, 2004.

Posen, Barry R. *Restraint: A New Foundation for U.S. Grand Strategy*. Ithaca, NY: Cornell University Press, 2014.

Potter, Lawrence G., ed. *The Persian Gulf in History*. London: Routledge, 2009. http://dx.doi.org/10.1057/9780230618459.

Prantl, Jochen. *The UN Security Council and Informal Groups of States: Complementing or Competing for Governance?* Oxford: Oxford University Press, 2006. http://dx.doi.org/10.1093/0199287686.001.0001.

Prezelj, Iztok. "Improving Inter-Organizational Cooperation in Counterterrorism." *Public Management Review* 15, no. 2 (2013): 1–27.

Putnam, Robert D. "Diplomacy and Domestic Politics: The Logic of Two-Level Games." *International Organization* 42, no. 3 (1988): 427–60. http://dx.doi.org/10.1017/S0020818300027697.

Putnam, Robert D., and Nicholas Bayne. *Hanging Together: Cooperation and Conflict in the Seven-Power Summits*. Cambridge, MA: Harvard University Press, 1987.

Rathbun, Brian C. *Diplomacy's Value: Creating Security in 1920s Europe and the Contemporary Middle East*. Ithaca, NY: Cornell University Press, 2014.

Renard, Thomas, and Sven Biscop, eds. *The European Union and Emerging Powers in the 21st Century: How Europe Can Shape a New Global Order*. Surrey, UK: Ashgate, 2012.

Reychler, Luc, and Thania Paffenholz, eds. *Peacebuilding: A Field Guide*. Boulder, CO: Lynne Rienner, 2001.

Richardson, James L. *The Great Powers since the Mid-Nineteenth Century*. Cambridge: Cambridge University Press, 1994. http://dx.doi.org/10.1017/CBO9780511559112.

Risse-Kappen, Thomas. "The Long-Term Future of European Security: Perpetual Anarchy or Community of Democracies?" In Smith and Carlsnaes, *European Foreign Policy*, 44–60.

Rosand, Eric. "The G8's Counter-Terrorism Group." Policy Brief 92, Center on Global Counter-Terrorism Cooperation, May 2009, accessed October 19, 2015. http://www.globalcenter.org/wp-content/uploads/2009/05/rosand_policybrief_092.pdf.

Rosecrance, Richard N. "Bipolarity, Multipolarity, and the Future." *Journal of Conflict Resolution* 10, no. 3 (1966): 314–27. http://dx.doi.org/10.1177/002200276601000304.

Rousseau, Jean-Jacques. *The Social Contract and Discourses*. London: Dent, 1973.

Ruggie, John G. "The Anatomy of an Institution." In *Multilateralism Matters: The Theory and Praxis of an Institutional Form*, edited by John G. Ruggie, 3–36. New York: Columbia University Press, 1993.

Sabatier, Paul. "An Advocacy Coalition Framework of Policy Change and the Role of Policy-Oriented Learning Therein." *Policy Sciences* 21, no. 2-3 (1988): 129–68. http://dx.doi.org/10.1007/BF00136406.

Sageman, Marc. *Leaderless Jihad: Terror Networks in the Twenty-First Century*. Philadelphia: University of Pennsylvania Press, 2008. http://dx.doi.org/10.9783/9780812206784.

Scherrer, Amandine. *G8 against Transnational Organized Crime*. Aldershot, UK: Ashgate, 2009.

Schrijver, Nino. "Reforming the UN Security Council in Pursuance of Collective Security." *Journal of Conflict and Security Law* 12, no. 1 (2007): 127–38. http://dx.doi.org/10.1093/jcsl/krm003.

Selznick, Philip. *TVA and the Grass Roots*. Berkeley: University of California Press, 1949.

Shanahan, Timothy. "Betraying a Certain Corruption of Mind: How (and How Not) to Define 'Terrorism.'" *Critical Studies on Terrorism* 3, no. 2 (August 2010): 173–90. http://dx.doi.org/10.1080/17539150903306139.

Sharma, Ruchir. *Breakout Nations: In Pursuit of the Next Economic Miracles*. New York: W. W. Norton, 2012.

Sharp, Paul. *Diplomatic Theory of International Relations*. Cambridge: Cambridge University Press, 2009. http://dx.doi.org/10.1017/CBO9780511805196.

Shaw, Zaria. "G8 Conclusions on Crime, 1975–2011." G8 Research Group, University of Toronto, June 9, 2011, accessed February 20, 2014. http://www.g8.utoronto.ca/conclusions/crime.pdf.

Sheehan, Michael. *The Balance of Power: History and Theory*. 2nd ed. London: Routledge, 1996. http://dx.doi.org/10.4324/9780203344613.

Shorr, David, and Thomas Wright. "Forum: The G20 and Global Governance: An Exchange." *Survival* 52, no. 2 (2010): 181–98. http://dx.doi.org/10.1080/00396331003764694.

Sievers, Loraine, and Sam Daws. *The Procedure of the UN Security Council*. 4th ed. Oxford: Clarendon Press, 2014. http://dx.doi.org/10.1093/acprof:osobl/9780199685295.001.0001.

Sil, Rudra, and Peter J. Katzenstein. "Analytical Eclecticism and the Study of World Politics: Reconfiguring Problems and Mechanisms across Research Traditions." *Perspectives on Politics* 8, no. 2 (2010): 411–31. http://dx.doi.org/10.1017/S1537592710001179.

Simma, Bruno, ed. *The Charter of the United Nations: A Commentary*. 2nd ed. New York: Oxford University Press, 2002.

Slobodchikoff, Michael O. *Strategic Cooperation: Overcoming the Barriers of Global Anarchy*. Lanham, MD: Lexington Books, 2013.

Smith, Courtney B. *Politics and Process and the United Nations: The Global Dance.* London: Lynne Rienner, 2006.

Smith, Gordon S. "The G8 and the G20: What Relationship Now?" In Bradford and Lim, *Global Leadership in Transition*, 48–54.

Smith, Gordon S., and Peter C. Heap, "Canada, the G8, and the G20: A Canadian Approach to Shaping Global Governance in a Shifting International Environment." *SPP Research Papers* 8, no. 3 (November 2010).

Smith, Martin A. *Power in the Changing Global Order: The US, Russia and China.* Cambridge: Polity, 2012.

Smith, Michael E. *International Security: Politics, Policy, Prospects.* Basingstoke, UK: Palgrave Macmillan, 2010.

Smith, Steve, and Walter Carlsnaes, eds. *European Foreign Policy: The EC and Changing Perspectives in Europe.* London: Sage, 1994.

Soda, Giuseppe, Alessandro Usai, and Akbaar Zaheer. "Network Memory: The Influence of Past and Current Networks on Performance." *Academy of Management Journal* 47, no. 6 (2004): 893–906. http://dx.doi.org/10.2307/20159629.

Solomon, Susan, ed. *Climate Change 2007: The Physical Science Basis: Part of the Working Group I Contribution to the Fourth Assessment Report of the Intergovernmental Panel on Climate Change.* New York: Cambridge University Press, 2007.

Spechler, Dine Rome. "Russian Foreign Policy during the Putin Presidency." *Problems of Post-Communism* 57, no. 5 (2010): 35–50. http://dx.doi.org/10.2753/PPC1075 -8216570503.

Sperling, James, ed. *Handbook of Security Governance.* Cheltenham, UK: Edward Elgar, 2011.

Stern, Nicholas. *The Economics of Climate Change.* Cambridge: Cambridge University Press, 2006.

Stone, Randall W. *Controlling Institutions: International Organizations and the Global Economy.* Cambridge: Cambridge University Press, 2011. http://dx.doi .org/10.1017/CBO9780511793943.

———. "Informal Governance in International Organizations: Introduction to the Special Issue." *Review of International Organizations* 8, no. 2 (2013): 121–36. http://dx.doi.org/10.1007/s11558-013-9168-y.

Suetong, Xan. *Ancient Chinese Political Thought and Modern Chinese Power.* Princeton, NJ: Princeton University Press, 2011.

Svendsen, Adam M. *The Professionalization of Intelligence Cooperation: Fashioning Method out of Mayhem.* Basingstoke, UK: Palgrave Macmillan, 2012. http://dx .doi.org/10.1057/9781137269362.

Tajfel, Henri, ed. *Social Identity and Intergroup Relations.* Cambridge: Cambridge University Press, 1982.

Tammen, Ronald, et al. *Power Transitions: Strategies for the 21st Century.* New York: Chatham House, 2000.

Thompson, Kenneth W. "The New Diplomacy and the Quest for Peace." *Interna-*

tional Organization 19, no. 3 (1965): 394–409. http://dx.doi.org/10.1017 /S0020818300012364.

Touval, Saadia. "Mediator's Flexibility and the U.N. Security Council." *Annals of the American Academy of Political and Social Science* 542, no. 1 (November 1995): 202–12. http://dx.doi.org/10.1177/0002716295542001013.

Trenkov-Wermuth, Calin. *United Nations Justice: Legal and Judicial Reform in Governance Operations.* Tokyo: United Nations University Press, 2010.

Tsebelis, George. *Nested Games: Rational Choice in Comparative Politics.* Berkeley: University of California, 1990.

Tsingou, Eleni. "Global Financial Governance and the Developing Anti–Money Laundering Regime: What Lessons for International Political Economy?" *International Politics* 47, no. 6 (2010): 617–37. http://dx.doi.org/10.1057/ip.2010.32.

Tucker, Richard, and David C. Hendrickson. "The Sources of American Legitimacy." *Foreign Affairs* 83, no. 6 (November–December 2004): 18–32. http://dx.doi.org /10.2307/20034134.

Vabulas, Felicity, and Duncan Snidal. "Organization without Delegation: Informal Intergovernmental Organizations (IIGOs) and the Spectrum of Intergovernmental Arrangements." *Review of International Organizations* 8, no. 2 (2013): 193–220. http://dx.doi.org/10.1007/s11558-012-9161-x.

Van de Graaf, Thijs, and Kirsten Westphal. "The G8 and G20 as Global Steering Committees for Energy: Opportunities and Constraints." *Global Policy* 2 (2011): 19–30. http://dx.doi.org/10.1111/j.1758-5899.2011.00121.x.

van Vliet, Jasper, Maarten van den Berg, Michiel Schaeffer, Detlef P. van Vuuren, Michel den Elzen, Andries F. Hof, Angelica Mendoza Beltran, and Malte Meinshausen. "Copenhagen Accord Pledges Imply Higher Costs for Staying below 2°C Warming." *Climatic Change* 113, no. 2 (2012): 551–61. http://dx.doi.org/10.1007 /s10584-012-0458-9.

Victor, David G. *Global Warming Gridlock: Creating More Effective Strategies for Protecting the Planet.* New York: Cambridge University Press, 2001.

Voeten, Eric. "Outside Options and the Logic of Security Council Actions." *American Political Science Review* 95, no. 4 (2001): 845–58. http://dx.doi.org/10.1017 /S000305540101005X.

Vogler, John. "The European Contribution to Global Environmental Governance." *International Affairs* 81, no. 4 (2005): 835–50. http://dx.doi.org/10.1111/j.1468 -2346.2005.00487.x.

Vosoughi, Mohammed Bagher. "The Kings of Hormuz: From the Beginning until the Arrival of the Portugese." In Potter, *Persian Gulf in History*, 199–227.

Walt, Stephen M. *The Origins of Alliances.* Ithaca, NY: Cornell University Press, 1987.

Watson, Adam. *The Evolution of International Society: A Comparative Historical Analysis.* London: Routledge, 1992. http://dx.doi.org/10.4324/9780203415726.

Weitz, Richard. *War and Governance: International Security in a Changing World Order.* Santa Barbara, CA: Praeger, 2011.

Wendt, Alexander. *The Social Theory of International Politics*. Cambridge: Cambridge University Press, 1999. http://dx.doi.org/10.1017/CBO9780511612183.

Westra, Joel H. "Cumulative Legitimation, Prudential Restraint, and the Maintenance of International Order: A Re-examination of the UN Charter System." *International Studies Quarterly* 54, no. 2 (2010): 513–33. http://dx.doi.org/10.1111/j.1468-2478.2010.00597.x.

White, Stephen K., ed. *Russia's Authoritarian Elections*. Abingdon, UK: Routledge, 2012.

Whitehead, Alfred North. *Process and Reality*. Corrected ed. New York: Free Press, 1978.

Whitfield, Teresa. *Friends Indeed? The United Nations, Groups of Friends, and the Resolution of Conflict*. Washington, DC: US Institute of Peace Press, 2007.

Wilkinson, David. "Unipolarity without Hegemony." *International Studies Review* 1, no. 2 (1999): 141–72. http://dx.doi.org/10.1111/1521-9488.00158.

Williams, Paul D., and Alex J. Bellamy. "Who's Keeping the Peace? Regionalization and Contemporary Peace Operations." *International Security* 29, no. 4 (Spring 2005): 157–95.

Winkler, Harald. "Measurable, Reportable and Verifiable: The Keys to Mitigation in the Copenhagen Deal." *Climate Policy* 8, no. 6 (2008): 534–47. http://dx.doi.org/10.3763/cpol.2008.0583.

Wohlforth, William C. "Unipolarity, Status Competition and Great Power War." *World Politics* 61, no. 1 (2009): 28–57. http://dx.doi.org/10.1017/S0043887109000021.

Wolfers, Arnold. *Discord or Collaboration: Essays on International Politics*. Baltimore, MD: Johns Hopkins Press, 1962.

Woods, Ngaire. "The Impact of the G20 on Global Governance: A History and Prospective." In Bradford and Lim, *Global Leadership in Transition*, 36–47.

Xue, Lan, and Yanbing Zhang. "Turning the G20 into a New Mechanism for Global Economic Governance: Obstacles and Prospects." In Bradford and Lim, *Global Leadership in Transition*, 55–64.

Yamashita, Hikaru. "The Group of 8 and Global Peacekeeping, 2004–2010." *Global Governance* 19, no. 3 (2013): 333–52.

Zagorski, Andrei. "Russian Approaches to Global Governance in the 21st Century." *International Spectator* 45, no. 4 (2010): 27–42. http://dx.doi.org/10.1080/03932729.2010.527099.

Zakaria, Fareed. *The Post-American World*. New York: Penguin, 2008.

Zarate, Juan C. *Treasury's War: The Unleashing of a New Era of Financial Warfare*. New York: PublicAffairs / Perseus Books, 2013.

INDEX

CPSIA information can be obtained at www.ICGtesting.com
Printed in the USA
BVOW05*0059160416

444252BV00002B/4/P